TEXT & PRESENTATION, 2009

TEXT & PRESENTATION, 2009

Edited by Kiki Gounaridou

The Comparative Drama Conference Series, 6

McFarland & Company, Inc., Publishers

Jefferson, North Carolina, and London

ISSN 1054-724X • ISBN 978-0-7864-4706-0

softcover : 50# alkaline paper ∞

Cover photograph: Teatro Greco in Taormina, Sicily, 2nd century B.C.
(photograph by Kiki Gounaridou)

Manufactured in the United States of America

*McFarland & Company, Inc., Publishers
   Box 611, Jefferson, North Carolina 28640
   www.mcfarlandpub.com*

Acknowledgments

This is my first volume as editor of *Text & Presentation*. I want to thank the Comparative Drama Conference Executive Board for appointing me to this position, as well as my predecessor, Stratos E. Constantinidis, with whom I worked as associate editor of *Text & Presentation* for the past few years. Stratos E. Constantinidis did an excellent job as editor (1999–2008) and left the Comparative Drama Conference Series in great shape and with extremely helpful organizing procedures in place. I also thank the past editors of *Text & Presentation*, Karelisa Hartigan (1980–1993), Bill Free (1993–1998), and Hanna Roisman (1998–1999) for establishing the reputation and high standards for this annual publication.

This issue of *Text & Presentation* and the 33rd Comparative Drama Conference were funded in part by the Department of Theatre and Dance, the College of Communication and Fine Arts, and the Bellarmine College of Liberal Arts at Loyola Marymount University, Los Angeles, as well as by Smith College.

This publication would not have been possible without the commitment and expertise of its editorial board: Marvin Carlson (City University of New York, Graduate Center), Miriam Chirico (Eastern Connecticut State University), Harry Elam (Stanford University), William Elwood (Southern Connecticut State University), Les Essif (University of Tennessee, Knoxville), Yoshiko Fukushima (University of Hawaii), William Gruber (Emory University), Jan-Lüder Hagens (University of Notre-Dame), Karelisa Hartigan (University of Florida), William Hutchings (University of Alabama, Birmingham), Baron Kelly (Chapman University), David Krasner (Emerson College), Jeffrey Loomis (Northwest Missouri State University), Helen Moritz (Santa Clara University), Jon Rossini (University of California, Davis), Elizabeth Scharffenberger (Columbia University), Laura Snyder (Stevenson University), Tony Stafford (University of Texas, El Paso), Ron Vince (McMaster University), Kevin J. Wetmore Jr. (Loyola Marymount University, Los Angeles), and Katerina Zacharia (Loyola Marymount University, Los Angeles). My thanks also go to all of the additional scholars who participated in the anonymous review of the manuscripts that were submitted for publication consideration. I would like to thank our associate editor, Graley Herren (Xavier University, Cincinnati), and our assistant editor, Joel Tansey (Five College Associate), both of whom provided very valuable assistance with various aspects of the editing of this volume, our book review editor, Verna

Foster (Loyola University, Chicago), who solicited and edited the book reviews, and our editorial assistant, Elizabeth McDonald-Zwoyer (Smith College), who contributed her hard work and exceptional intelligence toward the publication of this volume.

The inclusion of photographs in this volume was made possible with the permission of the following copyright owners: Kiki Gounaridou for the book cover photograph and Ping Chong & Company for the photographs in Yuko Karahashi's article.

Last but not least, I would like to thank the Director of the Conference, Kevin J. Wetmore, Jr. (Loyola Marymount University, Los Angeles), the Executive Board of the Conference, and the hundreds of scholars who presented and discussed their ideas and research at the Comparative Drama Conference in Los Angeles in 2008.

Contents

Review of Literature: Selected Books

Preface

Text & Presentation is an annual publication devoted to original work on all aspects of theatre scholarship and to diverse disciplinary and scholarly methodologies. For the past 32 years, The Comparative Drama Conference Series has been publishing a selection of the best papers presented at its annual meetings, thus making a valuable contribution to the international discussion and scholarship on theatre, drama, and performance by framing dramatic discourse, identifying emerging trends, and challenging established views. Participants at the Conference have come from over 35 countries in six continents: Australia, Austria, Belgium, Brazil, Bulgaria, Canada, China, Cyprus, Denmark, Egypt, England, Finland, France, Germany, Greece, Guam, Iceland, India, Iraq, Ireland, Israel, Italy, Japan, Jordan, Korea, Malaysia, New Zealand, Philippines, Russia, Saudi Arabia, Slovenia, South Africa, Taiwan, Tanzania, Turkey, United States of America. All the essays in *Text & Presentation* are indexed in the MLA International Bibliography.

This volume consists of 13 research essays (which have passed an anonymous peer review), one review essay, and seven book reviews. The 14 essays included here were among the 154 papers that were presented in 64 sessions and discussed by approximately 200 participants at the 33rd Comparative Drama Conference in Los Angeles, California, from 26 to 28 March 2009. Four of the sessions were devoted to staged readings of new plays including Terry Boyle's *Mourn Those Angel Faces*, Stratos Constantinidis's *Platonic Love*, Mariko Mitchem's *Stained Skin*, and Meron Langsner's *Seeing the Devil's Face*.

In addition to the daily concurrent sessions, there were also four plenary sessions and a show. The keynote address, "Reframing the Lens on Stage and Screen: Old and New Media Approaches to Mediated Theatres, from Shakespeare on BBC2 to Performances in *Second Life*," was given by Lizbeth Goodman (Director of SMARTlab Digital Media Institute & MAGICGamelab at the University of East London). David Greenfiel (Loyola Marymount University) and Beth Meszaros (Monmouth University) responded to the keynote address. The second plenary session, "30 Years of *Crimes of the Heart*," was a roundtable discussion with playwright Beth Henley and participants Theresia de Vroom (Loyola Marymount University), Verna Foster (Loyola University, Chicago), Sharon Friedman (Gallatin School, New York University), and Tony Stafford (University of Texas, El Paso).

The third plenary session, "Author Meets Critic," was devoted to *Oklahoma! The Making of an American Musical* by Tim Carter (University of North Carolina at Chapel Hill), who discussed his book with Mitch Hanlon (California State University, Fullerton) and Verna Foster (Loyola University, Chicago). The last plenary session, "Dramatic Monologues: Friel, Soyinka, and the Greek example," featured Wole Soyinka (Nobel Laureate playwright), Rush Rehm (Stanford University and Stanford Summer Theatre), Courtney Walsh (performer), and Katerina Zacharia (Loyola Marymount University, Los Angeles). The show that the conference attended on March 26, *Home Siege Home — Part 1 Clytemnestra*, was conceived and directed by Katharine Noon, devised in workshop by the Ghost Road Company Ensemble, and performed at the Ford Theatre in Hollywood.

The 14 papers in this volume are organized both thematically and chronologically: the volume begins with Mary Frances Williams's "Where's a Saint When You Need One? The Influence of Edmund Campion's *Ambrosia* on Shakespeare's *MacBeth*," that demonstrates that *Ambrosia* has significant parallels with *Macbeth* and that Shakespeare advocates Catholicism through the template of Campion's play. The two papers that follow discuss different aspects of Shaw's work: in "The Imperfect Wagnerite: Bernard Shaw and Richard Wagner," Christopher Innes argues that seeing Shaw's work in the perspective of Wagner, exposes a new dimension of subtextual political commentary in Shaw's plays. In "Gardens and Libraries in Shaw's *Widowers' Houses*: 'Life Here Is a Perfect Idyll,'" Tony J. Stafford claims that Shaw uses the garden and library settings in his plays in order to reveal that the surface problems among dramatic characters are in fact a reflection of the deep hypocrisy of social interactions.

The three papers that follow discuss contemporary playwrights who straddle modernism and postmodernity: Peter Leman, in "Relative Facts: Emergency Law, Northern Ireland, and Brian Friel's *The Freedom of the City*," argues that Friel's play, through its use of temporal discontinuity, demonstrates the extent to which fact is rendered relative by the extreme circumstances of life that emerge when the temporary provisions of emergency law in Northern Ireland become permanent. Les Essif's "The Totalitarian Non-Tragedy of American Business in the French Plays of Michel Vinaver" addresses Vinaver's dramaturgical investigation of the totalitarian mechanisms of American business culture and its appropriation of cultural space in France and the world. In "Attacking the Canon through the Corpse: Cannibalism and Surrogation in *Hamletmachine*," Sonya Freeman Loftis explores how cannibalism represents cultural surrogation in Heiner Müller's play.

The next two papers discuss adaptations of Ancient Greek stories for the contemporary stage. Francisco Barrenechea, in "Liberating Cruelty: Two Adaptations of Classical Tragedy for the Mexican Stage," discusses the productions of *Cruel Iphigenia* and *Real Andromache* in Mexico as particular ways of understanding the notion of the tragic and as transformations of the characters' identities through cruelty. Wen-ling Lin's "*Troy, Troy ... Taiwan (2005)*: Transformation from Epic to Elegy" examines how the public discourses of "oceanic culture" and "ocean country" influence the reworking of an intercultural adaptation of Homer's *Iliad* into a work of national imagination in Taiwan. John D. Swain's "Peeling Empire: Yū Miri's Performance of 'Resident Korean' in Japan" and Yuko Kurahashi's "Ping Chong's Postcolonial Historicism and Theatricalism: *Pojagi* in *The East-West Quartet*" both deal with Korean theatre. Swain discusses the case of Yū Miri, a Korean resident in Japan, who won the Japanese Kishida Drama Prize for her play *Festival of the Fish*, and Kurahashi contextualizes Ping Chong's play *Pojagi* as a description of a series of encounters between Korea and colonial powers and of the tragic result of the division of the Korean nation.

The two papers that follow delve into modes of contemporary performance: in "Great Souls, Big Wheels, and Other Words: Experiments with Truth and Representation in Verbatim Theatre," Donald McManus explains that verbatim theatre has roots reaching back to the early twentieth century, but has also enjoyed renewed interest since 2001, because of its historical and documentary approach to text. Sharon Friedman in "'Sounds Indistinguishable from Sights': Staging Subjectivity in Katie Mitchell's *Waves*" addresses Mitchell's multi-media ensemble production as a semiotic transposition of Virginia Woolf's novel *The Waves*. Sascha Just's "Down with Plot: Eisenstein, the Tramp, and the Subversiveness of Montage of Attraction" investigates the parallels between Sergei Eisenstein's theatre work and Charlie Chaplin's films and concludes that they both applied montage techniques in their productions to challenge authoritarian power structures. Lastly, Helen Moritz writes her review essay on Rita Felski's *Rethinking Tragedy*.

The Conference Executive Board also solicits nominations and self-nominations for the Philadelphia Constantinidis Essay in Critical Theory Award, endowed by Stratos E. Constantinidis and established in 2006 in memory of Philadelphia Constantinidis to encourage research and writing on Greek drama, theatre, and performance. The award is given to the best comparative essay on any aspect and period of Greek theatre that was published in English in any journal or anthology in any country during the calendar year previous to each conference. Essays and nominations should be sent to <compdram@lmu.edu> by 31 December each year. The winner is offered complimentary hotel accommodations, free registration to attend the Comparative Drama Conference, and a check for $1,000 during the awards ceremony.

The Executive Board welcomes research papers for the Comparative Drama Conference presenting original investigation on and critical analysis of research and developments in the fields of theatre, drama, and performance. Papers may be comparative across cultural, historical, disciplinary, and national boundaries, and may deal with any issue in theory, history, criticism, dramatic literature, historiography, translation, performance, or production.

Kiki Gounaridou
September 2009

Where's a Saint When You Need One?
The Influence of Edmund Campion's *Ambrosia* on Shakespeare's *Macbeth*

Mary Frances Williams

Abstract

St. Edmund Campion's neo–Latin Ambrosia *(1578) has significant parallels with Shakespeare's* Macbeth *(1606), including organization, structure, characters, scenes, imagery, themes, phrases, and vocabulary. Macbeth and Theodosius wonder if the blood will ever be washed off their hands. The Empress Justina sends two soldiers, who join with a madman, to kill St. Ambrose; Macbeth's two murderers join a third. Three demons sway Theodosius to violence; three witches influence Macbeth to kill. Evil, superstition, tyranny, injustice, and violence are intertwined. Macbeth's pattern and themes are Catholic, but Macbeth himself is not; he lives in a Protestant land without Catholic sacraments or healing saints, where the possessed must cure themselves (5.3.45–7). Macbeth is damned without means of redemption. But St. Ambrose absolves Theodosius the Great, who killed thousands and then destroyed paganism at Aquileia in 394. Shakespeare paradoxically advocates Catholicism through Campion's template and the absence of a saint.*

It has never previously been noticed that the Jesuit martyr St. Edmund Campion's neo–Latin play *Ambrosia* (performed at Prague in 1578)[1] is a potential influence on Shakespeare's *Macbeth* (1606) because of the numerous remarkable correspondences between the plays. *Ambrosia* is extraordinarily similar to *Macbeth* in its organizational pattern and structure, scenes, characters, imagery, religious references, themes, vocabulary, and meaning. However, Shakespeare neither copied *Ambrosia* nor is there a strict correspondence between the plays. Rather, Shakespeare absorbed and transformed his sources into something new. Substantial differences between the plays must be acknowledged in preface to this discussion: *Ambrosia* is very episodic with many seemingly extraneous scenes, a few comic and others overtly Catholic: miracles, exorcisms, processions, hymns, rituals, sacraments, etc. Valentin calls it "long et embarrassé" (2001:232). Many of its scenes, which are incidents from the life of St. Ambrose or events that are tangentially related to him, have no similarities with *Macbeth*. Shakespeare avoids comedy and omits Catholic ritual (although he quotes the Bible). Moreover, he is profoundly original in the Macbeths' intense self-examination and soliloquies (Elliott 1960:21) since Jesuit dramatists avoided both the soliloquy and psychological self-examination.

Nevertheless, *Macbeth*, like the Jesuit *Ambrosia*, contains a great deal of religious content, and *Macbeth*'s affinities with medieval religious drama have long been recognized. The Porter scene has similarities to "The Harrowing of Hell," part of the English Miracle Cycles (Wickham 1977; Asquith 2005), and *Macbeth* is somewhat like the medieval morality plays that enacted a pattern of temptation, fall, and repentance. In those plays, as in *Macbeth*, the protagonist was "surrounded by a group of characters who were allegorical embodiments of moral qualities bearing the relationship to him of either tempter or redeemer." These minor characters illuminated the protagonist and his internal struggle. But unlike *Macbeth*, the morality plays depicted salvation through contrition and penance (Rozett 1984:74–75). The continual progress towards damnation in *Macbeth* is instead more analogous to the Calvinist education-of-youth plays, such as W. Wager's *The Longer Thou Livest the More Fool Thou Art* (1559–1568), which inverted the traditional morality form by presenting a protagonist who is damned and cannot repent (Rozett 1984:87–88). Yet Shakespeare situates his damned, Calvinist reprobate in a play apparently based on a Jesuit model, organized in a Jesuit style, and with Catholic themes.

It is unclear how Shakespeare could have known Campion's play, which was not published until 1970. Shakespeare may have heard about it from an actor or someone who attended its performance in Prague for the Hapsburg Emperor Rudolf II in 1578 (where it was performed a second time) or at Munich in 1591. Or the play may have circulated in manuscript form. Since the surviving copy belonged to the German Jesuit playwright, Jacob Gretser (Simons 1970:xi–xii), whose *Timon* Shakespeare used for his *Timon of Athens*, manuscripts may have traveled between German playwrights and Shakespeare. Gregory Martin mentions the play by name in a poem published by Bridgewater (1588) (Simons 1970:ix–x), but it does not seem to have been known in England, where its Catholic content was dangerous. Another possibility is based on the argument that the teenaged Shakespeare might have taken part in theatricals at Hoghton in Lancashire in 1580 when Campion was there (Honigmann 1998; Milward 2003a:62–65; 1973:40–44; Wilson 2003:24–6; Honan 1998:60–70). Campion possibly taught Shakespeare Latin and dramatic technique at Hoghton (Milward 2003a: 62–65; 2005:11–12; 1973:44; Wilson 2003:24–26), and Shakespeare may have encountered *Ambrosia* there.

Shakespeare's source was Raphael Holinshed's accounts of Macbeth and King Duff's murder in his *Historie of Scotland* (1587). He possibly also consulted

George Buchanan's *Rerum Scotiarum historia* (1582) (Braunmuller 1997:13–15), Hector Boece, John Leslie, Seneca's *Medea*, and Matthew Gwinne's *Tres Sibyllae* performed for James I in 1605, in which three Sibyls mentioned James's ancestor Banquo (Paul 1950:17, 20–23; Bullough 1973:429–430; Braunmuller 1997: 5).[2] But Shakespeare made many changes; Bradbrook even declares that his use of Holinshed is slight (Bradbrook 1977:14). Braunmuller quotes Jones: "What [Shakespeare] did not find in Holinshed was any indication how to shape this narrative material for the stage, and this shaping must be our main concern" (Braunmuller 1997:15; Jones 1971:199).

Most notable of Shakespeare's "shaping" and alterations are his insertion of the murder of King Duff into the story of Macbeth; changing how Duncan died; turning Holinshed's and Buchanan's three women into witches (Paul 1950:255–274); changing the murder of Banquo; having only two (or three) murderers of Banquo; making Banquo innocent of crime; the alteration in Macbeth's character (Paul 1950:185; Bullough 1973:449); the reason for Macbeth's murder of Duncan (Shakespeare says ambition while Holinshed and Buchanan say that Macbeth was angry that Duncan made Malcolm his heir, and Donwald has malice against Duff because of injury); Duncan's greater age; Lady Macbeth's influence, her remorse (Paul 1950:191) and sudden death. Macduff is more important (Bullough 1973:449–450) and he learns about the murder of his family only after he flees Scotland. In Holinshed, Macbeth runs away before he is killed; but in *Macbeth*, he bravely fights in battle (Bullough 1973:467). Shakespeare also invents new scenes (Bullough 1973:448–451): Banquo's ghost; Lady Macbeth's sleepwalking; the execution of the Thane of Cawdor; Macbeth's letter; the doctor's diagnosis of Lady Macbeth; Lady Macbeth's illness and death; Macbeth's praise of Banquo; Macbeth's orders to two murderers; the healer Saint Edward the Confessor; the contrast between Lady Macduff and Lady Macbeth; the messenger who warns Lady Macduff; Macduff's refusal to kill Macbeth's soldiers; and his reluctance to kill Macbeth. These changes are incorporated into a dramatic structure that is embellished with themes, imagery, and vocabulary not found in the historical sources.

All these changes and inventions, Shakespeare's dramatic shaping, and the organization, themes, imagery, and language are paralleled in Campion's *Ambrosia*. The plays contain similar characters: the dominant, murderous Lady Macbeth resembles the Empress Justina; Lady Macbeth's perturbation is similar to Justina's anxiety. Macbeth's murderers are like those of Justina; Macduff's flight parallels the schoolteacher's; the witches equal Campion's demons; Theodosius is divided into both Macbeth and Macduff. *Ambrosia's* characters are types without depth, and *Macbeth* is noted for its "flatness" and undeveloped minor characters. Shared themes include: tyranny (both unjust government and political usurpation) and how it is an affront to God, manliness, cowardice, killing children, superstition, bloody hands and laments that blood is unable to be washed off (*Macbeth* 2.2.63–66; 3.4.138–140; 5.1), nature's response to human sin, blessings and references to heaven (Paul 1950:309, 313), and civil order versus disorder. There is the imagery of light and darkness (e.g., *Macbeth* 2.4.5–7), illness and healing, bloody banquets, weather, and beasts. Divine storms are important (a storm helped Theodosius defeat paganism at Aquileia in A.D. 394).[3] Shared words include: "fear," "blood," and "tyrant." *Ambrosia* contains demons, relics, visions, and miracles. *Macbeth* has witches, body parts, apparitions, and false "miracles." There are even similar lines: Macbeth says, "They have tied me to a stake. I cannot fly" (*Macbeth* 5.7.1). Theodosius laments: "I am bound fast among the spoils of hell" (*et cum inferni praedis ligor, Ambrosia* 5.3.1111). Above all, there is the focus on sin and damnation, and in *Ambrosia*, redemption.

Macbeth exhibits the organizational structure of *Ambrosia*. Ambrose is the hero of the first half of *Ambrosia* while Theodosius is in the second (Simons 1970:xvii). Macbeth is absent from much of the second half of the play (Braunmuller 1997:27), and the focus shifts from Macbeth as the "hero" in the first part to Macduff in the second (Heilman 1977:26). Both plays contain a powerful royal female, who is murderous, becomes agitated, and suddenly dies. Justina fades from view until Theodosius suddenly comments: "Justina's death has given back peace to all good men" (*Iustina mortua reddidit pacem bonis* 4.1.747). This is paralleled by the abrupt announcement of Lady Macbeth's death, "The Queen, my lord, is dead" (5.5.16). The murderous Empress Justina is contrasted with the pious Empress Flacilla, who helps homeless beggars, much as Lady Macduff is Lady Macbeth's opposite. Justina's agitation[5] differs from Ambrose's calm,[6] and is like the anxiety of Macbeth and Lady Macbeth.[7] The pattern of violence is similar: the execution of a traitor (Maximus; the Thane of Cawdor); a royal murder (Valentinian II; Duncan); other murders (the officials at Thessalonica; Banquo); a failed attempt at murder (Ambrose; Fleance); killing children (the massacre; Lady Macduff and her children); a warning about a murder (the schoolteacher; Lady Macduff); and a concluding battle in which tyrants are killed. Theodosius spares Maximus's troops (3.2.568–572); Macduff cannot kill Macbeth's soldiers (5.7.19). Theodosius briefly holds Maximus captive in Milan (3.2.595); Macduff offers Macbeth the option of being a captive (5.8.23–27). Theodosius orders the deaths of seven thousand, and Macbeth orders Macduff's family killed: "give to th' edge o'th'sword/His wife, his babes, and all unfortunate souls/That trace him in his line" (4.1.151–153). Even the ghost of Banquo may be broadly linked to *Ambrosia*: Macbeth sees the ghost, which reminds him of Banquo's unjust murder and unburied body: "safe in a ditch he bides" (3.4.27). Ambrose has a vision of St. Paul who tells him to find and move the bodies of the martyrs, Saints Protasius and Gervasius, to a basilica where they will be honored. Ambrose prays, "may the bodies of the saints lie buried" (Amb: *Cum pace divum corpora*/Cler: *Sepulta sint et gloria* 1.3.136–137). Macbeth exclaims: "If charnel houses and not our graves must send/Those that we bury back, our monuments/Shall be the maws of kites" (3.4.72–74); "Let the earth hide thee!" (95). Both Macbeth and Ambrose want bodies of the murdered to remain "buried."

But Ambrose does what Macbeth cannot: he restores the natural order disrupted by deaths of the martyrs by incorporating the innocent victims into religious ritual, revealing how they died, and publicly honoring them.

Both plays have healer saints: St. Ambrose is called a "physician of our maladies" (*medice morborum* 2.5.465) and he heals a blind man with the aid of the martyrs (1.6.267–268). St. Edward the Confessor miraculously cures the diseased. But Macbeth cannot find someone who will "minister to a mind diseased" (5.3.41) and he hopes for an antidote (5.3.44) and a physician for his country (5.3.50–57). Macbeth asks the doctor to "cast/The water of my land, find her disease,/And purge it to a sound and pristine health" (5.3.51–53). Macbeth's tyranny causes Scotland to be ill: Caithness says that Macduff's army is "the med'cine of the sickly weal,/And with him pour we in our country's purge" (5.2. 27–28). Illness is also linked to demonic possession: Ambrose exorcises a demon, and Lady Macbeth is possessed by demons who cause her sleepwalking.[7] The Doctor says about her, "Unnatural deeds/Do breed unnatural troubles" (5.1.62–63); "A great perturbation in nature" (5.1.8); "This disease is beyond my practice" (5.1.50); "More needs she the divine than the physician./God, God forgive us all" (5.1.65–66). Macbeth asks: "Canst thou not minister to a mind diseased,/Pluck from the memory a rooted sorrow" (5.3.41–42). The doctor answers, "Therein the patient/Must minister to himself" (5.3.46–47). The doctor's attitude towards Lady Macbeth is that of the Protestant England of James I, in which exorcism is forbidden and the possessed must cure themselves (Curry 1959:91–93; Paul 1950:97–98).[8] Lady Macbeth has no Ambrose to exorcise her demons.

The importance of fighting against tyranny is a common central theme. Theodosius calls the usurper Maximus a tyrant (*tyranne* 2.3.376) who must be subdued for "offending the Omnipotent" (*Pugnabit in te numen offensum Dei* 2.3.378) because (even though Maximus is Catholic) tyranny (whether usurpation or bad rule) is an affront to God and an insult to religion. Theodosius also declares that with divine aid he will fight the pagan tyrants and usurpers, Eugenius and Arbogast, who have treacherously killed Valentinian II (5.8.1307–1324). Ambrose calls Theodosius a tyrant because of his injustice: "Are you going to tread, as a despot (*more tyrannico*), on the threshold which curses you?" (5.4.1161–1162); "you dare present yourself in His dwelling, you, a servant whom He hates?" (5.4.1165–1166). Macbeth becomes a tyrant when he seizes power by murdering Duncan ("tyrant" 4.3.12, 37, 46, 105, 179, 186; 5.2.11; 5.4.8; 5.6.7; 5.7.11, 27; 5.8.27; "usurper" 5.8.55; "faith-breach" 5.2.18; "tyranny" 4.3.33; 5.8.67 "treason" 3.2.26). Macbeth knows the murder of Duncan offends the heavens ("his virtues/Will plead like angels, trumpet-tongued, against/The deep damnation of his taking-off" 1.7.18–21). Banquo declares he fights with God against Duncan's death: "In the great hand of God I stand, and thence/Against the undivulged pretense I fight/Of treasonous malice" (2.3.129–131); and Macduff leads an army to overthrow the "dead butcher and his fiend-like queen" (5.8.69).

An extraordinary parallel is the image of bloody hands. Ambrose prays for

Theodosius: "fallen by his felonious fury, not knowing how hideous his wound is, how full of blood his hands are" (*et lapsum gravi/Scelere furoris, neque scientem vulneris/Atrocitatem, sanguinis plenas manus* 5.1.996–998). He prohibits Theodosius from entering the basilica: "Stay outside, blood-stained prince!" (*Mane foris,/Sanguinee princeps!* 5.1.1011–1012) and asks "That hand, which is still dripping with shed blood, could it come into contact with holy things?" (*Haec quae cruorem stillat effusum manus,/Haec sacra contrectet?* 5.1.1020–1021). Theodosius laments: "Alas, I am sullied by an immeasurable misdeed, how dare I look at this flock attached to Christ? And at myself, a criminal, whose hands are shamefully red, my brothers, because they were steeped in innocent blood" (*Heu, sordidatus facinore immense, quibus/Oculis tuebor deditum Christo gregem?/Meme scelestum, cuius imbutae manus/Insonti sanguine turpiter, fraters, rubent* 5.6.1238–1241). He asks if "merciful God can perhaps bring himself, at your request, to wash my crime off" (*Si forte crimen eluerer clemens Deus/Per vos rogatus sustinet* 5.6.1244–1245).[9] Macbeth wonders: "Will all great Neptune's ocean wash this blood/Clean from my hand? No, this my hand will rather/The multitudinous seas incarnadine,/ Making the green one red" (2.2.63–66); "I am in blood/ Stepped in so far" (3.4.138–139). He tells Macduff: "But get thee back. My soul is too much charged/With blood of thine already!" (5.8.5–6). Lady Macbeth says; "What, will these hands ne'er be clean?" (5.1.37); "Here's the smell of the blood still. All the perfumes of Arabia will not sweeten this little hand" (5.1.42–43).

Both plays revolve around a bloody banquet: at the climax of *Ambrosia*, Ambrose refuses Theodosius entry into church: "stay outside, blood-stained prince!" (5.1.1011–1012); he asks: "That hand, which is still dripping with shed blood, could it come into contact with holy things? Shall the defiled tongue, which ordered death, venture to touch the bread of life?" (*Haec quae cruorem stillat effusum manus,/Haec sacra contrectet? Lingua quae iussit necem/Impura vitae tangere audebit cibum?* 5.1.1020–1022). Theodosius laments: "Christ's temple and table are accessible to slaves, who shudder at my crime.... They partake of sumptuous meals and heavenly banquets. But I am waiting here outside, filthy, repulsive, excommunicated, only fit for the underworld: I am bound fast among the spoils of hell" (5.3.1106, 1109–1111). But the absolved Theodosius is permitted to take communion ("he asked for the bread of life, because he was free from sins" (*vitae cibum/Purgatus expetit* 5.7.1284–1285); "he asked for the heavenly food" (*Coeleste quaerens pabulum* 1292); "nourished with the mystic meal" (*mystica plenus dape* 1294). The bloody ghost of Banquo confronts Macbeth and disrupts the banquet; the ghost and the bloodstained murderer spoil the feast. Lady Macbeth declares, "You have displaced the mirth, broke the good meeting/With most admired disorder" (3.4.111–112). Macbeth says, "anon we'll drink a measure/The table round./There's blood upon thy face" (3.4.12–14); "I have supped full with horrors" (5.5.13); "Ere we will eat our meal in fear, and sleep/In the affliction of these terrible dreams/That shake us nightly" (3.2.19–21). But the Lord hopes that with God's aid the overthrow of Macbeth's tyranny will purge their banquets of blood ("Give to our tables meat, sleep to our nights,/Free from our feasts and banquets bloody knives" 3.6.34–35).

The Three Murderers

A fascinating connection between the plays is found in a pair of remarkably similar scenes. *Ambrosia* opens with the Empress Justina, an Arian heretic,[10] expressing her hatred for Ambrose. Justina, who is a prototype of Elizabeth I, attacks Ambrose for teaching "doctrine which is nowhere taught by the Holy Bible" (1.1.40). She believes that she is the authority in matters of religious doctrine, and declares: "we will see who is master, Ambrose or I, Justina" (1.1.42–43). Justina is outraged that Ambrose opposes her ideas and power: "I am waging war against one single cleric" (1.1.8); "Ambrose shall pay dearly for a woman's wrath!" (1.1.13–14). She is annoyed by Ambrose's sanctity: "He rejoices in the piety of the people, his anointed hands and his high repute with the Supreme Head protect him. What is the use of my scepter?" (1.1.21–23). She wants to kill Ambrose and deplores her hesitation to kill: "never have I ventured to execute what my desire prescribes ... he whom I hate will never disappear" (1.1.18–19, 29–30).

When Macbeth prepares to kill Banquo, he praises his fine nature and says he fears him:

> Our fears in Banquo stick deep,
> And in his royalty of nature reigns that
> Which would be feared. Tis much he dares;
> And to that dauntless temper of his mind
> He hath a wisdom that doth guide his valor
> To act in safety. There is none but he
> Whose being I do fear; and under him
> My genius is rebuked, as it is said
> Mark Antony's was by Caesar [3.1.51–59].

Macbeth adds that the witches have "put a barren scepter in my grip" (3.1.64). Both Justina and Macbeth praise the wisdom and virtue of one man, who is the only one they fear, but resent receiving advice that they don't want to hear from him. Both decide to kill the only one who stands in the way of their desires because his opposition makes them seem powerless. Macbeth's deliberate evocation of ancient Rome provides further linkage between the plays.

Justina's general Furius agrees that Ambrose must be confronted: "This shall recoil upon his head, as I am a man!" (*Quod illius capiti, si ego vir sum, accidet!* 1.1.37) and asks for her orders. Justina tells him that if Ambrose continues to teach Catholicism, "he must be regarded as an enemy, and he must expiate that horrible crime" (1.1.41). Furius declares his loyalty, which is based both on military discipline and religious agreement: "I shall carry out your command; or rather, think of it as already executed" (1.1.44). Justina responds, "I shall be grateful to you! Go ahead, and remain firm!" (1.1.47). Furius tells the tribune Bambalio (who will be the "second murderer," along with Furius), "Have no conscientious scruples, execute the orders with dauntless courage" (1.2.49–50). Bambalio is equally resolute: "Let them beware!" (1.2.54).

Like Justina, Macbeth gives orders to two murderers, whom he questions to be certain of their reliability.[11] While Justina relies on military discipline and religious agreement, Macbeth uses knowledge of the murderers' disaffection and accusations that Banquo is the cause of their difficulties to make the men obedient. He raises the issue of religion when he asks if they "are so gospeled to pray for this good man ... whose heavy hand hath ... beggared yours forever?" (3.1.89–91). He then contemptuously likens them to dogs (3.1.93–102). After they insist that they are willing to kill: "I am reckless what/I do to spite the world" (3.1.111–112), he reminds them that Banquo is their enemy (3.1.116). They answer: "We are resolved, my lord" (3.1.140).

Yet in both plays, in spite of these protestations of loyalty and even though the murderers are motivated by strong religious, professional, and personal reasons, the intrigues of rulers and the attempts of their murderers fail. Furius and Bambalio arrive at the basilica. But before they can approach Ambrose, a third character, Madman, gets in their way, screaming that Ambrose is a "wolf! Kill that wolf!" and trying to kill him. Furius comments, "Everything has been arranged for that" (*composita res* 1.5.183). But he cannot kill Ambrose because the third "murderer" makes such a fuss. The possessed Madman is convinced that he is acting on Justina's behalf: "I shall knock your brains out, or I shall hand you over to Justina" (1.5.187); *Iustina, Iustina* (190). After Ambrose exorcises the demon and miraculously heals a blind man, Furius and his soldiers go over to Ambrose. But Furius wonders, "What will the Empress say to this?" His soldiers respond, "We will die in this faith!" (Fur: *Augusta quid dicet?* Mil: *Morimur ista fide!* 1.6.255).

In *Macbeth*, an unknown third murderer suddenly joins the other two, who ask: "But who did bid thee join with us?" His response, "Macbeth" (3.3.1), could be accurate or be merely his imagination.[12] The murderers attack Banquo and Fleance, but Fleance escapes when the torch is extinguished, possibly by the Third Murderer, who seems to have ruined the plot, like the madman in *Ambrosia*. These murderers also reluctantly report what has happened to the king: "We have lost best half of our affair./Well, let's away, and say how much is done" (3.3.23–24).

The Three Witches

Macbeth's witches are extraordinarily like *Ambrosia*'s demons. Three demons appear together in *Ambrosia*: Allecto, one of classical Furies, Mastix, and the deceased Roman Emperor Julian the Apostate. As befits a Jesuit drama, these demons explain their origin, motivation, and aims: they are demons from Hell (3.4.612) and "disseminate ... deceptions" (3.4.629). They intend to harm Theodosius by exploiting his weakness, but they have difficulty in determining it: "Caesar Theodosius shows a virile mind with great virtuousness; he curbs the passions of the flesh, of money, of pride, to which most men yield" (3.4.630–633). The demons want to injure Theodosius, not because of anything that he has done, or because God commands them, or because he is inherently evil, but because they don't like him and it pleases them to harm men. Julian has the further motivation of hatred for a Christian Emperor: "Why is Theodosius better than I myself was? He disdains the idols, he scoffs at you all; through Christ he triumphs, is feared, honored, respected" (3.4.623–625). The historical Ambrose similarly wrote to Theodosius: "The devil has been envious of your most outstanding merit. Overcome him while you still have the means" (*Ep.* 51 in Labriolle 1928:107). Campion's demons decide to encourage the Thessalonians to commit a crime that will provoke Theodosius's anger. Julian declares that they will call up "Wrath, who incites sudden goads of an irritation ... Let us spur her on; she will produce an immense calamity" (3.4.634–636). Allecto, the Fury who aroused anger in the *Aeneid*, says that if the people of Thessalonica commit murder, "When Caesar has learnt this he will be burning with anger, and beside himself with hatred, he will do something horrible, something wicked" (3.4.640–642). Mastix injects crime into the people's hearts; Allecto calls up rage. This leads to a riot at Thessalonica and the murder of three officials.

Shakespeare's three gender-ambiguous, bearded witches are similar to Campion's three demons since Julian was known for his philosopher's beard and Allecto is female in Virgil but may be male in *Ambrosia*. The demons are a model for the witches, and a demonic interpretation is facilitated since they are only once called "witch" (1.3.7) in the play.[13] The witches, who are recognized as evil,[14] were called demons as early as the Catholic historian John Leslie's account of Macbeth (1578), who said that the witches were demons in the likenesses of women and the "sure causes of treason, hatred and strife."[15] This interpretation of the witches as demons, which Curry persuasively argues, enables a close tie to *Ambrosia*. According to scholastic theology, demons or devils are fallen angels (Curry 1959:71–72); the witches are called angels: "the angel whom thou still hast served" (5.8.14). The witches, like demons, are subject to another power: "our masters" (4.1.63) (Curry 1959:60–63).[16] Demons cause storms and fog; the witches meet in foul weather (1.1.2, 11–12), manipulate nature's elements: "of nature's germen tumble altogether" (4.1.59), and cause storms (Curry 1959:74, 79–80). Demons are clairvoyant, provoke the imagination, inducing visions and hallucinations, and arouse desire (Curry 1959:75–77, 81–82). The witches are clairvoyant and prognosticate the future. They arouse Macbeth's passions by exploiting his weaknesses, and summon evil spirits that seem to speak (Curry 1959:77–79).

Although Greenblatt argues that the witches don't do anything beyond influence the weather (1993:123; 2001:192), they, in fact, set the play in motion through their attempts to exploit Macbeth's one weakness, his "vaulting ambition." Macbeth is an admirable man: a great warrior, noted for his bravery (1.2.15–23; 1.3.90–101), and a loving husband ("my dearest partner of greatness" 1.5.9; "love" 3.2.32; "dear wife!" 39; "dearest chuck" 48). He has a reputation for decency ("O valiant cousin, worthy gentleman!" 1.2.24; "Was once thought honest. You have loved him well" 4.3.13) and lacks vices. Macbeth has much natural good in him, as Lady Macbeth understands (Curry 1959:114–115), but he concentrates on his desire for worldly honors (Curry 1959:113; Elliott 1960:29) and aims for "th' imperial theme" (1.3.132). The witches prey on his weakness, "ambition" (1.7.27), arousing his passions, and perverting his reason (Curry 1959:116). The witches' prophecies are "responsive to thoughts already in Macbeth's mind" (Reed 1984:167; Moulton 1991:72; Wilks 1990:127); they tell Macbeth that the apparition "knows thy thought" (4.1.69). The witches, like demons, "pander to man's curiosity, and serve him solely with malicious intent, that he may 'dwindle, peak, and pine'" (1.3) (Bowden 1899:332–333). Macbeth does not deserve destruction, is not inherently evil, and is not marked for destruction by God. Rather, he lives in a world filled with demons who attempt to destroy his soul and against whom he must struggle.[17] The struggle is even greater for kings: Malcolm remarks, "A good and virtuous nature may recoil /In an imperial charge" (4.3.20–21).

The witches aim to encourage Macbeth "to his eventual destruction" (Milward 1990:128). They prevail in the same way as Campion's demons, who declare that they will arouse emotions and act through words: "Give their emotions free play, penetrate into their ears with a disturbing sound" (*Ambrosia.* 3.4.659–660). The witches' words affect Macbeth; he continually thinks about what they have told him, writes to his wife about it, and discusses it with Banquo. Their words infect his mind and that of Lady Macbeth, who invokes the "spirits/that tend on mortal thoughts" (1.5.38–39). But Banquo prays that his thoughts will not be so evilly influenced: "Merciful powers,/Restrain in me the cursed thoughts that nature/Gives way to in repose" (2.1.7–9). Macbeth finally realizes that the witches have lied: "damned all those that trust them!" (4.1.139); "I ... begin/To doubt th' equivocation of the fiend/That lies like truth" (5.6.42–43).

Campion's demons announce a second way they will harm Theodosius: bad advisors will influence him: "May hard-hearted leaders reign at his court. Let them instill into their master's mind horrible and frightful plans, worthy ... even of the calamities caused by Nero" (3.4.653–656). When Theodosius deliberates about his response to the murder of his officials, he considers Ambrose's advice to punish only the guilty and to "fear the progress of violent anger and refrain from impetuous acts" (*time/Praecipitis irae cursum et absiste impetu* 4.1.766–767). But Ruffinus exploits Theodosius's desire for order, arguing that the populace must be punished to prevent further riots. Theodosius agrees, and reveals a concern to be thought manly when he says that the people "[take me] for a king made of reeds, or perhaps they think of me as a branch cut away from the trunk, on which anyone may dance who wants to; if they had thought of me as a man, I think that they would have acted in a different way" (4.2.804–807).[18] Ruffinus eventually incites Theodosius to mass murder ("Seven thousand must expiate this atrocious crime" 4.2.824).

Macbeth contemplates murdering Duncan, but it is Lady Macbeth who persuades him to kill. She encourages Macbeth's ambition and taunts him; she knows her words have power: "Hie thee hither,/That I may pour my spirits in thine ear,/And chastise with the valor of my tongue" (1.5.23–25). She urges Macbeth to murder so that he will have glory ("Thou wouldst be great" 1.5.16; "the golden round" 26) and echoes Ambrose's advice to fear and Theodosius' rejection of weakness when she calls Macbeth a coward: "Art thou afeard/To be the same in thine own act and valor/As thou art in desire?" (1.7.39–41) "And live a coward in thine own esteem" (43); "This is the very painting of your fear!" (3.4.62); "Fie, my lord, fie, a soldier and afeard?" (5.1.31–32). Lady Macbeth raises Theodosius' theme of "manliness" when she accuses Macbeth of being "too full o'th' milk of human kindness" (1.5.15) and asks: "Are you a man?" (3.4.59); "What, quite unmanned in folly?" (3.4.75). Macbeth insists, "I dare do all that may become a man" (1.7.46); he says of the Ghost, "Being gone,/I am a man again" (3.4.109–110). But Lady Macbeth calls him a child: "'tis the eye of child-hood/That fears a painted devil" (2.2.57–58).

After Macbeth kills, the witches "go on to lure him to his destruction by fostering in him a feeling of security" through the apparitions that assure him that he is safe (Milward 1990:128–129). Again, bad advisors, this time supernatural apparitions, cloud Macbeth's judgment. He believes that he is invulnerable and becomes demonic himself ("treacherous" 4.3.18; "black Macbeth" 53; "Devilish Macbeth" 118; "fiend of Scotland" 237; "hell-hound" 5.8.3). Like Theodosius, whose anger caused him to be unjust, Macbeth is overly angry: "Some say he's mad; others that lesser hate him/Do call it valiant fury. But for certain/He cannot buckle his distempered cause/Within the belt of rule" (5.2.13–16). Ambrose, however, rebukes Theodosius and prays for him: "Safe in his high position, he has nobody to censure him. Hard is the lot of princes. For a man of lower rank will at once hear such things from his friends or enemies" (*Ambrosia.* 5.1.1000–1003). But Macbeth has no good advisor, only Lady Macbeth, who declares: "What need we fear who knows it, when none can call our power to account?" (5.1.32–33).

There is another set of demons in *Ambrosia,* those who caused the deaths of the martyrs, Saints Protasius and Gervasius. A letter hidden in their grave recounts their deaths (1.4.176–178):

> These two full brothers (lest anybody should be ignorant of their history) formerly lived in our city, when Nero was raging against the seed of the Chris-

tians sown by St Paul's exertions. But the wicked rabble, driven by impious instructions and a false oracle, demands from them absurd rites, empty dreams given by the gods, and that they should give good omens for a precarious war (*Quos turba profana,/Sacriegis acti monitis et numine falso,/Insanos poscunt ritus, et vana deorum/Somnia, difficili posituros omnia bello*). But the virtue of their noble characters could not allay that frenzy [1.3.95–102].

Nero unjustly executed them (1.3.103–109); and "Satan attacked their limbs" (1.4.172–173). Three hundred years before Theodosius, evil forces, impiety, and superstition incited an angry mob that caused innocent deaths at the hand of a tyrant.

The witches in *Macbeth* are equally motivated by false religion, practice absurd rites, and encourage Macbeth to empty dreams, but profess to give good omens for war. Banquo makes the witches part of pagan culture when he calls their predictions "oracles" (3.1.9). Macbeth's letter to Lady Macbeth, in which he informs her of the witches' prophecies, parallels the letter that recounts the martyrs' deaths. Both Macbeth's letter and the letter about the martyrs have a great impact: Lady Macbeth exclaims, "Thy letters have transported me beyond/ This ignorant present, and I feel now/The future in the instant" (1.5.54–56). Both letters deal with "impious instructions and ... empty dreams;" both have great power to affect their readers. But no saint interprets Macbeth's letter or warns about demons or injustice. Instead, Lady Macbeth immediately believes Macbeth's news and supports the witches' plans. She continually re-reads the letter while sleepwalking (5.1.3–7) and is equally "driven by impious instructions and a false oracle."

The tyrannical emperor Nero and the mob, which was devoted to impious rites, killed the martyrs. Likewise, the impious pagan tyrants (*impii* 5.7.1304; *Tyranni* 5.8.1317), Eugenius and Arbogast, killed the Emperor Valentinian, "an atrocious crime" (*Ingens facinus Eugenii* 5.7.1302), overthrew the government, and re-established "impious rites" (*sacrilegis ritibus* 5.8.1323). When Theodosius destroys the idols, Camillus asks: "How long, men, will this wicked superstition (*superstitio impia*) exercise your minds?" (5.9.1356–1357); "You ought to be ashamed to listen to the inventions of soothsayers" (5.9.1362–1363). Superstition and false religion lead to crime and tyranny. Similarly, the witches represent paganism and superstition; and they encourage Macbeth to become a tyrant through murder. When Macbeth trusts the apparitions, "The spirits that know" (5.3.4), and refers to "black Hecate's summons" (3.2.44), he links himself both to classical witchcraft and to pagan superstition. Macbeth, like the pagans in *Ambrosia*, follows a "diabolical" and impious religion of superstition, crime, and death.

Nevertheless, Ambrose says that Gervasius, through his death, "conquered the tyranny" (*victaque tyrannide* 1.3.108).[19] The martyrs suffered terrible deaths but were victorious because they helped end Nero's false religion. Likewise, the victims massacred at Thessalonica three hundred years later (a crime also motivated by demons who stirred up anger) prevail over Theodosius's tyranny because he ultimately submits to Ambrose. This significant idea is also found in *Macbeth*: six hundred years after the historical events of *Ambrosia*, Macbeth's murdered victims overcome his tyranny since their deaths impel the invasion of English armies that overthrow the Scottish tyrant. Macbeth echoes Ambrose when he says in bewilderment:

> The times has been
> That, when the brains were out, the man would die,
> And there an end. But now they rise again,
> With twenty mortal murders on their crowns,
> And push us from our stools. This is more strange
> Than such a murder is [3.4.80–85].

The historical pattern in *Ambrosia* is present in *Macbeth*: demons arouse emotion and encourage crime, which causes the deaths of innocents. But those deaths ultimately help to conquer tyranny.

All of these similarities emphasize a fundamental difference between the plays: in *Macbeth* there is no St. Ambrose who will cure Scotland of its illness and Lady Macbeth of her anxiety; no saint to exorcise demons, warn about injustice, honor dead victims, or absolve Macbeth. Although *Macbeth* similarly shows how tyranny arises from superstition, its characters do not recognize tyranny's connection with false religion even as they oppose it. Theodosius declares, "I confess that I deserve hell" (*Me fateor orco debitum* 5.1.1038) and begs Ambrose: "do not close to me the gates which Christ opens to those who show repentance" (*Quas poenitentibus aperit Christus fores,/Ne claude mihi* 5.4.1173–1174). After Ambrose absolves Theodosius, angels sing that he "has conquered the devils and atoned for his misdeed" (*Daemonum victor scelus expiavit* 5.6.1262). But Macbeth does not turn to confession for absolution of his sins (Milward 2003b:183; 1973:30). He rejects Roman religion concomitant with its culture: "Why should I play the Roman fool and die/On mine own sword?" (5.8.1–2); and his despair is that of the Calvinist reprobate.[20] The demons are not defeated — rather, they successfully destroy Macbeth. This is part of an overall diminution of religion in *Macbeth*. *Ambrosia* concludes with Theodosius thanking God for victory, embracing Ambrose, acknowledging God as Sovereign, and being hailed "long live our Glorious Caesar!" (5.10.1392). *Macbeth* ends less religiously: although Malcolm had asked "God above" to help him (4.3.121; cp. 3.6.46–50), he does not thank God at the play's end. Malcolm is hailed "King of Scotland!" (5.8.59), thanks everyone, acts "by the grace of Grace" (72), and will be crowned at Scone. The absent Ambrose is alluded to when Macduff greets Malcolm: "I see thee compassed with thy kingdom's pearl,/That speak my salutation in their minds" (5.8.56–57). St. Ambrose was famously called "the pearl glistening on the finger of God" (Labriolle 1928:xxix). But only nobles ornament Malcolm's kingdom; nothing has changed in Scotland.

INDEPENDENT SCHOLAR

Notes

1. For *Ambrosia* see Simons 1970; Shell 1996:103–118; Miola 2003:71–86; Valentin 2001: 232–234, 499–500. Citations and translations of *Ambrosia* are from Simons; citations of *Macbeth* are from Miola 2004.

2. Hector Boece in his *History of Scotland* (1527) invented the prophecy to Banquo. John Leslie, Bishop of Ross, an "ardent Roman Catholic," retold it in *De Origine, Moribus, et Rebus Gestis Scotorum* (Rome 1578) to promote Mary Stuart's claim to the throne (Paul 1950:171–172; Bullough 1973:441–443). In Boece, the sisters preface their salutations with "Salve" (Paul 1950:199), they are weird sisters and witches, Banquo is innocent, and the murder of Macduff's family and Macduff's killing of Macbeth are included (Bullough 1973:437–438). In Leslie, the women are devils, Banquo is innocent, and Macduff cuts off Macbeth's head (Bullough 1973:441).

3. Theodosius says that God performed a miracle (*miracli* 5.10.1384) by sending a storm against the enemy: "I am not worth so much ... that in order to rescue me, a violent rain from the sky, a mighty storm and a howling wind from the north should throw the horses of my opponents into disorder, and that Aeolus, called to arms out of his immense cavern, should overturn their haughty army, and that he should offer me the winds under his command as battle-signals" (5.10.1377–1382). Duncan's death causes storms and portents: "The night has been unruly. Where we lay,/Our chimneys were blown down, and, as they say,/Lamentings heard i'th'air, strange screams of death" (2.3.48–50). The witches are connected with bad weather (1.1.2; 1.3.39) and storms: "Though you untie the winds and let them fight/Against the churches, though the yeasty waves/Confound and swallow navigation up,/Though bladed corn be lodged and trees blown down,/Though castles topple on their warders' heads" (4.1.52–56).

4. Justina exclaims: "Justina, shall you never see a happy day? Shall you never be free from care? For me one grief follows the other" (2.1.272–273). Gratian is dead and Maximus has invaded Italy.

5. Ambrose preaches: "Whosoever, haunted with fear, is afraid of the vicissitudes to come and worries about fierce enemies who brandish their swords with threatening gestures, let him look at us, and at you, my sons" (1.4.142–145); "Unharmed admidst the evils, we are still alive. Behold our protectors [the martyrs]" (1.4. 146–148).

6. Macbeth is anxious when he learns of Fleance's escape ("Then comes my fit again. I had else been perfect ... But now I am cabined, cribbed, confined, bound in/To saucy doubts and fears" 3.4.22–26).

7. Curry 1959:88–91: demons invade Lady Macbeth's body and her sleepwalking is "demoniacal somnambulism." Both Catholics and Protestants accepted demonic possession.

8. Curry 1959:91–93: Protestants rejected saints, miracles, and exorcism and believed that the possessed should merely fast and pray. Diagnosis was left to physicians: "King James prepared ... a list of infallible symptoms, by which one might distinguish diabolical possession from ordinary insanity."

9. The historic Ambrose wrote to Theodosius, saying "I do not dare to offer the Sacrifice if you decide to be present. Can that which is not permissible when the blood of one man has been shed, be lawful when it is the blood of so great a number? I think not" (*Ep.* 51, in Labriolle 1928: 107). Theodoret (c. A.D. 450) reported that Ambrose forbade Theodosius to enter the church: "How can you lift up your hands still dripping with unjustly shed blood? How can you receive into those hands the most holy Body of the Lord? How can you carry to your lips His Blood after having poured forth so much blood unjustly in anger?" (Theodoret 5.17 in Labriolle 1928:111).

10. Ambrose opposed Justina's Arianism (Mitchell 2007:87, 273). He occupied a basilica to block Justina's attempts "to take over one of Milan's churches to hold an Arian Easter liturgy in 385 and 386" (Mitchell 2007:289; Ambrose *Ep.* 75–77 and 75a *Sermo contra Auxentium*; Liebe-

schuetz 2005:124–173; McLynn 1994:158–219; Moorhead 1999:132–134, 137–140; Labriolle 1928:40–65; Williams 1994:56; Williams 1995:202–203, 210–215).

11. Shakespeare invented Macbeth's meeting with the two murderers. It is often cut from modern performances. But Brown (2005:47) says it shows Macbeth's "convoluted" mind and Scotland's lawlessness.

12. Some argue that Macbeth sent the third murderer (e.g., Brown 2005:51; Elliott 1960:116); others think he is a mistake or is Macbeth. Williams 1972:261 rejects Macbeth as the third murderer.

13. Braunmuller 1997:28, 102: they are always Witch and Witches in the stage directions and speech headings. (The witch songs and Hecate passage are later additions to the play by Middleton. But the initial three witches are integral to the play.) The witches are women in Holinshed and Buchanan; in Shakespeare they are "three weïrd sisters" 2.1.20; "weïrd women" 3.1.2; "sisters" 3.1.59; "weïrd sisters" 1.5.7, 3.4.135, 4.1.136; "hags" 4.1.48, 115). Macbeth links them to witches when he says that they ride on the air (4.1.138) and that "Witchcraft celebrates/Pale Hecate's off'rings, and withered murder" (2.1.51–52). Wilson 2004:186: the three witches are the first time in an English drama when witches congregate and a witch conspiracy is new for the English stage.

14. Elliott 1960:29: in Shakespeare evil is "fundamentally devilish, created by 'the common Enemie of Man' (III.i.69), Satan." Macbeth knows the witches are supernatural: "what seemed corporeal,/Melted as breath into the wind" (1.3.82–83); "The supernatural soliciting/Cannot be ill, cannot be good" (133–134); they encourage murder, which is evil ("horrid image ... Against the use of nature" (138–140)). Banquo knows they are evil: "Or have we eaten on the insane root/That takes the reason prisoner?" (1.3.85–86); "can the devil speak true?" (108); "And oftentimes to win us to our harm,/The instruments of darkness tell us truths;/Win us with honest trifles, to betray's/In deepest consequence" (1.3.125–129); "And be these juggling fiends no more believed/That palter with us in a double sense,/That keep the word of promise to our ear/And break it to our hope" (5.8.19–22). Lady Macbeth summons demons ("you spirits/that tend on mortal thoughts" (1.5.38–39); "murd'ring ministers" (46)) to fill her with "cruelty" and stop "remorse" (40–45). She contrasts them with Heaven, which would stop murder (1.5.49–52). Duncan's "virtues/Will plead like angels, trumpet-tongued, against/The deep damnation of his taking off" (1.7.18–20).

15. John Leslie, *De Origine, Moribus, et Rebus Gestis Scotorum* 7.98 (Bullough 1973:519); Paul 1950:173.

16. Milward 1990:129 notes the "lingering presence of the devil, the prince of darkness, in Shakespeare's plays," e.g., "Angels are bright still, though the brightest fell" (4.3.23); "the common Enemie of Man" (3.1.71). Curry 1959:58–60: Catholics and Protestants believed in evil spirits, devils, demons, Satan, and witches.

17. The demons cannot force Theodosius to act: "Although the free will cannot be forced, when it is attracted it will possibly be overcome by evil" (*Amb.* 3.4.657–658; cp. 2.5.483–486). Macbeth has free will (Elliott 1960:29; Miola 2004:xv–xvi). But Protestant interpretations assume that the witches "compel" Macbeth to murder (Reed 1984:164–165, 167): "In some way Macbeth has offended against the harmonized structure of nature and, losing the protection of God, has exposed himself to demonic intervention. By almost every Renaissance demonologist ... we are told that a demon can work his mischief only by permission of God and, second, that a witch has no power to harm (or to prophesy) outside her partnership with the devil." Reed quotes King James I: the devil seeks to destroy the soul or the body or both, as God permits, and God draws out of that evil glory to himself. The Devil sees our "affections" and conforms himself to deceive us. Since God permits the evil behind the witches' intervention, the sin is in Macbeth's 'affection' that "thrusts him outside God's established order and protection."

18. Cf. "Let every soldier hew him down a bough/And bear't before him" (*Mac.* 5.4.4–5); "Who can impress the forest, bid the tree/Unfix his earth-bound root?" (4.1.95–96). Luther uses the image of the withered branch to describe the damned man and free will (Martin Luther, "An Attack on Free Will," in Miola 2004:115–116).

19. St. John Chrysostom similarly argued that dead Christian bodies can overwhelm emperors (Chrysostom, *On Babylas*, SC 367, Schatkin 274=Migne *Patrologiae Graecae* 50, 572; Shepardson 2009: 108–109).

20. Macbeth sold his soul to the devil ("mine eternall Jewell/Given to the common Enemie of Man" 3.1.70–71) (Elliott 1960:112–113). Although he fears the Ghost of Banquo (3.4.51–52, 69–70) and is reluctant to kill Macduff (5.8.5–6), he refuses Macduff's offer of captivity (5.8.23–27), a form of penance (Elliott 1960:223). While Macbeth may reject this out of pride (26, 223), he acts as if his death is deserved. His despair is that of the Calvinist reprobate who has been damned by God and cannot be saved (but compare Miola 2004:xvi).

References Cited

Asquith, Clare. *Shadowplay: The Hidden Beliefs and Coded Politics of William Shakespeare*. New York: Public Affairs, 2005.

Bowden, Henry Sebastian. *The Religion of Shakespeare. Chiefly from the Writings of the Late Mr. Richard Simpson, M.A.* London: Burns & Oates, 1899.

Bradbrook, M. C. "The Sources of *Macbeth*." *Aspects of* Macbeth. *Articles Reprinted from Shakespeare Survey*, edited by Kenneth Muir and Philip Edwards. 12–25. Cambridge: Cambridge University Press, 1977. [*Shakespeare Survey* 4 (1951)].

Braunmuller, A. R., ed. *Macbeth*. Cambridge: Cambridge University Press, 1997.

Brown, John Russell. *Macbeth*. Houndmills, U.K.: Palgrave, 2005.

Bullough, Geoffrey, ed. *Narrative and Dramatic Sources of Shakespeare*. Vol.7. London: Routledge and Kegan Paul, 1973.

Curry, Walter Clyde. *Shakespeare's Philosophical Patterns*. Second ed. Baton Rouge: Louisiana State University Press, 1959.

Elliott, G. R. *Dramatic Providence in* Macbeth. Princeton: Princeton University Press, 1960.

Greenblatt, Stephen. *Hamlet in Purgatory*. Princeton: Princeton University Press, 2001.

_____. "Shakespeare Bewitched." *New Historical Literary Study: Essays in Reproducing Texts, Representing History,* edited by Jeffrey N. Cox and Larry J. Reynolds. 108–135. Princeton: Princeton University Press.

Heilman, Robert B. "The Criminal as Tragic Hero: Dramatic Methods." *Aspects of* Macbeth. *Articles Reprinted from Shakespeare Survey*, edited by Kenneth Muir and Philip Edwards. 26–38. Cambridge: Cambridge University Press, 1977. [*Shakespeare Survey* 19 (1966)].

Honan, Park. *Shakespeare. A Life*. Oxford: Oxford University Press, 1998.

Honigmann, E. A. J. *Shakespeare the 'Lost Years.'* 2nd ed. Manchester: Manchester University Press, 1998.

Jones, Emrys. *Scenic Form in Shakespeare*. Oxford: Oxford University Press, 1971.

Labriolle, de, P. *The Life and Times of St. Ambrose*. Translated by Herbert Wilson. London: B. Herder Book Co., 1928.

Leibeschuetz, J. H. W. G., trans. *Ambrose of Milan. Political Letters and Speeches*. Liverpool: Liverpool University Press, 2005.

McLynn, N. *Ambrose of Milan. Church and Court in a Christian Capital*. Berkeley: University of California Press, 1994.

Milward, Peter. *The Mediaeval Dimension in Shakespeare's Plays*. Studies in Renaissance Literature 7. Lewiston, NY: The Edwin Mellen Press, 1990.

_____. *Shakespeare the Papist*. Ave Maria, FL: Sapientia, 2005.

_____. "Shakespeare's Jesuit Schoolmasters." *Theatre and Religion. Lancastrian Shakespeare*, edited by Richard Dutton, Alison Findlay, and Richard Wilson. 62–65. Manchester: Manchester University Press, 2003a.

_____. *Shakespeare's Meta-drama*. Hamlet *and* Macbeth. Tokyo: Sophia U, 2003b.

_____. *Shakespeare's Religious Background*. Chicago: Loyola University Press, 1973.

Miola, Robert. "Jesuit Drama in Early Modern England." *Theatre and Religion. Lancastrian Shakespeare*, edited by Richard Dutton, Alison Findlay, and Richard Wilson. 71–86. Manchester: Manchester University Press, 2003.

_____, ed. *Macbeth*. New York: W.W. Norton, 2004.

Mitchell, Stephen. *A History of the Later Roman Empire AD 284–641*. Malden, MA: Blackwell, 2007.

Moorhead, John. *Ambrose. Church and Society in the Late Roman World.* London: Longman, 1999.

Moulton, Richard G. "From *Shakespeare as a Dramatic Artist.*" Macbeth. *Critical Essays,* edited by S. Schoenbaum. 59–79. New York: Garland Publishing, 1991. [Richard G. Moulton. *Shakespeare as a Dramatic Artist.* Oxford: Clarendon, 1885, 144–167].

Paul, Henry N. *The Royal Play of* Macbeth. New York: The Macmillan Co., 1950.

Reed, Robert Rentoul, Jr. *Crime and God's Judgment in Shakespeare.* Lexington: University of Kentucky Press, 1984.

Rozett, Martha Tuck. *The Doctrine of Election and the Emergence of Elizabethan Tragedy.* Princeton: Princeton University Press, 1984.

Shell, Alison. "'We Are Made a Spectacle': Campion's Dramas." *The Reckoned Expense. Edmund Campion and The Early English Jesuits,* edited by Thomas M. McCoog, S.J. 103–118. Woodbridge: Boydell Press, 1996.

Shepardson, Christine. "Rewriting Julian's Legacy: John Chrysostom's *On Babylas* and Libanius' *Oration* 24." *Journal of Late Antiquity* 2.1 (2009):99–115.

Simons, Joseph., ed. and trans. *Ambrosia. A Neo-Latin Drama by Edumund Campion, S.J.* Assen: Van Gorcum, 1970.

Valentin, Jean-Marie. *Les jésuites et le theatre (1554–1680).* Paris: Éditions Desjonquères, 2001.

Wickham, Glynne. "Hell-Castle and its Door-Keeper." *Aspects of* Macbeth. *Articles Reprinted from Shakespeare Survey,* edited by Kenneth Muir and Philip Edwards. 39–45. Cambridge: Cambridge University Press, 1977. (Reprint *Shakespeare Survey* 19 (1966)).

Wilks, John S. *The Idea of Conscience in Renaissance Tragedy.* London: Routledge, 1990.

Williams, Daniel H. *Ambrose of Milan and the End of the Nicene-Arian Conflicts.* Oxford: Clarendon, 1995.

Williams, G.W. "The Third Murderer in *Macbeth.*" *Shakespeare Quarterly* 23 (1972):261.

Williams, Stephen, and Gerard Friell. *Theodosius. The Empire at Bay.* New Haven: Yale University Press, 1994.

Wills, Garry. *Witches and Jesuits. Shakespeare's Macbeth.* New York: Oxford University Press, 1995.

Wilson, Richard. "Introduction: a Torturing Hour — Shakespeare and the Martyrs." *Theatre and Religion. Lancastrian* Shakespeare, edited by Richard Dutton, Alison Findlay, and Richard Wilson. 24–26. Manchester: Manchester University Press, 2003.

_____. *Secret Shakespeare. Studies in Theatre, Religion and Resistance.* Manchester: Manchester University Press, 2004.

2

The (Im)perfect Wagnerite
Bernard Shaw and Richard Wagner

Christopher Innes

Abstract

Shaw is generally seen as in the school of Ibsen and naturalism. This disguises the true qualities of Shaw's plays, which are grotesquely realistic with strongly symbolic characterization. Seeing his work in the perspective of Wagner — in particular the interpretation of Wagner given in Shaw's book, The Perfect Wagnerite — *clarifies Shaw's work. In addition to scattered references to Wagner, or similar characters, a tetralogy analogous to the* Ring Cycle *can be found in Shaw's work; and the parallels expose a new dimension of subtextual political commentary in his plays.*

It is received knowledge that Bernard Shaw admired Ibsen, and emulated him in his own plays, addressing comparable themes in a naturalistic style. Delivered as a series of Fabian lectures in 1890 and published in 1891, *The Quintessence of Ibsenism* was put together while Shaw was working on his first play, *Widowers' Houses*. And indeed *Widowers' Houses* started out as a collaboration between Shaw and William Archer, the English translator of Ibsen, while some of the principles Shaw ascribed to Ibsen's drama in *The Quintessence of Ibsenism*— in particular the substitution of discussion for conventional dramatic climax, or the attack on conventional moral categories of hero and villain — apply directly to his own dramaturgy, possibly more so indeed than to Ibsen's. And the connections continue, even if at times coincidental. *Widowers' Houses* was performed in 1892 at J. T. Grein's Independent Theatre, which had opened with the first English production of Ibsen's *Ghosts* just earlier in the same year, while Janet Achurch who had played Nora in the London premier of *A Doll's House* (1889) went on to act the lead female roles in several of Shaw's plays, including *Candida* in 1897, which Shaw was later to describe as "a counterblast to Ibsen's *Doll's House*, showing that in the real typical doll's house it is the man who is the doll."[1] This view of Shaw as a follower and epigone of Ibsen has been the unquestioned standard.

Yet if one looks at Shaw's early plays with an open, objective eye, there seems to be remarkably little about them that could be called "Ibsenite." The "Ibsen

Club" in *The Philanderer* is presented as parody, despite the prominent bust of the whiskered Norwegian dramatist on display, while a play like *Widowers' Houses*— Shaw's very first play, which could therefore be expected to show Ibsen's influence at its most obvious, particularly with the involvement of William Archer — is filled with very un-naturalistic elements. Characters have symbolic and heavily moralized names: Cokane for a dandified procurer, Lickcheese for a creepingly obsequious evictor and slum rent-collector. Behavior is not motivated psychologically, but as a display of social determinism or even archetypal patterns: as with the young rich girl, Blanche's gratuitous physical torture of a serving maid, or her blatant sexuality, described as "a flush of undisguised animal excitement" and explicitly labeled as "this ferocity is erotic" (Shaw 1965:27).

So it is perhaps hardly surprising that Shaw and Archer proved incompatible as co-writers; and one can easily guess that the collaboration broke up because Shaw was pulling the play in directions quite alien to Ibsen. "Grotesque realism," the label with which Shaw identified this play in his preface to *Plays Unpleasant*, is a far cry from naturalism (Shaw 1986:12). However, there is a far nearer source than Ibsen for a play like *Widowers' Houses*— one which accommodates, even encourages symbolic characterization and archetypal behavior.

When the play was collected in 1898, and published together with *The Philanderer* and *Mrs Warren's Profession*, in *Plays Unpleasant*, the book Shaw was working on was *The Perfect Wagnerite*, published in exactly the same year. And when the Preface to *Plays Unpleasant* asserts that "the New Theatre," which Shaw's plays are intended for, "would never have come into existence but for the plays of Ibsen" then the very next reference is to "Wagner's Niebelungen tetralogy" (Shaw 1986:11–12). Ibsen and Wagner are equally responsible, in the view Shaw puts forward here, for the development of the modern drama in which his own plays are the prime example; and a few sentences further on "the Wagner Festival Playhouse at Bayreuth" is held up as an ideal example of the new stagecraft. While of course *The Perfect Wagnerite* was written some years later than *Widowers' Houses*, almost the whole time Shaw was working on that play, he was also producing a weekly column of music criticism, which was his main profession for almost 20 years, from 1876 all the way to 1894. And his music criticism is filled with articles about and references to Wagner and to *The Ring of the Niebelungs*. (In the index to the collected music criticism, for example, there are 216 entries under Richard Wagner — as opposed to the next most discussed composer, Wolfgang Mozart with 153.) The rationale for this emphasis on Wagner is explained by Shaw's preface, where Wagner is labeled "the Liberator" (Shaw 1981:1:59). As Shaw describes it, at the beginning of his career as a London music critic, Wagner "was then the furiously abused coming man" with the only pieces of his music ever played being "the Ride of the Valkyries at the Promenade Concerts" or "in pantomime harlequinades the clown produced a trombone, played a bit of the Pilgrim's March from Tannhäuser *fortissimo* as well as he could, and said 'The music of the future!'" (Shaw 1981:1:59). So, as a self-described "violent Wagnerite," Shaw was openly contributing through his music criticism to the battle over Wagner, and in a sense *Widowers' Houses* could be seen (among other things) as yet another provocative blow in this musical war.

Indeed, the original title for this play was — suggestively — *Rhine Gold*, and the first Act specifically takes place on the banks of the Rhine: "looking down the Rhine towards Bonn" with "the gate leading from the garden to the riverside ... on the right." In addition, just as in Wagner's *Rheingold*, the plot turns on the "theft" of gold, in the form of exploitive rents; while the major conflict in the play revolves around Trench's insistence that Love be separated from filthy lucre — which, as we shall see is the premise in Shaw's discussion of Wagner's opera — demanding that Blanche give up her father's "tainted money," only to find out that his own income comes from exactly the same source, so that he and Blanche's father Sartorius are "just as bad" (Shaw 1965:13, 18).

At first glance, of course, there is nothing remotely Wagnerian in the plot or characters. The sole candidate for Rhine Maiden is the only-too-human Blanche; and all the figures, including her, are relentlessly modern and very down-to-earth: slum-landlord, rent-collector, real-estate investor. However, for Shaw the mythical world of Wagner's Ring was a clear representation of nineteenth-century society in an allegorical disguise that simply revealed its essential nature underneath respectable bourgeois appearances. So in *The Perfect Wagnerite* the dwarf's discovery of the gold in the river is compared to the Klondike gold rush (a very contemporary allusion in 1898) while, referring to Alberich, Shaw remarks that "such dwarves are quite common in London" (Shaw 1923:8). In particular Alberich's exploitation of his own people, after forswearing love to gain the gold and welding it into a ring that gives him power, is presented as "a poetic vision of unregulated industrial capitalism as it was made known in Germany in the middle of the nineteenth century by Engels's *Condition of the Labouring Classes in England.*" So that Alberich's gloomy mine "might just as well be a match-factory, with yellow phosphorus, phossy jaw, a large dividend, and plenty of clergyman shareholders. Or it might be a whitelead factory, or a chemical works, or a pottery, or a rail-shunting yard, or a tailoring shop, or a little gin-sodden laundry ... or any other of the places where human life and welfare are daily sacrificed in order that some greedy foolish" plutocrat may pile up riches (Shaw 1923:17–18). Indeed, from the perspective of the perfect Wagnerite, Wagner was the ideal Shavian revolutionary. As Shaw points out, in 1848-1849, Europe's year of revolution, Wagner had been one of the leaders of the Dresden uprising (together with the anarchist Bakunin — whom Shaw at one point identifies with Wagner's Siegfried) (Shaw 1923:60). As a direct result, Wagner had to flee to Switzerland before taking refuge in Paris. He also wrote numerous socialist pamphlets, including one on "Art and Revolution" which Shaw called "the pamphlets and manifestoes of a born agitator" (Shaw 1923:30). As Shaw pointed out, Wagner wrote *Rheingold* in direct response to the failure of the year of revolution.

However, the correspondences between the world of the Niebelungs and the system of industrial capitalism are by no means one-to-one, because—as Shaw reminds us—no allegory can have exact parallels if it is going to be artistically effective. And Shaw's point about Wagner is even more applicable to his own reverse allegory, where modern characters in the setting of late nineteenth-/early twentieth-century capitalism are given shifting analogies to figures in the Ring cycle. Indeed Shaw's Wagnerian reference is still more sub-textual than Wagner's nineteenth-century parallels, and is made vaguer by pointing rather to Shaw's highly political interpretation of the Ring, than to Wagner's original operas. In addition, Shaw deliberately makes the references in his plays a partial echo, instead of setting up any detailed parallels in either character or plot. So they function as subliminal suggestion.

An example of the way this Wagnerian analogy works is Blanche, the anti-heroine from *Widowers' Houses*. As a single figure from an ambiguous social background, she is a quasi-realistic updating of Wagner's three identical and biologically ambiguous females, half-human, half-fish. The purity of the Rhine Maidens is represented solely by her name (Blanche ironically signifying "white"), while their innocent sexuality is transformed into her "animalistic" vitality and erotic "ferocity"—yet this could be seen as the equivalent of the Rhine Maidens' tantalization of Alberich and their devastating rejection of the dwarf whom they have aroused. At the same time, in representing Blanche as completely self-centered, Shaw is simply transcribing his take on the Klondike equivalent of the Rhine Maidens, who do not care what effect their seduction and rejection may have on the dwarf. His characterization in *Widowers' Houses* follows the opening metaphor of his Rhine Gold discussion:

> Try to imagine yourself [as a young and good-looking woman] at Klondyke five years ago. The place is teeming with gold.... Now suppose a man comes along: a man with common desires, cupidities, ambitions, just like most of the men you know.... So long as he is preoccupied with love of you, the gold and all that it implies, will escape him.... Not until he forswears love will he stretch out his hand to the gold, and found the Plutonic empire for himself. But ... he may be an ugly, ungracious, unamiable person, whose affections may seem merely ludicrous and despicable to you. In that case you may repulse him.... What is left to him then but to curse the love he can never win, and turn remorselessly to the gold? [Shaw 1923:6].

And Trench's demand that Blanche give up Sartorius's gold—only to discover that the money he himself lives on comes from the same source—is a clear variation of the dialectic between love and the plutonic system set up by Wagner's *Rheingold*.

The Wagnerian dimension to Shaw's plays has of course been discussed by others, and indeed the notion has been around for some considerable time. Among the first was Arthur Ganz, who in the 1970s suggested parallels with a wide range of Wagner operas—for instance noting the similarity in dramatic situation between *Lohengrin* and Shaw's *Caesar and Cleopatra*, or between *Tannhäuser* and the Hell scene of *Man and Superman* (187–207). Ganz was followed a decade later by Robert Coskren, who searched for echoes of Wagner's "naive hero," Siegfried, claiming that "Shaw's 'Siegfried' plays include *Widowers' Houses, Candida, Major Barbara, Back to Methuselah* and *Saint Joan*" (Coskren:27). However, as a result of this narrow focus, Coskren concluded that Shaw's main purpose in setting up Wagnerian parallels was parody. So the frail poet Marchbanks in *Candida* becomes a parody of Siegfried, or (after her death) St. Joan's appearance in the dreaming king's bedchamber is presented as a gender-reversed image of an impotent Siegfried (Joan herself) unable to wake Brunhilde (in the shape of King Charles). But if, instead of a specific figure, one searches for patterns of action or relationship, then something very different and far more interesting emerges. Instead of parody, the Wagnerian parallels serve to shadow-in a wider significance for otherwise everyday characters, suggesting an archetypal dimension to their activities, or showing the glimpse of another perspective in which they become carriers of destiny.

In general Wagner's mythical figures move in pairs: Wotan accompanied by the cunning Loki; Alberich and his henchman-brother, Mime—building on this, in Shaw's view, the action is grounded in a dialectic of Love versus Plutonic power. (So Alberich has to foreswear love in order to be able to grab the gold, as indeed do the giants, while Wotan has to give up the gold to keep Freia, the Goddess of youth and desire.) And, Shaw carries over the same inversion of standard values that he asserts in Wagner: "let us not forget that godhead means to Wagner infirmity and compromise, and manhood strength and integrity" (Shaw 1923:33). (As a sign of which, Wagner's human heroes are singular: Siegfried and Brunhilde.)

So in *Widowers' Houses*, the weak-willed Trench, as a tourist in the opening scene, like Wotan a wanderer, is accompanied by the insinuating Cokane (a sly equivalent to Wagner's manipulative Loki), while the plutocratic exploiter of the poor, Sartorius, dependent on his rent-collector Lickcheese, clearly echoes Alberich and his henchman-brother, Mime—with Sartorius's apparent respectability expressing Shaw's perception that "though Alberich in 1850, [when Wagner started on *Rheingold*] may have been merely the vulgar factory-owner portrayed in Friedrich Engel's *Condition of the Working Classes*, in 1876 [when Wagner finished *Götterdammerung*] he was well on the way to becoming a model philanthropic employer and financier" in order "to make money on the *modern* scale" [My emphasis] (Shaw 1923:103–104). This model is still more developed in Shaw's 1905 *Major Barbara*, where "merchant of death," Undershaft is an exact equivalent to the arms manufacturer "Krupp of Essen" cited by Shaw in the 1913 edition of *The Perfect Wagnerite*. Similarly, when Lickcheese arrives with "a silk hat of the glossiest black" on his head, it is Shaw's equivalent of the Tarnhelm manufactured by Mime, the magic helmet which allows its possessor to appear in any shape. As Shaw put it in *The Perfect Wagnerite*: "This helmet is a very common article in our streets, where it generally takes the form of a tall hat. It makes a man invisible as a shareholder, and changes him into various shapes, such as a pious Christian, a subscriber to hospitals, a benefactor to the poor ... when he is really a pitiful parasite..." (Shaw 1923:18–19).

Where in *Widower's Houses* the analogies are subtextual, Shaw specifically referred to his 1922 five-part *Back to Methuselah* in terms of Wagner's *Ring Cycle*, and indeed there are all sorts of Wagnerian echoes scattered fairly randomly through all five of the sections in this "metabiological Pentateuch"— as Shaw subtitled his eight-hour history of the world from the Creation to "As Far As Thought Can Reach" (AD 31,920, the date of the concluding play) in conscious superemulation of Wagner's four-part mythos. So, for example, the Biblical Cain, depicted as "natural man," can be seen as equivalent to Siegfried, but in a crude and solely physical parody of Wagner's hero. However, the individual parallels are relatively insignificant in thematic terms; and where Shaw undoubtedly intended his audiences to draw the comparison with Wagner would have been in terms of sheer scale: both *Back to Methuselah* and the *Ring* being outsize, massive, multi-part works, constructing a new mythology based on existing archetypes.[2] But *Back to Methuselah* is more a recapitulation and recuperation of isolated Wagnerian elements on a very general level. Over the two previous decades Shaw wrote four plays that correspond directly to Wagner's tetralogy, and in the same order — even if not consecutively. Viewed from the perspective of Shaw's book, *The Perfect Wagnerite*, there is a comparable *Ring Cycle* embedded in Shaw's dramatic works.

Shaw's "Wagnerian" tetralogy starts, of course — as we have seen — with *Widowers' Houses* (1892) as *Rheingold*. Slightly more separated than the four sections of Wagner's *Ring*, since the hyper-prolific Shaw wrote other plays in between, I would argue that *Mrs Warren's Profession* (1902) in important ways echoes *Die Valkyrie*, while *Major Barbara* (1905) is — as has been very generally recognized — Shaw's *Siegfried*, and *Heartbreak House* (1919) is the equivalent of *Götterdammerung*.

Mrs Warren's Profession, the next major play after *Widower's Houses*, can also be seen as the next play in Shaw's Wagnerian cycle. One major theme is the parentage of the daughter of the one-time prostitute turned wealthy brothel owner — and the possibility of incest with the men who propose marriage to her. Vivie Warren's father, it turns out, may be either the family friend Sir George Crofts — the major investor in Mrs Warren's business, who makes her a business proposal of marriage — or the local clergyman, the Rev. Samuel Gardner, a former customer of Mrs Warren, whose son offers a sentimental proposal. At first glance, in the beginning of the play, Vivie echoes Wagner's Sieglinde, with a (in Shaw's play, clichéd) romantic relationship to Frank Gardner, who may indeed, like Wagner's Siegmund, be her brother. And indeed, although juvenile, Frank, shotgun in hand, has a stand-off with Croft (as Wagner's Siegmund does with

Wotan, sword against spear). Later Vivie, the mathematical "wrangler" from Cambridge University who rejects her putative father — the half-blind Wotan in the shape of Sir George Croft, the major stakeholder in Mrs Warren's brothels — and ends up (by her own choice) in isolation in an enclosed office, rejecting life and love in favor of chartered accountancy, has clearly evolved into Shaw's Brunhilde (shut away on a flame-circled mountain-top). Typically, given his contempt for the popularity of "The Ride of the Valkyries," this part of Wagner's opera is omitted from *Mrs Warren's Profession*. But the brothels of the play are clearly the equivalent of the slum-business of *Widowers' Houses*, or the white-lead factories mentioned by Shaw in his analysis of the analogy between Wagner's *Ring Cycle* and nineteenth-century Capitalism. In the same way, Mrs Warren herself is both the morally outraged Fricka, Queen of Valhalla (which in Victorian terms precisely equates to the luxurious palaces of dreams, her brothels), and also — as a proponent of women's rights — one of the Valkyries.

Jon Wisenthal has convincingly argued that all Shaw's plays are strongly operatic — quoting specifically from Shaw's 1935 autobiographical preface written for the first edition of his music criticism, *London Music in 1888–89 as Heard by Corno di Bassetto* (1937), where Shaw recounts that "Harley Granville-Barker was not far out when, at a rehearsal of one of my plays, he cried out 'Ladies and gentlemen: will you please remember this is Italian opera.'"[3] The actors being so addressed were rehearsing *Man and Superman* (1904), where the third act (the hell scene) figures Tanner — the role played by Granville-Barker — as Mozart's *Don Giovanni*, with the heiress pursuing him, Ann Whitefield, as Donna Ana. The operatic orchestration of Shaw's plays in general, scored as they are for soprano, alto, tenor and bass voices, with operatic rhetorical tropes, has long been recognized. Wisenthal has also written a long essay on *Major Barbara*'s connections to *Siegfried* taking Barbara herself as a warrior maid (her Salvation Army uniform substituting for the Wagnerian steel cuirass and horned helmet). Indeed it is so much a commonplace that *Major Barbara* is an almost point-to-point updated equivalent of Wagner's third episode in the *Ring Cycle*, that it hardly now needs stressing.[4] The triumphant march (itself yet another operatic motif: the wedding march from *Lucia di Lammermoor*) which leaves Barbara in despair, can be seen as the Ride of the Valkyries. Undershaft himself is generally agreed to represent Wotan — needing an orphan to redeem Valhalla, in the shape of Undershaft's factory town on a hill: "white walls ... tall trees, domes ... beautifully situated and beautiful in itself" with his partner Lazarus as Alberich (Shaw 1965:493). The outsider, Cusins (loosely associated with Shaw's friend, the classicist Gilbert Murray) as Siegfried. Both are children from incestuous marriages (with Cusin's claim to be an orphan because his mother is his "father's deceased wife's sister," their marriage thus being illegal in England, as the comic equivalent to the Siegmund/Sieglinde, brother/sister pairing) (Shaw 1965:495). And Cusins indeed emerges as the hero to win his Brunhilde on the hilltop of Undershaft's armaments factory, by cutting through social conventions just as Siegfried walked through the fires surrounding Wagner's Brunhilde (both of which for Shaw are "a lie, an illusion, a mirage" — Wotan's flames being an obvious allegory, symbolizing that the fire of "hell was a fiction devised for the intimidation and subjection of the masses"), and so on (Shaw 1923:45).

By contrast, Wagner has never been mentioned in terms of *Heartbreak House*. Yet this is clearly Shaw's *Götterdammerung*. Looking at his introduction to the 1922 edition of *The Perfect Wagnerite*, the total destruction of the First World War had made Shaw rethink the status of Wagner's final play in the *Ring*, which Shaw had earlier dismissed as "grand opera": a romantic and conventional piece that failed to measure up to the revolutionary potential of the first three operas. Instead Shaw declares:

> As to the sociological aspect of The Ring ... it seems to challenge the so-called Great War to invalidate it, if it can.... The Ring ends with everybody dead except the three mermaids; and though the war went far enough in that conclusive direction to suggest that the next war may possibly even kill the mermaids with 'depth charges,' the curtain is not yet down on our drama, and we have to carry on as best we can [Shaw 1923:x–xi].

This is certainly the situation at the end of *Heartbreak House*. A poetic depiction of the self-destruction of the leisured classes, whose lack of responsibility has been responsible for the First World War, and will destroy them too, the play ends with Heartbreak House (which, with nautical echoes in its architecture, represents the ship of state, or England) as the target of bombs from the German Zeppelins. The plutocrat Mangan, who has tried to buy the hand of the young Ellie Dunn, and the Burglar, who has tried to blackmail the owner of the house, the superannuated inventor Captain Shotover, are both killed by a bomb when taking refuge in Captain Shotover's munitions store, situated in a neighboring quarry. This is the exact equivalent of Wagner's removing Günther, the ruler of the Gibichungs who tricks Siegfried into giving him Brunhilde, and Alberich's surviving son Hagen, who has stolen the dead Siegfried's ring. During the same Zeppelin raid in *Heartbreak House* the priest's house has also been destroyed, representing both the ending of the manipulation of religion by the elite to rule over the masses, and the destruction of the Gibichung Hall. When the characters draw back the curtains and light all the lights in the House to attract the Zeppelins, they are metaphorically at least (as the stage directions explicitly state) keeping "*the home fires burning*" (Shaw 1965:802). It is the burning of Valhalla, even if delayed (as Shaw's comment has suggested) until the Zeppelins return, perhaps the next night. Further, *Götterdammerung* has three females trios: the Norns, and the Rhinemaidens, as well as Brunhilde, Gutrune (Günther's sister whom Siegfried is drugged into loving), and Valtruta (the Valkryie who comes to beg Brunhilde's aid). *Heartbreak House* also has a trio: Shotover's daughters, Hermione Hushabye, and Lady Utterword, plus Ellie Dunn who becomes the ancient Shotover's mystic wife. Shaw also referred to this play as his *King Lear*, who famously had three daughters; and the Shake-spearian echo combines with the Wagnerian. Siegfried is split into two heroes, each of whom lacks something to make them truly heroic: Hector Hushabye (personally brave, with a drawer full of medals to prove it, but incapable of intervening to change the system), and Mazzini Dunn, named after the Italian revolutionary, who is a romantic idealist. As for the decrepit and superannuated Captain Shotover, being under the control of the millionaire Capitalist Mangan, who doubles for Hagen, Alberich's son, Shotover fits the pattern of Wagner's Günther, King of the Gibichungs, more than he does Shakespeare's Lear.

Throughout these four plays there is nothing parodic in the Wagnerian parallels. The analogies are reversed so that where Wagner's mythical Gods, Giants, Dwarves and Human Heroes refer indirectly to the social structure of nineteenth-century industrial capitalism, Shaw's modern plutocrats, arms manufacturers and shareholders relate sub-textually to the archetypal figures of Wagner's Ring. The effect of Shaw's parallels is to emphasize that the realistic and contemporary individuals in his plays have a wider status. Glimpsing their mythic aura, we see them as representatives of Capitalism. They become no less significant in the history of humanity than Wagner's superhuman beings are in the rise and fall of the whole of creation.

YORK UNIVERSITY

Notes

1. Shaw, *Evening Standard*, 28 November 1944. For a more extended discussion of this relationship, see my *Modern British Drama* (Innes 2002:14–22).
2. The Wagnerian parallels have been explored by Coskren (39–43). See also Wisenthal, (1974:207 ff.).
3. See J. L. Wisenthal, "'Please Remember This is Italian Opera': Shaw's Plays as Music-Drama" (1998:283–308).
4. The points here are summarized from a wide range of critics: J. L. Wisenthal (1972); Arthur Ganz, Robert Coskren (33–38), and Alfred Turco (117–119).

References Cited

Coskren, Robert. "*Siegfried* Elements in the Plays of Bernard Shaw." *Shaw* II (1982):39–43.
Ganz, Arthur. "The Playwright as Perfect Wagnerite: Motifs from the Music Dramas in the Theatre of Bernard Shaw." *Comparative Drama* 13 (Fall 1979):189–201.
Innes, Christopher. *Modern British Drama: The Twentieth Century*. Cambridge: Cambridge University Press, 2002.
Shaw, Bernard. *The Complete Bernard Shaw: Plays*, edited by Dan Laurence. London: Paul Hamlyn, 1965.
_____. *The Perfect Wagnerite*. London: Constable & Co, 1923.
_____. *Plays Unpleasant*. Harmondsworth: Penguin Books, 1986.
_____. *Shaw's Music: The Complete Musical Criticism in Three Volumes*, edited by Dan Laurence. London, Toronto: Bodley Head, 1981.

Turco, Alfred. *Shaw's Moral Vision*. Ithaca: Cornell University Press, 1976.

Wisenthal, J. L. *The Marriage of Contraries*. Cambridge: Harvard University Press, 1974.

_____. "'Please Remember This Is Italian Opera': Shaw's Plays as Music-Drama." *The Cambridge Companion to George Bernard Shaw*, edited by Christopher Innes. 283–308. Cambridge: Cambridge University Press, 1998.

_____. "The Underside of Undershaft: a Wagnerian Motif in *Major Barbara*." *The Shaw Review* 15.2. (May 1972):56–61.

Gardens and Libraries in Shaw's *Widowers' Houses*
"Life Here Is a Perfect Idyll"
Tony J. Stafford

Abstract

Many scholars praise Shaw's first play for its propagandistic and social criticism values, but Shaw insisted that Widowers' House *is not a "pamphlet in dialogue" but a "work of art as much as any comedy by Moliere." This is not to say that the play is not a virulent attack on greed, exploitation, tainted money, and the class system, but Shaw's artistic completeness of conception leads us into a deeper understanding of the causes beneath the surface of the social evils, and he uses the garden and library settings as a way of developing the idea that the surface problems are a reflection of the system of hypocrisy and pretense which lie deeper in society and the individuals who make up this society. For Sartorius, as a way of gaining entrance into higher social levels, appearance is of prime importance, and the garden and library function as vital tools in his achievement of that goal.*

Even though *Widowers' Houses* is Shaw's first play, it has an artistic completeness of conception and a surprising sophistication in style, technique, and content. Some critics, ignoring the artistic issue, have chosen to focus on the satiric and propagandistic elements in the play, labeling it Shaw's "darkest and bleakest" comedy, concerned more with "human depravity" rather than the traditional comedic subject of "human folly" (Marker 1998:110), and calling it an "insistent piece of economic propaganda" (Ganz 1983:81). But others have argued for its artistic qualities, qualities as McDowell says that "compensate for the flaws that its detractors ... have overemphasized" (1994:231). McDowell continues by pointing out that for a beginning playwright, Shaw exhibits an expertise in "directness of approach, subtlety of implication, master of the tensely drawn scene, and remarkable terseness and economy of line" (1994:239). Indeed, Shaw himself insisted that *Widowers' Houses* is not a "pamphlet in dialogue" but a "work of art as much as any comedy by Moliere" (McDowell 1994:238). Shaw was justifiably proud of its artistic worth and was cognizant of the fullness of its conception, of its "viability in the theater" and the "subtlety and the range of implication present in it" (McDowell 1994:238). This is not to say that the propagandistic element does not make a strong presence in Shaw's play, as it does in all of his plays, and is indeed a virulent attack on greed, exploitation, tainted money, and the class system. But the artistry, while not perfect, also rewards study. By examining Shaw's use of garden and library settings in *Widowers' Houses* in meticulous detail, one gains an appreciation of the complexity, subtlety, and mastery which Shaw therein reveals, as well as an insight into the play's deeper textual implications.[1]

As with any viable piece of dramatic literature, critics have noted a number of different themes in *Widowers' Houses*. Some have focused on Shaw's attack on society, on the exploitation of the poor, on slum-landlordism, on greed, and indifference toward the destitute. Charles Carpenter, for example, notes that the "broad target is the prevalent assumption that capitalism is the best of all possible economic systems," that "poverty and its consequences are inevitable," and that "the slum mortgagee and landlord are powerless to alter the state of society" (1969:36). As Marker puts it, "its theme is ruthless exploitation of the destitute and homeless by the mercantile and the upper classes alike" and its intent is "to implicate every member of the audience in that social crime" (1998:104). Carpenter adds that Shaw "puts the blame squarely on society as a whole" (1969: 35). But, on the level of the individual characters, Shaw inculcates an entirely different theme. While these statements which the play makes about society in general, as noted by the critics, are true, a far more stinging indictment arises from the fact that these evils exist because they are supported by a system of hypocrisy and pretense as practiced by those who are trying to gain respect and acceptance into a class which they yearn to be a part of. Thus, Shaw uses the settings of gardens and libraries as one means by which he is able to develop and dramatize in a subtle and powerful way his major theme involving hypocrisy and pretense.

Although the garden and library are merely stage settings, much of Shaw's intent is contained in his stage directions, and his descriptions support and eventually merge with the action and characters. It has long been recognized that Shaw's stage directions contain vital insights, that his "stage directions are more revelatory than the characters' speeches" (Ganz 1983:85) and, even as a beginner, Shaw exhibits his determination "from the outset to direct his plays on paper, down to the smallest movement or inflection" (Marker 1998:106). In a study of the influence of Shaw's stage directions on a playwright such as Oscar Wilde, Morrison points out that Shaw "continued to develop stage directions into a combination of psychological analysis, political documentary, and philosophical discourse, shaping flesh and blood characters and their whole moral universe, with a vigour and artistry unmatched by any other playwright" (1981:9). The same may be said of his physical descriptions as well.[2] Nothing in Shaw is unimportant, and everything down to the smallest detail has significance, such as his use of gardens and libraries, a study of which is rewarded with an understanding of his intent and an awareness of the interrelatedness of all the parts in his plays.

In *Widowers' Houses*, the very first words which Shaw wrote for the dramatic form, preceding the rest of his canon, was "*the garden.*" This particular garden happens to be "*the garden restaurant of a hotel at Remagen on the Rhine*" (1981:31). He continues by saying that it is "*a fine afternoon in August.*" Generally, the action of Shaw's comedies takes place in splendid weather, a point which Shaw usually emphasizes. There are rarely storms, clouds, darkness, and oppressive conditions. This is not coincidental, but rather an essential part of Shaw's satiric statement. Shaw takes pains to present a surface, in a lovely garden, with delightful weather, pleasant, tranquil, and, almost, an "idyllic" world (Cokane's description), which belies the ugliness underneath, foulness composed of greed, pretense, falsity, hypocrisy, and selfishness. *Widowers' Houses* initiates the precedent for this. Underneath the pleasant August afternoon in the garden restaurant, the powerful, unwritten laws of upper echelon British society are at work.

The nature of a garden, in this case in a foreign country, the inhabitants of the garden, and the attitudes exhibited in the garden are clues to the meaning generated from such a setting. The fact that this particular garden is located in a foreign country with Englishmen there immediately establishes the fact that the people present are tourists and therefore, likely, persons of some means. Present at the beginning are Trench, the nephew of Lady Roxdale, and Cokane, a gentleman who is obsessed with propriety and all the inviolable rules of upper class England, and the subject of their opening conversation is "appearance," a common garden topic in Shaw's plays. Cokane, in point of fact, encapsulates the very essence of Shaw's gardens where appearances, acceptability, and proper conduct prevail. When Trench, who cares little for form and appearances, begins to sing a rousing drinking song, Cokane is scandalized and delivers a scalding reprimand to Trench, "in the name of common decency, Harry, will you remember that you are a Gentleman, and not a coster on Hampstead Heath on Bank Holiday," and "either you travel as a gentleman, or you travel alone," as well as "I have been uneasy all the afternoon about what they [the other English couple] must think of us. Look at our appearance" (1981:32). After Trench's casual rejoinder "what's wrong with our appearance," Cokane stresses that "how are they to know that you are *well connected* [emphasis added] if you do not shew it by your costume?" Trench concedes that "I suppose I ought to have brought a change" (1981:33). With Cokane's emphasis on social class, appearances, respectability, and proper conduct ("tact" is Cokane's favorite word for it), the theme of the garden, as well as the play itself, is established.

Cokane presents the very epitome of British garden behavior: formal, proper, prudish, and rule-bound. When Trench, who ironically is the one with the upper class connections, calls Cokane "Billy," Cokane recoils with "do stop calling me Billy in public, Trench. My name is Cokane. I am sure they were persons of consequence: you were struck with the distinguished appearance of the father yourself" (1981:32). Later, Cokane, exposing his true values, "how am I to preserve the respect of fellow travelers of position and wealth, if I am to be Billied at every turn?"(1981:42). Also, Cokane, ever the invoker of the aristocracy, turns to Trench, with no seeming motivation, and asks him, within hearing distance of the Sartoriuses, "I have often meant to ask you: is Lady Roxdale [whose name also connotes a garden, or at least the idea of a pleasant place in nature] your mother's sister or your father's" (1981:34), and when Cokane, always knowledgeable about upper class behavior, suggests that Lady Roxdale "looks forward to floating your wife in society in London" and Trench scoffs at the idea, Cokane tries to instruct him with, "you dont know the importance of these things; apparently idle ceremonial trifles, really the springs and wheels of a great aristocratic system" (1981:35). Cokane, always the picture of politeness, affability, and sometimes archness, as though he himself were a member of the aristocracy, stresses "good manners," "morals," "tact," and "delicacy! good taste! Savoir faire!" (1981:42). In the middle of the act, Sartorius and Cokane depart to visit a church, during which time the audience discovers that Trench and Blanche have already conversed and are in the process of establishing a relationship and sealing it with a kiss, which act Cokane witnesses and, alone with Trench, begins to berate Trench *"with the severity of a judge"*:

> No, my dear boy. No, no. Never. I blush for you. I was never so ashamed in my life.... No, my dear fellow, no, no. Bad taste, Harry, bad form! ... She a perfect lady, a person of the highest breeding, actually in your arms.... Have you no principles, Trench? Have you no religious convictions? Have you no acquaintance with the usages of society? [1981:42].

After Sartorius has requested that Trench receive letters from his family to the effect that Blanche would be acceptable to them, Cokane's sense of etiquette and good breeding shows once again. He knows, for example, that Lady Roxdale will want to know what Sartorius's wealth is derived from. When Trench tries to shrug off such issues, Cokane admonishes him once again with "when will you begin to get a little sense," Trench asks him not to be "moral," and Cokane cites the rules to him again with "if you are going to get money with your wife, doesnt it concern your family to know how that money was made?" (1981:47). Toward the end of the act, Shaw creates a tableau of Cokane composing a letter to Lady Roxdale on behalf of Trench, which is being dictated by Sartorial, a visual representation of Sartorius's power of control and dominant voice.

Scholars have of course been intrigued with the implications of Cokane's name. McDowell offers that Cokane's name suggests "a mindless hedonism deriving from a drug-induced lethargy and also a man who is at home in a world of illusion and false appearances, a dweller in the land of Cockaigne" (1994:238) while Woodfield asserts his name suggests "Cockaigne, the fabulous land of lux-

ury and idleness, signifying what he represents" (1991:55). But in a garden of
aristocratic behavior, what is required is a narcotic to keep ugliness, disturbance,
impoliteness, indiscretion, and abrasiveness at bay, and the drugs which provide
this are tact, good taste, delicacy, politeness, diplomacy, and proper conduct, all
of which Cokane is a master of. These drugs make social interaction function
more gently, softening the harshness of reality.

In this same garden of respectability where Cokane flourishes, Sartorius
dominates by his mere presence. Although Sartorius is not a member of the aristocracy, he is comfortable in a social setting and a garden because he has culti-
vated the manner of the upper class, the word "gentleman" being connected with
him over a half dozen times in the first act alone. It is pretense at its fullest and
the garden often is a place of great hypocritical practice. Shaw notes that Sartorius's *"incisive, domineering utterance and imposing style, with his strong aquiline
nose and resolute clean-shaven mouth, give him an air of importance"* (1981:33).
The impeccable details of his aristocratic dress, appropriate to his name and
appearance, are significant: *"he wears a light grey frock-coat with silk linings, a
white hat, and a field-glass slung in a new leather case,"* and, Shaw adds, is *"formidable to servants, not easily accessible to anyone"* (1981:33). The message is clear:
he is a man to whom appearance, and consequently acceptance, is tantamount,
and the name "Sartorius" bespeaks the importance of clothing to him (this in
ironic contrast to Trench, a member of the upper class, whose attitude toward
dress is quite casual). In short, here and throughout the play, Sartorius behaves
as though he is a member of the upper class, even though he is not. When Sartorius's porter places the packages on a table and the waiter tells him that that
table is already taken, Sartorius's reaction is extreme and revelatory, speaking
"severely" and *"with fierce condescension"* (1981:33).When Cokane attempts to
smooth things over, Sartorius arrogantly and *"coldly turn[s] his back on him"*
(1981:34). He mimics an attitude of privilege and haughtiness and is only too
willing to display what titles he can, telling Cokane, "I am a vestryman" (1981:37).

Although Sartorius has made it into the social garden, having one of his
own at Surbiton as well, he wants more, and through the rest of the garden scene,
Sartorius manifests his determination to gain upper-class acceptance through his
powerful control, especially by means of Trench's relationship with his daughter, Blanche. Shaw describes her as a *"well-dressed, well-fed, good-looking, strong-
minded young woman, presentably ladylike"* (1981:33), a Pygmalion-like creation
of Sartorius. Clearly, these two seek entrée into upper class British gardens, even
though their present search is in a foreign garden. In due time, it becomes clear
that Trench and Blanche have an attraction for each other, but Sartorius will not
let it advance until he has assurance that he gets what he wants. When Sartorius
asks Trench if there will be any objections from his family, Trench demurs that
they have nothing to do with it. Sartorius's response reveals his position, his
determination, and the importance of upper class acceptance to him: "Excuse
me sir: they have a great deal to do with it" (1981:44). Trench assures him that

she will be accepted, but Sartorius says that "that wont do for me, sir" and that "I must have a guarantee on my side that she will be received on equal terms by your family" (1981:44). He says that Trench's relatives, belonging to a social class who, in Sartorius's words, "turn their backs on newcomers whom they may not think quite good enough for them" (1981:44), will not do the same to Blanche. Trench is uncertain how to guarantee such an attitude, but Sartorius does: "When you can shew me a few letters from the principal members of your family, congratulating you in a fairly cordial way, I shall be satisfied" (1981:44). This is the crux of the play, Sartorius's prime motivation, and the essence and symbolic meaning of the garden. Sartorius has pulled himself up from extreme poverty by making a fortune in slum dwellings, and now he craves nothing more in the world than for him and his daughter to be accepted by aristocratic society, and it begins in and is defined by the garden.

On the subject of Sartorius's control, several critics have complained that "the entire play is founded on the vast coincidence that on a continental vacation the youthful hero, Dr. Harry Trench, should meet and become desperately infatuated with the daughter of a great slum landlord," who manages the very property from which his own income derives (Ganz 1983:81). Woodfield calls it "stretching both coincidence and probability; that the father has a connection to the hero through his aunt stretches both even further" (1991:55). This is inverted logic. Sartorius is not the kind of man who leaves things to chance; it is just as possible, and more than likely, that Sartorius planned this trip for him and his daughter with the full knowledge that Trench would be on the same trip, on the same boat, and staying in the same hotel, hoping that nature would take its course, and what appears to be a coincidence may well not be a chance encounter at all. As Sartorius himself tells Cokane, "the truth is, Mr. Cokane, I am quite well acquainted with Dr Trench's position and *affairs* [emphasis added]; and I have long desired to know him personally" (1981:50). By his own admission, Sartorius keeps a close eye on Lady Roxdale's family and its "affairs." It is more believable and likely that he has created this situation, and, as would be typical of him, Sartorius may have carefully calculated and anticipated everything: the "chance" meeting of Blanche and Trench, Trench's objection to Sartorius's source of income (even though he could not have foreseen Lickcheese's informing Trench about his business, he could have surmised that with the ongoing parliamentary and clerical investigations and the publication of the "blue book" sooner or later Trench would find out), Trench's complicity in the business, and Blanche's reaction.

In a performance of the play, one other graphic depiction of Sartorius's control is created by the tableau of Sartorius dictating a letter to Cokane, who is composing the letter on Trench's behalf which will be sent under Trench's name to Lady Roxdale who will actually be hearing Sartorius's voice when she reads it. Such are the convolutions necessitated by the hypocrisy of garden behavior. The scene ends with Sartorius reading the letter, which he has just dictated, although Cokane finished it, "*nodding gravely over it with complete approval*" (1981:52). The scene displays Shaw's mastery of irony and performance values.

Aside from his desire to amass wealth, Sartorius's most powerful longing is to have his daughter, Blanche, accepted into higher societal levels, and his efforts have been designed to create a young lady who will be at home in the English garden environment, even though he appears, through his determined insistence, insecure about her acceptability (known in psychology as the "reaction formation" principle or, in common parlance, "overcompensation"). When Blanche is reluctant to visit yet another church, Sartorius convinces her by reminding her that "I would like you to see everything. It is part of your education" (1981:37), a point on which she will not cross him: "Oh, my education! Very well, very well: I suppose I must go through with it" (1981:38). He has gone to great pains and expense to make her well educated and well bred. When Sartorius gives his reasons to Trench about his need for proof of acceptance by Trench's family, he makes a very revealing point when he says, "I am resolved that my daughter shall approach no circle in which she will not be received with the full consideration to which her education and her breeding (*here his self-control slips a little, and he repeats, as if Trench has contradicted him*)—I say, her breeding—entitle her" (1981:44). Shaw's stage directions communicate the depth of Sartorius's feelings on the subject. And again, a few lines later, Shaw's directions establish the importance to Sartorius of Blanche's status when Trench says "Blanche is a lady: thatll be good enough for them [his family]," and Sartorius, "*moved,*" says, "I am glad you think so" (1981:44). Blanche reveals her knowledge of the rules of polite society when she scolds Trench for speaking "to me without any introduction" (1981:38), and "you had no right to speak to me that day on board the steamer" (1981:39). But her true self lurks just below the surface. Her hypocrisy is unintentionally established when Trench reminds her that "it was you who spoke to me" (1981:39), and again later when Trench says, "here they [Sartorius and Cokane] are back again" and Blanche, her mask almost slipping, starts to curse with "Oh, d—." Again and again we see through the false façade which she maintains. A few lines later, when Cokane reprimands Trench for his behavior with her and insists that "she [is] a perfect lady, a person of the highest breeding" (1981:41), Cokane's words ring hollow.

In terms of the meaning of characters' names, Blanche's name is obvious, the implication being that it is ironical, since she is anything but pure, but it also conveys her father's attitude toward her and, as a verb, to blanch is to whiten, which is what Sartorius has tried to do through her education and breeding. Moreover there could also be a garden connection in that "to blanch" is to scald garden vegetables to make them lighter and more flavorful, which is another way of describing the process which Sartorius uses.

Critics have assigned various associations to Trench's name. McDowell says that Trench "suggests an individual who is 'entrenched' in his society and who becomes a 'blocking' character set against radical change" (1994:238), while

Woodfield notes that "'Trench' has a heavy sound which suggests that his initial *'rather boyish'* manner overlies an unappealing stodginess (he also digs himself a 'trench' from which there is no escape") (1991:54). Further, Vogeler speculates that by assigning the name of Trench, Shaw "perhaps meant to suggest how entrenched were London's land and tax systems" (1986:5). In actuality, the name "Trench" suggests several possibilities, culminating in a garden connection. We know first of all that Sartorius has chosen the villa at Surbiton because, as he says, "I chose the house because it is on gravel. The death-rate is low" (1981:57), which means that it has good drainage which helps prevent the infestation and disease of bogs, sewers, and swamps. We also know that this is in contrast to the conditions in the slums which Sartorius owns, for as Lickcheese says, "you come down with me to Robbins's Row, and I'll shew you a soil and a deathrate, I will!" (1981:60).[3] We also know that a trench is one means by which soil is drained and which we also know in Sartorius's scale of values is of great importance to him. Perhaps Trench's name signifies Sartorius's expectations of living above the swamp of poverty on a higher, well-drained social level by means of Trench. Secondly, a trench is also a means by which two bodies of water are connected or which connects a body of water to a target area, and Trench will be Sartorius's connecting trench to the aristocracy. Thirdly, although Trench's family is already a member of the aristocracy, a fact which Trench handles with aplomb, Trench, through his name, is nevertheless associated with the garden. A trench is also a means by which a garden is irrigated, and Trench will serve as the means by which Sartorius will grow his own upper class garden of respectability and acceptability.

One final connection regarding gardens should be noted. When Cokane reads from the Baedeker about Rolandseck, describing it as surrounded with "numerous villas and *pleasant gardens*" [emphasis added] (1981:36). Blanche says that it "sounds civilized and comfortable. I vote we go there," to which Sartorius responds, "quite like our place at Surbiton, my dear," and "quite," Blanche concurs (1981:60). With the introduction of the villa at Surbiton into the text, this passage serves as a bridge to the garden motif in Act II located at Surbiton.

The garden motif appears again in Act II, but there it is contextualized in such a way as to make a powerful ironic contrast. After Sartorius discharges Lickcheese and leaves the room, Lickcheese is then left alone with Trench and Cokane and proceeds to describe to them, in a discussion of the source of Sartorius's wealth, the abominable conditions which exist in the "tenement houses," "houses that you wouldn't hardly look at without holding your nose" (1981:60), which Sartorius owns and which serve as an ironical contrast to Sartorius's world of gardens and villas. Lickcheese points out the contrast himself: "Just look how he lives himself, and youll see the good of it to him. He likes a low deathrate and a gravel soil for himself, he does" (1981:60). When Cokane invokes the old cliché, "the love of money is the root of all evil," Lickcheese makes the connection for us: "Yes, sir; and we'd all like to have the tree growing in our *garden*" (1981:61).

When Sartorius returns, he invites Cokane with, "what do you say to a stroll through the garden, Mr Cokane? We are celebrated here for our flowers," to which Cokane replies, "Charmed, my dear sir, charmed. Life here is an idyll — a perfect idyll. We were just dwelling on it" (1981:62), which is a blatant prevarication in that what they had just been "dwelling" on before Sartorius entered is the inhumane condition of Robins Row. Sartorius, having heartlessly and with haughty indifference dismissed Lickcheese, turns to Cokane, the epitome of English garden manners, and invites him into his pleasant garden while Lickcheese faces his four starving children "looking to me for their bread" (1981:58). Sartorius, eager to become accepted into upper class British society, has acquired, in addition to an aristocratic demeanor, a garden of his own, a garden in which he takes obvious pride, being "celebrated for our flowers." In fact, Sartorius moves through the play from a tourist's restaurant garden in Act I in Germany, to a villa in Act II, with a garden, in the resort place of Surbiton, to, in Act III, their house in Bedford Square, London, moving all the while through a world of opulence. But the play has a fourth setting, the squalid tenement houses on Robins Row which contrasts with Sartorius's settings and which incriminates, with biting irony, the pretense, the hypocrisy and the foundation on which Sartorius's wealth is founded. In fact, Sartorius will not even go anywhere near his slum properties, for, as Lickcheese phrases it, "catch him going down to collect his own rents! Not likely!" (1981:61). The garden law again is decorousness, acceptability, respectability, and indifference to the suffering of those less fortunate. Or as Lickcheese states it, "many another daughter has been turned out upon the streets to gratify his affection for Blanche" (1981:61).[4]

The other status symbol, along with gardens, in *Widowers' Houses,* which Shaw uses to visually support and develop his message is the library and books. Act II begins with the stage directions, *"In the library of a handsomely appointed villa at Surbiton on a sunny forenoon in September"* (1981:53). Shaw notes that *"all the walls are lined with shelves of smartly tooled books, fitting into their places like bricks"* (1981:53). The books are obviously expensive editions, beautifully decorated, of the classics — and untouched (*"fitting into their places like bricks,"* having never been taken off the shelves and "obviously unread," as Marker puts it) (1983:108). When Cokane comments later that "you must be happy here with all these books, Mr. Sartorius. A literary atmosphere," Sartorius, unaware of the irony of his words, says that "I have not looked into them. They are pleasant for Blanche occasionally when she reads" (1981:57). Sartorius's words are belied by Shaw's opening stage directions where he points out that as the scene opens, *"Blanche, in her prettiest frock, sits reading* The Queen" (1981:53), a periodical covering court life and the clothing fashions of the day and suggesting Blanche's social ambitions. Blanche is not interested in the beautiful, tooled classics on the library shelves. They are there, as with so many things in Sartorius's world, for appearances, in this case to give an impression of "education and breeding," which he emphasizes about Blanche's upbringing several times. In *Widowers'*

Houses, the library is present for the same reason the garden is, as a powerful and subtle revelation of the hypocritical attitudes in British society.

Since, from Sartorius's point of view, the expensive library is there for Blanche, it is by means of Blanche that the irony and hypocrisy of the situation is presented. While a reader of the printed text of the play may forget these opening stage directions, fading naturally from consciousness as action, character, and dialogue subsequently get more of the reader's attention, a live audience sitting in a theatre facing the stage with the library set in prominent view throughout the act could not ignore the set so easily. A performance of the play would elicit the irony of the contrast and the incongruity between the setting, an established symbol in western civilization of learning, education, breeding, literacy, and culture, and the action of the characters, especially as performed by Blanche. As her true character begins to be revealed, the hypocrisy of her behavior is emphasized by the backdrop of culture and enlightenment. Her father tells her at one point, "you will of course not meet him until he has spoken to me," to which she responds "*hypocritically*" (Shaw's description), "of course not, papa. I shouldn't have thought of such a thing" (1981:54). We find out later that Trench has already shown the letters from his family to her before Sartorius sees them, this, in direct disobedience of her father's command and a sign of her duplicity.

When Trench and Blanche have a conversation alone and he announces to her that he will not accept money from her father and that they will have to live on his seven hundred pounds a year, Blanche begins, from that point on to the end of the act, to lose all self-control, and her violent temper begins to emerge, right in front of the beautifully tooled books. Shaw traces her progress. At first she fights against it, "*her face and voice betray the beginning of a struggle with her temper*" (1981:64). When Trench takes her hand away at one point, "*she flushes angrily; and her voice is no longer even an imitation of the voice of a lady*" (1981:65). This is the person who is reputed to be "a perfect lady" and is regarded as such by her father. Trying to win Trench over, her "*voice softening and refining for the last time,*" and, that failing, she becomes "*white with anger*" (1981:66). After this, she is out of control, "*too angry to care whether she is overheard or not*" (1981:67).

After she angrily breaks off the relation with Trench, we see her real vicious nature emerge in the scene, in the library, with the parlormaid. She scolds the maid in the most humiliating and cruel way, "*seizing her by the hair and throat*" and shouting "stop that noise, I tell you unless you want me to kill you" (1981:78). The maid can hardly speak "*as Blanche's fingers tighten furiously on her*" and is saved only by the arrival of Sartorius, who tries to coax Blanche into controlling her temper. In a live performance, the visual irony of Blanche's abnormal behavior being played out in front of "her" library would be evident to an audience. Gardens and libraries in conjunction in Shaw's early plays are used to establish the value of appearance, and the inevitable hypocrisy, to the upwardly ambitious, as Shaw perceived it, in British society.

With no garden nor library present, the last act takes place in Blanche's parlor ("this is my daughter's room"), fire burning, curtains drawn, and lamps lighted. Bernard Dukore points out that traditionally the time sequence in comedy is from Winter to Spring, but that in *Widowers' Houses*, the first act occurs in August, the second in September, and the third in Winter (1974:31). Dukore concludes that "the increasingly bleak seasonal ambience ironically contrasts with the surface gaiety of the play's conclusion, and it supports Shaw's mockery" (1974:31). Sartorius and Blanche have also seemingly withdrawn more into themselves and are now alienated from the world. We have also penetrated deeper into the heart of the Sartorius family where the truth is revealed about the true and cynical nature of society and their participation in it. Shaw, nevertheless, visually emphasizes again their hypocrisy by noting that the pianoforte has "*a sort of bedspread which covers the top, shewing that the instrument is seldom, if ever, opened*" (1981:78).

Since it is January in London in Act III, a garden setting would not be appropriate and, while it is Blanche's parlor and not a library, the book motif, nevertheless, is present, resonating in a different way, and lies at the heart of several motifs and important moments. When Lickcheese returns to Sartorius's house, now as a prosperous investor with a new business proposition about the slum dwellings, he begins by producing a book which contains the results of the Royal Commission on Housing of the Working Class, in which Sartorius is described as "the worst slum landlord in London." Lickcheese "*doubles back the book at the place indicated, and hands it to Sartorious* (1981:85) and this is the means by which Blanche will discover what the book says about her father. But Sartorious is indifferent to the publication: "I dont care that for my name being in bluebooks. My friends dont read them and I'm neither a cabinet member nor a candidate for Parliament" (1981:82). But Blanche a little later discovers the book and reads. The tableau of her as she "*sits down and begins to read*" contrasts with the opening tableau of Act II where she sits in the library of expensive books reading a journal about court life and fashions for amusement. Three critical actions result from her discovery of the "bluebook," as the Commission's book is called. First, she comes to understand the reason why Trench "would not touch the money" of her father's which caused her to break off the engagement. She tries to rip the book and, failing that, tosses it into the fender in the fireplace. Second, it is by means of this book that Blanche's duplicitous nature is revealed yet again. As Sartorius looks about for the bluebook and finally spies it in the fender, he asks Blanche, "have you seen it?" Blanche, still furious over what she has read, replies, "No. Yes. (*Angrily*) No. I have not seen it. What have I to do with it?" (1981:85). Sartorius, as well as the audience, sees his daughter's true nature. Third, when Blanche confronts her father about the book, it is an opportunity for her father to explain the rationale of his business, for him to discuss the nature of poverty, and for him to inform her, and the audience, of his own impoverished background. The book provides the occasion for Shaw to practice his "drama of discussion" at this point in the play. It also provides the opportunity for Blanche to express her, and her father's, basic value system: "How can you expect any one to think well of us when such things are written about us in that infamous book?" (1981:86). In all instances, her true inner self, sitting by the fire in her parlor in the heart of the house, emerges. She states the she "hates" the idea of poverty, does not wish to know about the poor, and that "I love you because you brought me up to something better ... [and] I should hate you if you had not" (1981:86). Not realizing the implications of his own remarks, he boasts that "I have made a real lady of you" and that "it is natural for you to feel that way, after your bringing up. It is the ladylike view of the matter" (1981:87).

The purpose of Lickcheese's visit is to make a business proposal to Sartorius, which basically involves fixing up the slum dwellings so that a higher compensation can be gained when they are torn down for highways and other renewal projects. It is the height of hypocrisy, cynicism, and inhuman values and best perhaps summed up in Sartorius's mendacious, oily, and cynically hypocritical statement that "I certainly feel, as Mr Cokane puts it, that it is our duty: one which I have perhaps too long neglected out of regard for the poorest class of tenants" (1981:88). This statement is put into clearest perspective when compared to the conversation at the beginning of Act II when Sartorius discharges Lickcheese for spending "one pound four" for fixing a stair case. While *Widowers' Houses* exposes the heartlessness and injustices of British society, it is the underlying hypocrisy and pretense that is really at the heart of the problem, and this is communicated poignantly by Shaw's use of gardens and libraries.

UNIVERSITY OF TEXAS AT EL PASO

Notes

1. In a book-length study entitled *Shaw's Evolving Art: From Gardens to Libraries and Back Again,* the present author exams Shaw's use of these two settings through a number of plays, including *Mrs. Warren's Profession* (primarily gardens), *Arms and the Man* (a library and a garden), *Candida* (a garden — a vast park, actually — and a library), *Man and Superman* (a library and a garden with books on a garden table), *Major Barbara* (a book motif and contrasting nature scenes), *Misalliance* (book motif and an ever-present garden), and *Heartbreak House* (a book motif and the final scene in the garden, awaiting destruction). The study traces Shaw's evolving use of the settings as he moves from play to play, changing the significance of them as he perfects his art and integrating them more and more into the text.

2. In Morrison's study, she quotes from a letter from Wilde to Shaw about his reading of and admiration for *Widowers' Houses,* "with its detailed character descriptions," after which "Wilde for the first time used such descriptions in a play of his own" and "they sound just like Shaw's" (1981:8). The play under discussion is *An Ideal Husband,* which, according to Morrison, "abounds in this kind of Shavian detail [the description of Lickcheese] for both major and minor characters," and, she continues, "these interpretive stage directions represent the influence of Shaw" (1981:9). Before Wilde's encounter with *Widowers' Houses,* this was not Wilde's "custom" (1981:7).

3. Raymond S. Nelson, "Shaw's *Widowers' Houses,*" *Research Studies* 37 (1969):27–37 quotes from the Rev. Andrew Mearns, *The Bitter Cry of Outcast Land,"* which is quoted in J. A. R. Pimlott, *Toynbee Hall: Fifty Years of Social Progress, 1884–1934* (London, 1935):30. Talking about a slum he visited, Mearns writes, "To get into them you have to penetrate courts reeking with poi-

sonous and malodorous gases arising from accumulations of sewage and refuse scattered in all directions and often flowing beneath your feet; courts many of them which the sun never penetrates and which are never visited by a breath of air. Drains and sewers were bad if they existed, and most tenements like those in Robbins's Row had poor drainage and high death rates" (Nelson 1969:24). Nelson adds, "Shaw knew these conditions well" (1969:24).

    4. McDowell notes that Blanche's "indifference toward the unfortunate, her possessiveness, and her cruelty are not only personal qualities, they are also symbolic of a demoralized, unjust society" (1994:237).

References Cited

Carpenter, Charles. *Bernard Shaw & the Art of Destroying Ideals: The Early Plays.* Milwaukee: University of Wisconsin Press, 1969.
Dukore, Bernard. "*Widowers' Houses:* A Question of Genre." *Modern Drama* 17 (1974):27–32.
Ganz, Arthur. *George Bernard Shaw.* New York: Grove Press, 1983.
Marker, Frederick J. "Shaw's Early Plays." *The Cambridge Companion to George Bernard Shaw,* edited by Christopher Innes. 103–123. Cambridge, U.K.: Cambridge University Press, 1998.
McDowell, Frederick P. W. "*Widowers' Houses*: A Play for the 1890s and the 1990s." *Shaw: The Annual of Bernard Shaw Studies* 14 (1994):231–40.
Morrison, Kristin. "Horrible Flesh and Blood." *Theatre Notebook: A Journal of the History and Technique of the British Theatre* 35.1 (1981):7–9.
Nelson, Raymond. "Shaw's *Widowers' Houses.*" *Research Studies* 37 (1969):27–37.
Shaw, Bernard. *Widowers' Houses* in *Plays Unpleasant.* New York: Penguin, 1981. 31–96.
Vogeler, Martha. "*Widowers' Houses* and the London County Council." *The Independent Shavian* 24 (1986):3–11.
Woodfield, James. "Shaw's *Widowers' Houses.*" *Shaw: The Annual of Bernard Shaw Studies* 11 (1991):47–64.

Relative Facts
Emergency Law, Northern Ireland, and Brian Friel's *The Freedom of the City*

Peter Leman

Abstract

Brian Friel's play The Freedom of the City, *an imaginative rendering of Bloody Sunday and of the legal, political, and cultural responses that followed, raises a number of significant questions about the mechanisms or "coercive networks" that are deployed by the state during an emergency and the representational strategies of the state, of culture, and of art by which different institutions or individuals attempt to make sense of tragedy. Drawing upon theorizations of the "state of exception" by Giorgio Agamben and others, I argue that Friel's play, through its use of perspectivalism and temporal discontinuity, demonstrates the extent to which fact is rendered relative by the extreme circumstances of life that emerge when the temporary provisions of emergency law become permanent. Under such conditions, the status of political subjects with respect to the law is determined not by relevant facts (so important to the normal rule of law), but by the relative facts created or imagined by the state.*

Brian Friel's *The Freedom of the City* was first performed in Dublin's Abbey Theatre on 20 February 1973. The play portrays a scenario that closely resembles the events of 30 January 1972 — better known as Bloody Sunday — when 13 civil rights marchers were killed in Derry, Northern Ireland, by British soldiers. However, Friel has made it clear that he began *The Freedom of the City* long before Bloody Sunday and insists it is not about Bloody Sunday or its aftermath, which may be one reason he sets the play in 1970. He was initially interested in writing a play about poverty and had been working on it for 10 months or so; but, he says, "then Bloody Sunday happened, and the play I was writing, and wasn't succeeding with, suddenly found a focus" (1999:57). Commentary on the play generally disregards (or at least takes with a grain of salt) Friel's denial of a direct representational connection between his play and Bloody Sunday, reading the work's portrayal of three civil rights marchers killed by British troops as a definite response to the event and to the subsequent tribunal overseen by Lord

Widgery, who cleared the military from any blame. Indeed, it is difficult to read *Freedom* as anything other than a Bloody Sunday play, or at least a "Troubles" play, as Stephen Watt describes it (2006). Whatever its "true" subject matter, the play raises a number of significant questions about the event, but also about the nature of emergency, the mechanisms or "coercive networks" that are deployed by the state during an emergency, and the representational strategies of the state, of culture, and of art by which different institutions or individuals attempt to make sense of tragic events. Given these wider concerns, I am inclined to agree with Friel that, in a sense, *The Freedom of the City* is not about Bloody Sunday. This is true in the same sense that Bloody Sunday is not about Bloody Sunday. The event, in other words, was not isolated — it did not happen out of nowhere. It was, at the time, the most recent tragedy in a long history of tragedies inflicted on Northern Irish soil and we must understand the event in the context of this history. Friel's play guides us in this process, thematizing the tyrannies of time and history alongside a plot that illustrates the forms of power that have shaped that history — namely the forms of law deployed during the state(s) of emergency.

To begin with the work's critical deployment and its state(s) of reception: *The Freedom of the City* is not one of the most popular of Friel's plays in performance, and initial reviews were quite negative, dismissing it as mere anti–British propaganda (see Dantanus 140). However, the play has received substantial critical attention in large part because of its controversial subject matter and the political preoccupation that it implies. Despite Friel's attempt to distance *Freedom* from its immediate political context, many critics, such as Elizabeth Winkler (1981) and F. C. McGrath (1999), see the play as representing a crucial moment in Friel's growth as a playwright, when he developed a more critical view of nationalism and began to expand his social concerns to the realm of the political, recognizing and even fulfilling (however reluctantly) the political potential of drama. While critics often address the question of politics as if a debate existed — as McGrath does in noting the ways some critics have oversimplified the play by focusing on its "overt political content" (100) — the consensus, apart from the early reviewers, is that while *Freedom* deals with political issues, it does so in a non-propagandistic way in large part through its inclusion of multiple voices and perspectives. For example, Winkler, whose reading McGrath includes among the oversimplified, argues that the play's form and "dramatic juxtaposition" of characters makes its political message indirect at best (1981:13), while Moray McGowan insists that Friel "is no dogmatist," despite his concern with serious social issues facing Catholics in Northern Ireland (301). Further consensus holds that *Freedom*, in its use of competing discourses, is one of Friel's earliest "language" plays, a designation most often associated with his better known *Translations* (1980); thus Helen Fulton contends that *Freedom* demonstrates the principle of hegemony through its use of discourse, vividly illustrating the "power of language to impose control and contain opposition" (63).

I would concur with many of these observations: *The Freedom of the City* is deeply political, even (or especially) if it doesn't resort to propagandistic or Manichean distinctions along the lines of British-Bad/Irish-Good. Importantly, acknowledging its political interventions is not to say that the play fails aesthetically or formally—quite the opposite, in fact. The aesthetic and formal qualities of the play, composed of complex and competing linguistic registers, contribute significantly to the political; or, put differently, the aesthetic is political in *The Freedom of the City* as the play reveals the ideological nature of law, insists on the more truthful (because ambiguous) nature of fictional representation compared to the "factual" representations of the state, and encourages the disjunction or interruption of temporal progression—the play, in other words, draws attention to time and the role of history in present struggles. The particular history that the play looks toward and interrogates, I argue, is that of Northern Ireland's experience of emergency law. No critics have yet substantially read the play in this context, although many recognize the centrality of the character of the Judge in *Freedom* as an expression of state authority and some, particularly McGrath, have correctly read the Judge and his inquiry in relationship to Lord Widgery's Bloody Sunday tribunal. Scott Boltwood describes some of the immediate legal contexts important to the play, but he does not relate this specifically to the history of emergency law in Northern Ireland (98–99); and Ulick O'Connor argues in reading *Freedom* that the "fundamental fact" of the British Government's response to Bloody Sunday "is that they failed to apply the Rule of Law to their own army and administration" (9). However, this reading, like the others, does not recognize the crucial role of emergency law in this situation: it was not a failure to apply the Rule of Law, but a deliberate authorizing of the army and Widgery through the suspension of the Rule of Law.

In this paper, I relate the history of emergency law in Northern Ireland to both Friel's play and the tragic events to which it responds. Ultimately, I argue that through the use of perspectivalism and temporal discontinuity, Friel demonstrates the extent to which fact is rendered relative by the extreme circumstances of life that emerge when the temporary provisions of emergency law become permanent. Under such conditions, the status of political subjects with respect to the law is determined not by relevant facts, but by the *relative* facts created or imagined by the agents of the state. Friel has expressed an ongoing interest in the relationship between fact and fiction, between history and imaginative literature, describing in a brief autobiographical essay that the lines between fact and fiction become blurred in the process of remembering one's life (1999:38), and stating in a program note to *Making History* (1988) that "history and fiction are related and comparable forms of discourse" (1999:135). In *Freedom*, Friel demonstrates how the lines between history and fiction are not simply the concern of the artist, but of the state as well—in other words, the "official" history of Northern Ireland and of Bloody Sunday has in many ways been a fiction, and a more accurate representation of the truths of history can emerge through dramatic fiction.

Before looking closely at these ideas in Friel's play, it will be helpful first to define emergency law (which, depending on the context, can go by a number of names: exceptional powers, special powers, emergency provisions, martial law, etc.), and then sketch a brief history of states of emergency in Northern Ireland leading up to Bloody Sunday. Although Giorgio Agamben notes that the concept of "emergency" or the "state of exception" is difficult to define, emergency law is (essentially or supposedly) the means by which a state protects itself in the face of an internal or external threat of some kind, like "terrorism" (2005:1–2). The state of emergency temporarily suspends the normal rule of law and constitutional order as it grants "special powers" to the sovereign or government for the sake of restoring law and order; such powers may include the ability to "impose curfew, close premises, roads and transportation routes, detain and intern, proscribe organizations, engage in censorship, ban meetings, processions and gatherings, alter the court system, ban uniforms, weapons and the use of cars" (Donohue 2001:xix). This list actually comes from the 1922 Civil Authorities (Special Powers) Act, used in Northern Ireland. "Amongst other provisions," Laura Donohue writes, this Act "granted extensive powers of entry, search and seizure, and, in a Draconian catch-all phrase, empowered the Civil Authority 'to take all such steps and issue all such orders as may be necessary for preserving the peace and maintaining order'" (2001:xix). In *State of Exception* (2005), Agamben analyzes the phenomenon of states of emergency in modern government, showing that the provisions of emergency law, by definition "exceptional" measures meant to be temporary, frequently become permanent. Quoting Benjamin, Agamben says that since "the state of exception ... has become the rule, ... it not only appears increasingly as a *technique* of government rather than an exceptional measure, but it also lets its own nature as *the constitutive paradigm of the juridical order* come to light" (2005:6–7, emphasis in original). Clinton Rossiter warns that because there are no effective "safeguards available for insuring that emergency powers" be used properly and temporarily, the "quasi-dictatorial provisions of modern constitutional systems ... are liable to be transformed into totalitarian schemes if conditions become favorable to it" (qtd. in Agamben 2005:6). Northern Ireland is certainly one of these areas where conditions became favorable to the transformation of temporary emergency provisions into a totalitarian scheme. "The story of Irish history," Donohue says, "is a tale punctuated by the assumption and exercise of extraordinary State power ... Political forces repeatedly turn to the codification of emergency powers as a means to secure the State, North or South" (2001:xix).

As mentioned, in 1922, the Unionist government in Northern Ireland passed the Special Powers Act in response to political violence between Catholics and Protestants. Though the measure was temporary, it was renewed annually from 1923 to 1927 and extended in 1928 through the Civil Authorities (Special Powers) Act (Northern Ireland) (Donahue 16). The emergency provisions were then made permanent through a similarly named act in 1933. The government's justification for this extreme measure was, essentially, that *it worked* in suppressing and deterring violence; it was effective. And, they claimed, its "interference with the ordinary principles of law" was "in practice comparatively trifling" (Donahue 39). In 1936, the National Council for Civil Liberties issued a report stating that although the emergency situation in 1922 may have justified the Special Powers Act (SPA), such conditions no longer existed and, therefore, the emergency measures lacked justification (Donahue 114). The government responded by shifting the emphasis of the Act's purpose — previously, the SPA was intended to restore law and order; now, they claimed, it was necessary for maintaining peace (Donahue 115). Taken together, emergency laws were in effect in Northern Ireland for over 80 years. The events preceding Bloody Sunday were directly related to the entrenchment and codification of these emergency powers — the Civil Rights March that began on that Sunday morning was, among other things, a protest against an increasing use of internment without trial and certain "interrogation techniques" (which became the subject of a case filed by Northern Ireland against England in the European Commission on Human Rights in 1973). These conditions, in which exceptional measures had become the norm, provide the backdrop for the events of Bloody Sunday and for Friel's play. His work, I argue, can be understood as a response to the extreme conditions of life (which include poverty) that develop under permanent emergency rule.

The Freedom of the City opens with the tragic outcome of a clash between a Civil Rights March and the British military. While Bloody Sunday escalated to violence and bloodshed in the streets of Derry, Friel's play takes us into a fictional outcome of the dispersal where three strangers — Michael, Lily, and Skinner — involved in the march accidentally stagger into the Mayor's parlor in the Guildhall in an effort to escape the conflict outside. The play begins with the three of them lying dead on the ground in front of the Guildhall: a moment that, Boltwood says, "announces the disruption of both chronological and naturalistic mimesis" (102). The drama then shifts primarily between flashbacks of their short time in the Guildhall to the inquiry following the event, roughly based on Lord Widgery's inquiry into the events of Bloody Sunday. A judge narrates his purpose, interviews witnesses, and, near the play's end, offers his conclusions. In addition, the priest who, in the beginning, has administered last rites to the three enters occasionally to offer his interpretation of the events; a drunk balladeer shows up to praise the three deceased as "republican" heroes; and, among others, an American Sociologist expert on the culture of poverty appears now and then to provide academic commentary. The play is temporally nonlinear and formally perspectival as these various voices attempt to interpret the three characters and their deaths — attempt, in other words, to determine the facts and their meaning.

"Fact" is, of course, an important concept in the law. The initial question asked when a case is brought before a judge is whether it concerns a question of fact or a question of law. Cases that are questions of law are generally decided without the assistance of a jury because the facts of the case are not in question — the only question is: how does the *law* apply to the facts? And this is something that only a judge can determine. A question of fact, on the other hand, concerns "an issue that is material to the outcome of the case and requires an interpretation of conflicting views on the factual circumstances surrounding the case" ("Question"). It must, therefore, be decided by a jury following witness and expert testimonies. The matter before the Judge in Friel's play is clearly a question of fact (as is the matter before Widgery as well as before Lord Saville, whom former Prime Minister Tony Blair appointed to revisit the case in 1998). Indeed, the Judge in the play insists that this is a "fact-finding exercise" (109). However, because he is conducting a mere "tribunal" or "inquiry," the only one allowed to interpret the conflicting views is the Judge himself. This is perhaps symptomatic of the judiciary under an emergency, in which the executive, legislative, and judicial powers are lumped together or dissolved; the Judge does not have to subject himself and his interpretation of the facts to the "objectivity" of a jury's consideration because the rule of law has been suspended. The question of fact is, therefore, already in a problematic frame from the beginning.

In an odd moment after the three protestors have settled more or less comfortably into the Mayor's parlor, waiting for the trouble outside to die down, Michael — the serious one of the three, committed to the nonviolent aims of the civil rights movement — lectures Lily (a mother of 11 children) and Skinner (judged by Michael as lacking seriousness):

> MICHAEL: But as I say to Norah, the main thing is to keep a united front. The ultimate objectives we're all striving for is more important than the personalities or the politics of the individuals concerned.
> SKINNER: At this point in time.
> MICHAEL: What's that?
> SKINNER: And taking full cognizance of all relative facts.
> MICHAEL: What d'you mean? [127].

Before Skinner replies with another cryptic statement, Lily interrupts them by asking about Norah, Michael's fiancé. A few critics have drawn attention to this passage in which Skinner parodies Michael's serious way of speaking (suggesting a resemblance, perhaps, with military or legal diction), but the focus tends to be on Michael's civil rights discourse or Lily's tendency to mediate tension between Michael and Skinner. Critics have failed to recognize that instead of saying "relevant facts," which would be the convention, Skinner uses the strange term "*relative* facts."[1] The phrase could simply mean all of the facts concerned with a particular matter, but the statement is followed by Michael's question and is then ignored entirely. The matter is left unresolved, which, paradoxically, even as the characters ignore it, only serves to draw attention to it. I do not think the phrase "relative fact," then, is merely an idle or flippant comment on Skinner's part — Michael sees him as flippant, but there is a seriousness or a realism concealed by his flippancy that exceeds even Michael's and encourages us to read Skinner's word choice more closely rather than to dismiss it as a parodic or unconscious malapropism.

Later, after there have been various shifts from the "holy of holies" in the Guildhall to the statements of the tribunal judge and others, Lily makes one of her many comments that tend to interrupt Michael's somber (often one-sided) conversations. In this case, Michael observes that more tanks have arrived outside. At this point, he and the others do not know that they are actually the target of the security forces, who presume that a band of 50 or more terrorist republicans have taken Guildhall as a symbolic act of resistance against the Unionist government. Skinner then asks Lily if she is asleep and she replies, "D'you know what I heard a man saying on the telly one night? D'you see them fellas that go up into outer space? Well, they don't get old up there the way we get old down here. Whatever way the clocks work there, we age ten times as quick as they do" (144). Lily is referring here to Einstein's special theory of relativity and to the theoretical scenario in which time slows down the closer one comes to traveling at the speed of light. This conversation takes place (in the dramatic, not chronological, order) immediately following the testimony of Winbourne, a forensic chemist, regarding the essential question of fact at the center of the inquiry, and of both Widgery's and Saville's: that is, whether or not the deceased possessed firearms and used them when they exited the building. Widgery used a similar expert to discuss the "paraffin test," which suggests the likelihood of a person's having fired a weapon based on the amount and the pattern of lead particles found on that person's hands or body. Although Winbourne admits ignorance as to "what constitutes conclusive evidence," the Judge's insistent questions ultimately persuade Winbourne to agree that he is "personally convinced" that Michael did fire a weapon, given the lead deposits found on his body (142–143). It is following this expert testimony on the primary question of fact that we get Lily's reference to the theory of relativity and this throws us back, I suggest, to Skinner's "relative facts."

Fact, by definition, is that "which has really occurred or is actually the case" ("Fact"). However, Lily's invocation of Einstein's classic principle and Skinner's oxymoronic "relative facts" imply that different perspectives and different conditions can render facts disputable, subject to interpretation, and therefore relative, *or* that under certain conditions the disputed can be rendered factual, as seen in the Judge's re-forming of Winbourne's inconclusive evidence as conclusive. There are significant and problematic implications to these suggestions. They draw attention to the very structure of the play, which is based on the principle of perspectival variation, and reinforce the play's preoccupation with time and history. In terms of the perspectival, the play's form is essentially a dramatic instantiation of Heisenberg's famous version of the relativity principle, which demonstrated that "the process (or method) of observation determines our definition of the object of observation" (Craige 1983:2). We, as the audience, see Michael, Lily, and Skinner directly, but we also see and hear from the tribunal judge and his witnesses (including Brigadier Johnson Hansbury, who gave the order to fire, Dr. Winbourne, and Professor Cuppely, a pathologist who vividly and very "factually" describes the victims' wounds), the Priest who administered last rights to the dead, a drunk Balladeer who sings of the dead as "republican heroes," the reporter Liam O'Kelly, and, among a few minor voices, the American sociologist, Professor Dodds. Each of the interpretations of the events offered by these characters is determined by their relative perspectives, which are both specific to the observers and tied to particular points in the chronology of events: there are no facts, as Nietzsche has said, "only interpretations" (267). The exception in terms of chronology is Dodds, whose speeches are not tied to the diegetic world of the play: he addresses the audience directly (he is tied to the viewer's moment, in other words) and lectures on the "culture of poverty." I will examine his character in detail shortly, but first it is crucial to acknowledge a potential problem with Friel's thematic and formal invocation of scientific relativity: Einstein and Heisenberg posited theories of relativity that applied universally to the physical world, not to historical conditions brought about by political force; put differently, they were concerned with the forces of nature, not the forces of the State. From this the question follows, if *all* is relative and there are only interpretations, does it not imply that even Friel's representations of events within the Guildhall are interpretations? My response to this question is twofold and contradictory — no and yes. On the one hand, neither Friel nor the characters through which he invokes relativity are interested in the general physics or metaphysics of the universe, but they are interested in history. Given the *fact* that people actually died on Bloody Sunday, something not subject to interpretation by any account, and the effect that this and the subsequent inquiry had on Friel and others, it is safe to assume that the relativity with which Friel is concerned is of a specific, politico-historical, and not universal, kind. Friel, therefore, asserts a form of relativity delimited by the political conditions of emergency in Northern Ireland *by analogy* with the universal relativity of Einstein and Heisenberg. In the play itself, there are "fictional facts," or things which have really occurred or are actually the case within the fictional world of *Freedom* (Dolezel 149). The Guildhall scenes are to be taken (initially, a complication I will soon address) as a baseline of fictional fact to which Friel as author and we as audience have privileged access and against which the relative facts produced by the interpretations of other characters are repeatedly defined. On the other hand, and this is the "yes" response to the question, the factual baseline is complicated when Friel introduces what we might call counterfactuals: firstly Dodds, who, as far as we know, has no factual existence in the world of the main storyline; then the factually impossible post-mortem speeches of Michael, Lily, and Skinner; and finally the moment of their deaths with which the play ends and in which they do not die. I will examine each of these in turn suggesting ultimately that one of the aesthetic virtues of Friel's play is its deep ambiguity, expressed most importantly through these factual/counterfactual metatheatrical slippages in which universal relativity creeps in on Friel's delimited relativity; but in the most ambiguous of these, the final scene, Friel makes a decisively unambiguous political statement.

In addition to the main characters, Dodds and the Judge are, in many ways, two of the most important voices in the play (which is not to diminish the importance of the other voices), and their respective discourses are not unrelated. And in terms of illustrating both the effect of perspective on the "facts" and the problem of time and its suspension, Professor Dodds is an illuminating figure. Dodds has been variously interpreted in the criticism since it is not entirely clear how we, as the audience, are supposed to respond to him. On the one hand, Dodds seems to be replicating another discourse that, like the Judge's, is detached from the facts of the "real" lives of those who suffer under poverty, but on the other hand many of his observations seem to be accurate. Dodds (whose theories closely resemble those of American anthropologist Oscar Lewis, as McGrath has shown [112]) explains to the audience the nature of "inherited" poverty and how the "culture of poverty" has both physical (i.e., economic and social) and psychological effects. We cannot help but think of Michael, Lily, and Skinner in the terms that Dodds presents, so he could be seen as guiding the audience in their interpretation of the events depicted in the play. Indeed, one could even suggest, as Ulf Dantanus does, that Dodds is Friel's attempt to "direct the attention of the audience to the subject of poverty" and away from immediate politics (1988:136). I hardly think this is the case, however, and rather argue that Dodds is a metatheatrical and meta*hermeneutic* device meant to entice us into an interpretation of the events which we are not, ultimately, supposed to accept. The scenes in the Guildhall remain factual, at this point, but Dodds by stepping out and addressing us directly forces us to question the role that our own perspectives as audience members play in what we take those facts to mean. He illustrates how one's perspective can, in Heisenbergian fashion, alter and determine the definition of the object of observation, a concept that applies to the various perspectives, ours included, that "read" the factual deaths of the protagonists.

Further, and beyond Dodds's role as "relative" hermeneutic device, critics have yet to acknowledge the historical role that anthropologists like Dodds have played at different times in the colonial legal establishment. McGrath does note that Dodds consistently appears between scenes of the Judge and the protagonists in the Guildhall (though he sees this as evidence that Dodds somehow mitigates the Judge's bias and refusal to consider sociological facts) (115–116); and Stephen Watt correctly observes that Dodds speaks of the poor "As if describing colonized or primitive 'Others'" (37). When taken together, however, these observations reveal that Dodds could be read as a supportive and not corrective intermediary between the law and the object of study/control. Anthropologists influenced, directly and indirectly, the legal establishment during the colonial

period in India, Africa, and elsewhere according to this very model: as interme-
diaries who provided "expert" interpretations of the culture under consideration,
or expert knowledge (of traditional practices or languages) used to craft or jus-
tify colonial policy (see Asad 1973).[2] The historical complicity between anthro-
pological forms of knowledge and colonial states allows us to further question
Dodds's status in the play, particularly given his proximity in the drama between
the Judge and the protagonists. The Judge, as McGrath recognizes, does insist
at the beginning of the play that "We are not conducting a social survey" in
response to a policeman's reference to Lily's impoverished living conditions (108).
However, this insistence does not necessarily reject the importance of such information to the law; while explicit sociological information is not needed for the
present inquiry, it can normalize the law's assumptions about the poor. Dodds's
theories provide a context in which the Judge's assumptions make sense: Dodds
argues that the "culture of poverty" is inherited and passed on, as if inherent in
the colonized "Other" rather than the consequence of a politically oppressive history. For the Judge, the condition of the poor and reasons for their condition do
not need to be discussed because they are already a given. Dodds draws attention away from the fact that the poverty represented through the play's characters is in large part a product of the oppressive laws and policies that have
conditioned Northern Ireland. However, Dodds also stands between the audience and the three Derry citizens, placing us in the position of judge — we are,
therefore, again challenged to question our own perspectives and our own complicity in the interpretation of the events portrayed.

   One of the key concepts that Dodds — and through him, Friel — challenges
us to consider is related to time. He asserts that the poor have "very little sense
of history" and tend to be "present-time orientated," never planning for the
future (133). Here Dodds introduces another image of temporal suspension that
resonates with Lily's invocation of Einsteinian relativity and the concept of emergency as a "*tempor*ary" suspension of law. For Dodds, poverty as a condition is
one of temporal suspension, tied to the present, neglecting both history and
time to come. Time is not frozen for the poor, but they are frozen in time, fet-
tered by their present-time orientation, unable to critically view their condition
in the context of past and future. From what we see of the characters, this appears
to be true. Lily, in particular, seems to be a strong candidate for present-time
orientation, not only introducing the image of suspended time, but asking repeatedly about the time (139, 158); narrating "At this minute" what her family and
neighbors are doing while she sits in the parlor (141); and reveling with Skinner
in their present situation by partaking of "municipal booze" and playfully donning the Mayor's robes as if without thought of the consequences (129, 136).
Indeed, according to Dodds, such behavior is characteristic of present-time orientation because the poor have a "sharper aptitude for spontaneity and for excitement" and "have a hell of a lot more fun than we [the middle-class] have" (135).
Michael is less bound to the present than Lily and Skinner; his efforts to emerge

from poverty through education and hard work indicate a developing ability to plan for the future and, therefore, join the middle-class. Several times, Michael tries to keep time moving forward by preparing to leave the parlor and face the consequences outside. He believes that by cooperating, they will not be blamed severely for their accidental intrusion upon the Guildhall. However, each time he tries to leave, Lily and Skinner hold him up. Skinner interrupts their movement toward the door early on by insisting on having another of the Mayor's cigars (139); he again interrupts Michael's gesture toward departure with a performative "last call" for drinks (156–157); much to Lily's delight, he later erupts into a lengthy performance of a "meeting of the corporation," speeding through a parodic municipal agenda (159–160); and eventually both Skinner and Lily do their best to defer having to leave by telling stories and playing games, with Lily demanding of Michael shortly before they are forced to leave, "Would you give me one second, young fella?" (165). Indeed, the mayor's parlor functions as a sort of outer space for these characters where time, in relativistic fashion, seems to slow down for them. (Interestingly, Widgery mentions in his report that in one of the photographs taken on Bloody Sunday, the clock of Guildhall is frozen at 10 past 4 [2001:40].) This repeated insistence on remaining in the present, then, would seem to illustrate and confirm Dodds's notion of the present-time orientation of the poor.

However, despite the apparent applicability of this theory, Lily and Skinner's preoccupation with time does not confirm it; rather, their obsession with deferring any plans for the immediate future reads more like a parody of Dodds's abstract academic concepts when we understand Lily and Skinner's reason for not wanting to leave the Guildhall. These efforts at present-time orientation and temporal suspension reveal the characters' growing sense of what awaits them outside. They are not ignorant of history, as Dodds suggests — in fact, only an understanding of history, of how the state has behaved in the past toward people like them, would allow Skinner and Lily to realize how it will treat them for their desecration of the Mayoral sanctuary: with death. In Act II, the three characters address the audience directly, describing for us their respective thoughts in the moment of their deaths. They enter Dodds's extra-diegetic space at this point (suspended outside the temporal framework of the rest of the play) and provide us further insight into their characters. This is the second counterfactual moment referred to above: within the fictional world of the play, this is factually impossible and here we begin to see something of Friel's perspective emerge through the dramatic fabric. In a sense, this is an extension of the fictional fact to which we are given privileged access and against which others' interpretations are shown to be relative: these are portrayed as the (f)actual thoughts that occurred in the characters' minds in the moments immediately preceding their deaths. At the same time, however, the circumstances in which their thoughts are made known to us are entirely counterfactual — a fiction within a fiction — and, therefore, begin to expose Friel, who as author has departed from verisimilitude and chosen to have them speak to us in this way. Their thoughts are crucial, however, to demystifying Dodds's perspectives (which threaten to become ours) on the absent historical sense of the poor.

Ironically, Michael, who speaks first, reveals the most underdeveloped sense of history despite his growing emergence into Dodds's middle-class and his invocation of historical figures like Gandhi in advocating nonviolence. Not only does he continue to express his faith in the civil rights movement, but up until the moment they are shot, he believes they will be fine if they cooperate. Though Skinner has warned Michael that they may be shot if they leave the building, Michael tells us he knew for certain that they wouldn't be shot because "Shooting belonged to a totally different order of things" (149). When the guns fire, he still cannot believe it, saying, "I knew a terrible mistake had been made.... My mouth kept trying to form the word mistake — mistake — mistake. And that is how I died — in disbelief, in astonishment, in shock. It was a foolish way for a man to die" (149–150). Even in the moment of his death, Michael refuses to acknowledge their fate, trying but failing to insist that the fact of this outcome is incorrect. He remains willfully suspended in disbelief. In contrast, and although Lily is not as serious as Michael — constantly telling anecdotes about her family, drinking and playing with Skinner, and displaying a degree of innocence — certain statements she makes indicate her growing awareness of their fate. Talking with Skinner about being buried by the "welfare people," Lily says: "Isn't that peculiar? All the same, to be put down in style, that's nice" (152). Here "put down" could doubly refer to being buried or killed. Later she talks about coming into the hall sick with the tear gas and going out drunk: "God, I come in reeling and now I'm going out reeling" (158). Again, her words here have a double meaning: "come in" and "going out" could also refer to birth and death. And seemingly out of nowhere, Lily says during one of Michael and Skinner's arguments, "I want the chairman to go before me," as if she knows she will die before her already lifeless husband (160). Even Lily's reference to Einstein and the suspension of time seems to hint at this subtle awareness of the tragedy that awaits; she keeps telling stories, much like Scheherazade, trying to prolong having to leave the parlor. Finally, in her death statement, her "instinct" makes explicit their fate: "The moment we stepped outside the front door I knew I was going to die, instinctively, the way an animal knows. Jesus, they're going to murder me" (150). Whereas Michael never realized what would happen to them, Lily begins to understand and then fully realizes their fate the moment they leave the Guildhall — that is, the moment they step outside the suspended time of the parlor and into a scene of repeated history. Finally, again despite apparent flippancy and glibness, Skinner demonstrates an awareness of their fate long before the others:

> A short time after I realized we were in the Mayor's parlour I knew that a price would be exacted. And when they ordered us a second time to lay down our arms I began to suspect what the price would be because they leave nothing to chance and because the poor are always overcharged. And as we stood on

the Guildhall steps, two thoughts raced through my mind: how seriously they took us and how unpardonably casual we were about them; and that to match their seriousness would demand a total dedication, a solemnity as formal as theirs [150].

Skinner's playfulness and Doddsian present-time orientation in the parlor are products not of his poverty, but of his acute understanding (which, I argue, is evidence of his understanding of history) of how the state treats people like them: they "are always overcharged." The poor are always treated more harshly than they deserve. In this way, then, while Dodds has encouraged the audience to interpret the characters a certain way (as flippant and ignorant of history), Skinner in particular dismantles this theory and sheds light on the true source of poverty in their situation: the conditions and forms of political subjectivity generated by years of emergency rule. In *Homo Sacer*, Agamben asks, "What is the *form of life* ... that corresponds to the *form of law*?" (1998: 52). Skinner's last thoughts provide a way of answering this question with respect to emergency law in Northern Ireland. While he does not refer to emergency law directly, Skinner recognizes the conditions and states of being that are a direct result of the long duration of "temporary" emergency powers.

When a state of emergency is first declared and the exception is still considered temporary, all citizens are treated as potential victims of whatever threatens the state. The people forfeit their rights for the sake of protection and the restoration of law and order, after which it is understood that rights will be restored. However, when the emergency becomes permanent — when the exception becomes the norm — all "citizens" become potential threats. Everyone becomes a suspect and, therefore, can be treated as such regardless of concrete evidence ("facts") proving their criminality. We see this attitude in the Judge from the beginning of the play. Just as he tells us that his objective is to find the facts and not to pass judgment, he states that "our concern and our only concern is with that period of time when these three people came together, seized possession of a civic building, and openly defied the security forces" (110). "The facts" that the inquiry will gather, he says, will ultimately help to determine whether the terrorists planned ahead or acted in the heat of the moment. He never asks, were these three actually terrorists? And this is because under the state of emergency, all people, or at least all people of a certain kind (who, in this case, would include the poor, Catholic minority of Northern Ireland), are criminal. They are automatically suspect and very easily presumed guilty — not innocent until proven guilty, just guilty. And the facts about which the judge speaks so grandly will indicate this guilt because they are made relative through the absolute gravitational pull of the state's special powers. From the State's perspective, to the exclusion of all others, the non-factual is factual. This automatic presumption of criminality manifests itself in different ways in the three characters who, as we have seen, each understand at different moments the consequences of their presence in the Guildhall. Two of them, but particularly Skinner, understand or are honest about what it means to be a subject in a state of permanent emergency — they are automatically suspects and identified not only as criminals but as immediate threats at the first hint of dissent. This is what it means to be "taken seriously" and "overcharged." Agamben states that "modern totalitarianism can be defined as the establishment, by means of the state of exception, of a legal civil war that allows for the physical elimination not only of political adversaries but of entire categories of citizens who for some reason cannot be integrated into the political system" (2005:2). Michael, Lily, and Skinner (and the victims of Bloody Sunday) fall into one such category. Therefore, they are shot the moment they leave the building, despite the fact that none of them have guns.[3]

After the three death speeches, the drama returns to the inquiry, where other witnesses are heard, and then back and forth again, from Guildhall to inquiry to media reports on the funeral. After the funeral, the Judge sums up, and the play concludes with the three alone on stage with their hands above their heads, suspended in the fatal moment. A gun fires for fifteen seconds, but they do not move. After the gun stops, the stage directions read: "The three stand as before, staring out, their hands above their heads" (169). Thus the play ends with the idea and the image (or even the literal space) of suspension visible on stage, significant in a number of ways because emergency is a suspension of the rule of law, a suspension of order and civil society and fact, because Lily tries so desperately to suspend time in the parlor, but ultimately cannot, and because the facts were suspended by Widgery. However, this image complicates the play's adherence to what I have called a baseline of fictional fact in representations of Michael, Lily, and Skinner in and outside the Guildhall. Here we have the final counterfactual in which the protagonists do not die in the moment of their deaths, even though we saw the gunfire's fatal aftermath in the first scene of the play. There was an element of fictional fact in the death speeches, but in this final scene, fictional fact is radically suspended as Friel refuses to maintain verisimilitude. This departure fully reveals his role as author and artist in crafting the story — this, he seems to say, is a work of fiction and I can change the facts to suit my needs. This is a moment of supreme honesty on Friel's part, and it causes us to reflect back on the entirety of the play and see that it has all been his interpretation of the "facts" of Bloody Sunday. This does not challenge the reading of the other perspectives as relative, but it adds further complexity and ambiguity, something characteristic of Friel's work (though not always characteristic of "political" literature). An important difference with the other perspectives, however, is that while the Judge and others "read" the significance of the deaths, Friel rewrites them. The message is both artistic and political: he reveals that this is fiction and interpretation and he can, therefore, suspend fact and keep the characters alive despite the gunfire and the inevitability established in the beginning scene. Were he to keep with fictional fact, the three would fall and the circular momentum would conclude the play by disappearing into the darkness of the past, the chronologically subsequent scene which we saw, in the past, at the beginning of the play and toward which our minds would naturally turn. However this would repeat what the State has done after burying the dead of Bloody Sunday beneath a mass of relative facts; the State has said, in effect, "The facts are established. It is now in the past. Leave it in the past and move on." Friel's response, at the expense of formal or aesthetic unity: "We must suspend the State's established facts — keep the dead alive. No matter what the State says in the name of emergency, do not let them die. Rewrite the 'official' facts." That people died is a fact, recognized even by the state; that cannot be rewritten. What is open to interpretation, however, is how they died and why. Friel's play, by formally and thematically exploring the relativization of fact in the context of emergency rule, argues that these questions were not adequately answered by Widgery and that it would be necessary to suspend the State's conclusions in order to discover the truth, or an interpretation of the deaths that more truthfully reveals the abuses perpetuated in the name of restoring order and maintaining peace. The opening of a new inquiry into Bloody Sunday in 1998 brought hope for the victims' families, demonstrating that the impulse, of which Friel's play is a powerful expression, to refuse the State's facts and search for the truth has remained alive. Lord Saville's inquiry promises to free the dead from the relative facts of the State, but the problem of suspension persists. Saville has repeatedly deferred the deadline for his final report, frustrating to so many perhaps, in part, because the facts over the passage of time become increasingly both relevant and relative.

UNIVERSITY OF CALIFORNIA, IRVINE

Notes

Acknowledgments. I have received generous advice at different stages of this paper's evolution and express my sincerest gratitude to Kevin Whelan, members of the Southern California Irish Studies Colloquium, the "Irish Drama" panel participants and attendees at the 33rd Comparative Drama Conference, Laura O'Connor, Annie Moore, Judy Joshua, Julia Obert, and, of course, *Text & Presentation*'s anonymous reviewers.

1. Indeed, McGowan even misquotes the passage, including "relevant" instead of "relative" (1980:290). The 1974 edition she quotes does use the word "relative" (Friel 1974:42). The 1984 edition published in Friel's *Selected Plays* also uses "relative," and unless otherwise noted, my page references are to this later edition.

2. As Asad et al. demonstrate, the relationship between anthropologists and colonial administrations was, at times, vexed, but the former's expert knowledge became increasingly important, especially in Africa with the development of Indirect Rule. The British-Kenyan anthropologist Louis Leakey, for example, served as an interpreter during a portion Jomo Kenyatta's 1952 trial and famously withdrew under accusation of prejudiced mistranslations (Slater 1957:116–117); and a colonial-era report from a Judicial Advisors Conference insisted that "team-work between a trained anthropologist and someone with a more legal approach" would benefit the study and administration of "customary law" in Africa ("Native" 1953:22).

3. One of the few conclusions made public by the Saville Inquiry in recent years was that the

Bloody Sunday victims were not armed, thus discrediting Widgery's claim, backed by "forensic evidence," to the contrary (see Erwin 2004). Friel replicates Widgery's forensic evidence by having the Judge persuade Winbourne that the paraffin test definitively proves Michael had a gun, but then we see that this is simply another instance of the State's relative facts when none of the three victims holds a gun when they exit the Guildhall. Though Friel could not have known this for certain about the actual Bloody Sunday victims at the time, he imagines it to be so for his characters in order to demonstrate the State's process of creating fact.

References Cited

Agamben, Giorgio. *Homo Sacer: Sovereign Power and Bare Life*. Stanford: Stanford University Press, 1998.
_____. *State of Exception*. Chicago: University of Chicago Press, 2005.
Allen, Erwin. "Bloody Sunday victims cleared of being armed." *Irish Examiner*, 8 June 2004. <http://archives.tcm.ie/irishexaminer/2004/06/08/story489194636.asp>
Asad, Talal, ed. *Anthropology and the Colonial Encounter*. New York: Humanities Press, 1973.
Bloody Sunday, 1972: Lord Widgery's Report of Events in Londonderry, Northern Ireland, on 30 January 1972. London: The Stationary Office, 2001.
Boltwood, Scott. *Brian Friel, Ireland, and the North*. Cambridge: Cambridge University Press, 2007.
Craige, Betty Jean. "What Is Relativism in the Arts?" *Relativism in the Arts*, edited by Betty Jean Craige. 1–20. Athens: University of Georgia Press, 1983.
Dantanus, Ulf. *Brian Friel: A Study*. London: Faber, 1988.
Dolezel, Lubomir. *Heterocosmica: Fiction and Possible Worlds*. Baltimore & London: The Johns Hopkins University Press, 1998.
Donohue, Laura K. *Counter-terrorist law and emergency powers in the United Kingdom, 1922–2000*. Dublin: Irish Academic Press, 2001.
"Fact." Def. 4.a. *Oxford English Dictionary Online*. 2nd ed. 1989. Oxford English Dictionary. <www.oed.com> (accessed 1 May 2009).
Friel, Brian. *Essays, Diaries, Interviews: 1964–1999*, edited by Christopher Murray. London & New York: Faber & Faber, 1999.
_____. *The Freedom of the City*. London: Faber & Faber, 1974.
_____. *Selected Plays*. London: Faber & Faber, 1984.
Fulton, Helen. "Hegemonic Discourses in Brian Friel's *The Freedom of the City*." *Language and Tradition in Ireland: Continuities and Displacements*, edited by Maria Tymoczko and Colin Ireland. 62–83. Amherst & Boston: University of Massachusetts Press, 2003.
McGowan, Moray M. "Truth, Politics and the Individual: Brian Friel's *The Freedom of the City* and the Northern Ireland Conflict." *Literatur in Wissenschaft und Unterricht*. Vol. 12 (1980): 287–303.
McGrath, F.C. *Brian Friel's (Post)Colonial Drama: Language, Illusion, and Politics*. Syracuse, NY: Syracuse University Press, 1999.
"Native Courts and Native Customary Law in Africa." *Judicial Advisers' Conference*. Special supplement to the *Journal of African Administration*. (Oct. 1953).
Nietzsche, Friedrich. (1881) *Will to Power*, translated by Walter Kaufmann and R.J. Hollingsdale. New York: Vintage, 1968.
O'Connor, Ulick. *Brian Friel: Crisis and Commitment*. Dublin: Elo Publications, 1980.
"Question of Fact." *West's Encyclopedia of American Law*, edited by Jeffrey Lehman and Shirelle Phelps. 13 vols. 8.200–201. 2nd ed. Detroit: Gale, 2005. *Gale Virtual Reference Library*. University of California, Irvine. 14 May 2009.
Slater, Montagu. *The Trial of Jomo Kenyatta*. London: Secker & Warburg, 1957.
Watt, Stephen. "Friel and the Northern Ireland 'troubles' play." *The Cambridge Companion to Brian Friel*, edited by Anthony Roche. 30–40. Cambridge: Cambridge University Press, 2006.
Winkler, Elizabeth Hale. "Brian Friel's *The Freedom of the City*: Historical Actuality and Dramatic Imagination." *The Canadian Journal of Irish Studies* 7.1 (1981):12–31.

The Totalitarian Non-Tragedy of American Business in the French Plays of Michel Vinaver

Les Essif

Abstract

*Michel Vinaver, the former business executive and arguably the most cel-
ebrated living French dramatist, wrote four plays from 1970 to 1998 dealing with the imposition of American business culture on France and the
world, a takeover that established a new global corporate capitalism, which
Vinaver refers to as the "System." In this essay, I will address Vinaver's
dramaturgical investigation of the "uncultured," totalitarian mechanisms
of this new world order and its appropriation of cultural space and the
consciousness of characters who are equally "crushed by the system and in
perfect communication with it." Paying special attention to the structural
and thematic evolution of the plays, my discussion will be informed by a
variety of cultural theories (Guy Debord, Jean Baudrillard, Will Hutton)
and by the dramaturgical insight of David Bradby and by Vinaver himself.*

If anyone had any doubts about the fundamental flaws of American-style
global capitalism, the hitherto unimaginable depth of the most recent global
economic crisis and its ongoing fallout should dispel those doubts. Make no
mistake, the eyes of the world point to the American way of life, its *weltan-
schauung*, as the ideological epicenter of the collapse. Among the *homo sapiens*
cast of millions, the protagonist of the story leading to this unhappy end is not
just any *homo sapiens* per se but, as Régis Debray puts it, "*homo americanus*" (203).
In our globalizing world, what I call, after Baudrillard, "American unculture" (Essif
2004) extends well beyond the geographical location of the U.S. Debray's *homo
americanus* is both a creature and a perspective which is dominant in the U.S.
but encountered throughout the world (this and all further translations from the
French are mine). There is no other foreign culture that the French take more
seriously than the American one; there is no identity more *homo americanus* than
the American free-market capitalist businessman or entrepreneur. The French
know something is wrong — very wrong — with the Americano-global capital-

ism that they admittedly have guardedly adopted and have been complicit in proliferating around the world.

Since World War II, and more definitely since 1960, most European states have maintained democratic political systems, multiparty systems that are in many ways even more democratic than the one we have in the U.S. They have also pursued a more or less free-market economy, but one mixed with a strong dose of socialism and consequent limitations of corporate power and wealth — a power which leads inevitably to abuse. One of the most essential divergences between the U.S. and Europe in general is, according to Will Hutton, that "Europeans dislike inequality more than Americans" (51). Hutton argues persuasively that the major difference between American society and European societies is this belief in the social contract. The fact is, even as Europeans have largely adopted and supported an Americano-global capitalist economic system, they maintain deep reservations about it and have taken different cultural and social paths. The French stand out in this regard. The American individualistic pursuit of an obviously materialistic source of happiness stands opposed to the importance of equality and fraternity for the French. Ideologically, the French can still discern the culture and society through the proliferating stuff and fluff of the totalizing capitalist economy. In short, the French have a problem with American capitalism, in particular with what the Americano-global capitalist system has more or less imposed on the world, the term "Americano-global" referring to global capitalism viewed as the U.S.'s design and projection of a new world order, the world as a free-market extension of the U.S. (When American politicians speak to the world about freedom and democracy, they have capitalism in mind as a litmus test.) Unlike the Americans, the French maintain — or believe they maintain — a dialectical awareness of the contradictions of capital and they pursue the ideological means to recognize, expose, and attempt to resist the dictatorship of capital, its totalizing tendencies. In part because there is something theatrical about dictatorship and totalizing systems — something which lends itself to experimentation with a wide variety of dynamic stage imagery — French dramatists have participated in the examination of American-style capitalism. Chief among these dramatists is Michel Vinaver.

Michel Vinaver is the most celebrated living French dramatist. He also has produced a remarkable body of critical writings on world drama, including his own. What is even more unique about him is that he spent nearly 30 years as an international business executive who has also lived in the U.S. He has a broad understanding of U.S. culture as well as the culture of the international business world. As a CEO of a multinational company, he directed major corporate takeovers, a business practice which is prominent in his plays about America. Vinaver wrote five "American" plays from 1969 to 2001, the latest play being *September 11, 2001*, which I have written about elsewhere in terms of hyperreality and I will not treat here (Essif 2007). The first four works, extremely complex and quite long, cover various stages of Americano-global capitalism, examining its effects on French culture and on the world. They belong to Vinaver's "theatre of the everyday" style of dramatic writing, characterized by a seemingly random, fragmented interlace of utterances, representing multiple points of view and unveiling the fundamental disorder of reality. Punctuation is largely absent. Vinaver says he seeks to evoke the magma of human communication and contemporary reality, "the disarticulated elements of the uprooted everyday" (1982:241–242).

Vinaver has maintained that as a dramatist he assumes no political position and that in writing these plays he never had any intention to "attack the system." On the contrary, he says, his only objective was to "capture the here and now of capitalism," to reveal the "new consciousness" it imposed on French society in particular and on the globe in general (1982:303–304). In his first American play, one of the characters acts as a metatheatrical spokesperson for the author. Like Vinaver in life, the character, named Passemar, deals in both business and art, as an executive in a French company who is also writing and directing the play about the company. Early in the play, Passemar asks a rather ingenuous question which seems to reflect Vinaver's pretention to neutrality: "Is the takeover of a medium-sized French company ... by a powerful American company a good thing or a bad thing?" (1986c:398).

Vinaver's disavowal has considerably influenced the readings of most critics of these plays, especially the Anglo-American critics. Despite evidence to the contrary, many tend to mitigate the very dark image of the social consequences of Americano-global capitalism that appears in his plays. In fact, all of Vinaver's "America" plays are about the failure of the System in terms of the destructive new world view it imposed on French society, in which social relationships were reconfigured according to the imperatives of what Guy Debord has termed the "society of the spectacle." Debord defines spectacle succinctly as "a social relationship between people that is mediated by images" (12) "that are superior to the world" (26). Thus social relationships become "pseudo-social" relationships that stem not from the collective interaction of social individuals but from a "society of the spectacle" and its "totalitarian rule over the conditions of existence" (19), a socioeconomic system which identifies individuals primarily as producers-consumers, the identity which motivates all their relationships. As Vinaver admitted out of the other side of his mouth, all of the characters of the plays and all the players in the System, the corporate execs as well as the workers, and the Americans as well as the French, find themselves "both crushed by the system and in perfect communication with it" (1982:286).

The most notable British admirer of Vinaver's work, David Bradby, finds that Vinaver's second play about American business, *It Bowls You Over*, "presents capitalism as a dynamic, self-perpetuating system that can turn its own defeat into the principle of a new advance" (1993:86). Reviewing Vinaver's reflections on his third American play, *High Places*, Bradby insists that Vinaver refused to present a "simple denunciation of the system" and so the structure of the work "needed to show how the most intimate details of human behavior can serve the interests of 'the system' or be conditioned by it" (1993:101). In other words, Bradby is speaking about a totalizing, totalitarian system which cannot be stopped. Yet he concludes that "the result aimed for is a comic vision" (1993: 102). In a somewhat more negative tone, Janelle Reinelt questions the joyfully comedic tone and what she identifies as the theme of reconciliation in Vinaver's first play about American capitalism, a tone and a theme which she feels are "somewhat dissonant with the corporate take-over battles of the 90s and the transnational movement of capital which is now [at the turn-of the-century] characterizing the present state of play" (44). In other words, Reinelt is insinuating that Vinaver's vision of capitalism came up short. I disagree. I think the overall dramaturgical effect of all of Vinaver's America plays, though non-tragic, is very dark comedy indeed, and also remarkably prophetic.

I will limit the following discussion to an overview of the narrative and spatial structures (especially the relationship of characters to space) of Vinaver's four full-length American plays with some reference to samples of the magma taken from the dialogue in order to show the evolution in Vinaver's totalitarian view of Americano-global capitalism and his portrayal of the socioeconomic system as both antisocial and indestructible. This wholly negative vision of capitalism coincides with French theories of the society of the spectacle and hyperreality (Baudrillard; Essif 2007). Hyperreality, a consciousness in which everyday reality has become indistinguishable from its mediated, commodified representations, is the cultural consequence and the logical end of an American-style consumer society, an economic system produced by undialectical unculture (Essif 2007). Vinaver was supremely aware of the sociocultural significance and consequence of capitalism. Consequently, his plays as well as his critical writings reveal with astonishing accuracy the evolution of the Americano-global system. Since, as Vinaver contends, all players in the System are both crushed by it and in perfect communication with it, as is the case in a hyperreal society of the spectacle, the sense of tragedy, contained within and filtered as it is through a new pseudo-social consciousness, is not obvious at the fictional level of the work, which becomes non-tragic. Yet what reasonable spectator-reader could contemplate the non-tragic, portentous fictional reality of Vinaver's plays without experiencing a tragic sense of loss?

Finally, the present discussion says something about the role of theatre — the theatrical image — in creating this vision of American capitalism. In the theatre, our perception of space is largely determined by our perception of the character's relation to the space. Vinaver's plays challenge the categories of social space as well as character in terms of social relationship. Places of work, home, and leisure acquire meaning through the character's social use of the space, through the interaction of the social-subjective identities that occupy and use these spaces. In contrast, the totalitarian business spaces of Vinaver's theatre subsume, exclude, and/or complicate community and social relationship. Vinaver's characters do not belong to the places they occupy because they belong more to the System than they do to one another, and consequently, the spaces are not places in the conventional sense of the term. Ultimately, they do not belong to a space because, in the end, in light of the reconfiguration of their subjective identity which is overdetermined by their profession to the detriment of their social identity, there is no place to belong to. Moreover, morality being a value which implies social relationship, since capitalism has no morality independent from individual profit (from a business relationship), morality is excluded. The characters' private lives too are eradicated. Vinaver's drama broaches some pretty potent subject matter.

Overboard

Vinaver has agreed with critics that three of his plays form a kind of trilogy representing and covering three stages of capitalism, examining its intensifying effects on Vinaver's home culture and the world. The first American play is *Overboard (Par-dessus bord*, 1970). An American conglomerate, the United Company, is trying to take over a medium-sized, family-run, French toilet paper manufacturer. The family business, Ravoire & Dehaze, consists of the father and his two sons, one of whom, Olivier, shares the father's conventionally French approach to the business world. He aspires to continue the family business by employing more or less unaggressive, traditional marketing tactics. The other son, Benoît, manifests an Americanized, aggressive business personality. When early in the play the father dies, Benoît winds up in control. He calls in two extreme (hypertypically market-worshipping) American consultants who preach to his managers the totalitarian American religion of marketing, and Benoît begins to beat the Americans at their own game. In the end, however, almost imperceptibly, the American conglomerate acquires and devours not only the French company but the lifestyles of the executives as well.

America and the American firm have a very limited *physical* presence in this play. But this fact does not reduce the firm's totalitarian control of the action. David Bradby speaks of "the constant switching from the level of macrocosm ... to the level of microcosm," the former being represented by "the large institutional body of Radé [Ravoire & Dehaze]," but it equally covers the corporate personality and the machinations of the American conglomerate that are reflected in the dialogue of the French executives. The level of microcosm is represented by "the separate individual existences" (1993:38) of the managers and employees of the company, present and future. It is difficult to separate the macrocosm from the microcosm, largely because the System speaks through the mouths of executives who constitute the institutional bodies, the workers, and those characters who will be conscripted into the firm, all of whom are every bit as "crushed by the system and in perfect communication with it."

The numbers of characters and spaces are huge and the action/dialogue constantly shifts from one scene and one group of characters to the next. Characters include the French family that owns the business, an array of business executives, Benoît's American wife Margerie (who eventually becomes the wife of the other brother), a banker, a priest, a client of the business, the executives from the American firm, and the owner of a jazz club and his musicians. The two American consultants, Jenny and Jack, who are brought in to help the French compete against the Americans, occupy an intermediate space between the French characters and the Americans. Juxtaposed with these physically present characters, there are also diegetic mythical characters evoked by Monsieur Onde, a college professor who presents a rolling lecture at a Paris university lecture hall on the mythical gods involved in a struggle that eventually turns out to be one of "the triumph of evil over good." While American business is evoked, other than the American consultants who ostensibly work for the French, the only additional mimetic (visually presented) American character is Ralph Young, vice-president of the United Paper Company, which will take over the French firm. But through his readiness to adapt, Benoît too acts as a spokesperson for the Americans. Tying all these characters together is Passemar, Vinaver's double. Passemar is the author and director of this play who also happens to be a newly hired executive with the French company. We remember that this is a play within the play, a play about the takeover of the French firm and that Vinaver was a corporate executive working for an American firm when he wrote this play. Throughout the action of the play Passemar intervenes to reveal to the audience his dramaturgical brainstorming, including his indecision over the kind of theatre he wants this to be, conventional or experimental. In the end, theatrical art is metatheatrically treated as a consumer product as Passemar raises the question of the potential cost and marketability of certain "total theatre" production techniques.

Despite the number of characters, or perhaps in part owing to it, Vinaver speaks of the "erasure of character" and the prominence of landscape in this play: "there is no central character other than the company itself, and, on the inside of the company, there are figures rather than characters ... the place formerly occupied by the character or characters is now occupied by a site, and by a population that inhabits this site ... the landscape has really, only now, taken center stage from the agents, from the actors" (1998:110). Still, landscape and character are interdependent categories of drama and performance. There is no instance where the one does not accommodate the interpretation of the other.

The landscape comprises, from the very beginning of the play, a number of disparate spaces that are "catapulted together" as Vinaver puts it: the Lépine storehouse, Passemar's office, Dehaze's workshop, the party room, the lecture hall (1998:208). Along the way, in the second and third movements (Vinaver uses "movements" instead of acts), Vinaver adds many other spaces, including the offices of the French executives, the hospital room where Dehaze the father expires, Benoît's and Margerie's bedroom and later their living room, the office of Professor Onde, and, most notably, the space of the jazz club, the Infirmary.

In short, the characters "disappear" into the landscape, the no man's land, the dystopian no-place and the non-space of the Americano-global marketing world. There is, then, a great irony in this "multiplicity" of spaces which, at the expense of the depleted character identities, sets up the constellations of characters, sets the tone of the dialogue, and moves the macrocosmic theme of an undifferentiated corporate space. Yet there are, in effect, two macrocosmic spaces in this work in addition to the corporate space: metatheatrical space — represented, articulated, manipulated, and pondered by Passemar — and mythical space — diegetically referenced by Professor Onde. The metatheatrical space both extends the mythical space and counterposes the "real" corporate space. All are spaces of abstraction. Marketing has become the new mythology, the new religion, and one which has as intimate a relationship with theatre as the old mythology. Yet the tragedy of the old mythologies will become the non-tragedy of the new corporate consciousness.

To remain within the scope of this discussion, I would like to focus on one particular relatively concrete space. Benoît's Americanized vision leads us to the Infirmary, whose centerpiece is the jazz band in which the owner-musician Alex participates. As a uniquely "anti-totalitarian" American art form, jazz has a special place in this story. In a book about the meaning of life, Terry Eagleton asks us to:

> Take, as an image of the good life, a jazz group. A jazz group which is improvising obviously differs from a symphony orchestra, since to a large extent each member is free to express herself as she likes. But she does so with a receptive sensitivity to the self-expressive performances of the other musicians.... There is no conflict here between freedom and the "good of the whole," yet the image is *the reverse of totalitarian* ... (my emphasis). There is self-realization, but only through a loss of self in the music as a whole [171–173].

When the French and other Europeans opened their hearts and their minds to American jazz, we would like to think that it was because of what Eagleton describes as a sort of laboratory for social symbiosis enriched by the intellectual and artistic freedom it espoused. We get a glimpse of these qualities of jazz at the beginning of the play. Vinaver first introduces the space of the jazz club — with its resonance of the U.S. — in the third movement, titled "Seizing Power." The three musicians are Alex, at the piano, Butch, a black bass player, and Art, a black tenor saxophonist. Throughout the movement they play mostly brief pieces, "music at the extreme limit of tension, sometimes of audibility." But these jazz musicians, representatives of an American counter-culture, seem like cool, carefree dudes, the exact opposite of Benoît and his business partners: "relaxed behavior, nonchalant and serious, they keep in contact with each other through gestures, looks, and laughter at times" (1986c:417). Their music and their comportment infuse the atmosphere with an anti-materialistic, anti-authoritarian, counter-cultural alternative to the other spaces of the story. However, toward the end of the movement, the Infirmary fills up with customers in their twenties, who drink beer and Coca-Cola. The introduction of Coca-Cola into the jazz club, evidence of American corporate culture and its preliminary incursions on both the (original) American counter culture of jazz and on French culture in general, prefigures the wholesale takeover of the French system. The ambiance attracts cool, trend-setting capitalists. At the end of the movement, Benoît and Margerie enter the Infirmary because, as Benoît puts it, "It's a cool little club that's on the way up" and "Jazz is back in fashion." To which Margerie replies, "It makes me blue like everything that comes from America why do all of you have to copy everything that comes from the U.S.?" (1986c:433). Jazz becomes the "fashionable," "cool little" import from the U.S. that infects French culture, first perhaps as an artistic outlet but ultimately as a business. By the fifth movement of the play, the jazz club will become purely a place of and for business. The black musicians will have returned to the U.S., but not to rehabilitate or rejoin the American jazz scene. Butch is fighting "the man" in the civil rights culture wars — and, as Alex and Jiji his girlfriend-partner put it, he will "get himself massacred ... by the police ... of the United States of America" (471–472). The music at the club will no longer be live but recorded. Alex, the owner, will serve drinks and Jiji will continue her "little happenings," but jazz "is finished," as Alex remarks rather bluntly and certainly untragically (473). By the end of the play, Alex will essentially sacrifice his alternative jazzman identity and become an executive in the new, fully Americanized company. The jazz club loses its identity as an alternative cultural space and essentially becomes an extension of the nowhere of the corporate world.

The sixth and final movement of the play is short. Its title: "The Wedding Banquet." The wedding banquet echoes the annual company party that took place rather spontaneously ("the stage fills with people and becomes animated") in the second half of the first movement (1986c:394). For the first party the corporate-capitalist magma still evidenced overtones of French hierarchical, family-style, yet top-down system of business. Fragmented, disjointed, isolated, unattributed short utterances constitute a polylogue of company workers sketching out the mundane, "office-party" types of concerns about the food, personal lives, office rumor, and shop talk about inter-company relationships, allusions to the balancing act between family and work ("office work housework more office work the bistrot"), pot shots at the bosses, and the usual disgruntlement with the management: "They give you a party in order to spit on you after.... Exploiting us is normal, it's the role they play; what would you do if you had the bucks?" (396). The magma of this final company party scene, however, reflects the fundamental changes in the company profile and the System that controls professional and family life: the workers, the managers, the families of all.

The space is, for the first time in the play, clearly singular, consolidated, unified — and, dare I say, totalizing — and it takes up the entire sixth movement. Elaborate stage directions describe the scene of the banquet room:

> buffet tables with mountains of food and barrels of Beaujolais and Black and White, and everyone is there, eating, drinking, dancing, talking; two carpenters are completing the construction of a small stage which an electrician is equipping with spotlights, microphones, and speakers; the stream of music is a mixture of pop, free jazz, Mozart piano sonatas; flowers are everywhere; the managers are handing out plates, filling glasses, passing out food trays and clearing dirty dishes, when they're not dancing. Words mix with random moments of clarity: it is a magma with occasional eruptions [1986c:492].

A magma indeed: the "everyone" (simultaneously corresponding to and contrasting with the everywhere/nowhere of space) of the play is backgrounded by a seemingly hybrid, or multicultural, or eclectic array of food and music, in abundance: "mountains" of food, "barrels" of French wine and Anglo-Saxon scotch, pop, free jazz, and Mozart. Flowers are everywhere. This clearly anticipates the celebration of a new society and a new system, a new corporatized social system. In the new system where marketing is everything, the company managers market themselves to the workers, playing at the subservience of waiting tables, at being servants of the great family of workers. We get the impression that everything is either interconnected or interconnectable, and definitely alterable to suit the needs of the evolving system. In a bit of American fanfare, Ralph Young, the vice president of the American firm, finally makes his physical on-stage appearance to cheer the "new addition to the family of the United Paper Company: U-P-CO, rah! rah!" (503). Benoît takes the opportunity to call an array of company players to the microphone to tell their stories. In what follows, the truth of what the audience has experienced up to this point about relationships among the company executives and employees flies out the window. Attitudes of indifference among co-workers, managers, and clients transform into emotionally charged tributes, bitter rivals become best friends. Marketing contaminates the social and psychological realms.

The festivities continue with various utterances from "the people." Finally, drawing to a conclusion of the play Passemar issues a trite, simplistic formula for the new capitalist paradigm: "Keep a cool head don't let yourself get off track make the first move...." Then, stepping away from his internal, executive role: "I'm coming to the end of my play and I'm beginning to think that it's a little too lavish.... I'm a little skeptical when I hear the vice president from United say nothing will change [in Ravoire et Dehaze] of course everything will change soon enough for better or worse who knows?" (505–506). Such a simple, seemingly inconsequential, yet profound remark. How can we notice change if the reality we are supposed to be changing is generated and perpetuated by an illusion, by a series of lies and self deceptions? Yet lies are undetectable and irrelevant. In the new system there is an absence of conflict and contradiction. The new extreme system of capitalism cannot lose. People lost their jobs, their communal lives, but they have also lost the intellectual and emotional clarity to claim or even feel this loss: totalitarian control, untragic consequence.

Thus, despite its physical "distance," America has practically a ubiquitous presence in the magma of the dialogue of this play. Let me conclude the discussion with reference to a particularly telling morsel. Early in the play, one of the executives of the French company almost too casually presents the following statistic: in the 1960s, at the time of the action, the French were consuming about one tenth the amount of toilet paper that the Americans were consuming, and what is more, the toilet paper they were wiping themselves with was almost all of rough stock rather than the quilted padding (*ouate de cellulose*) being produced by the American Company, named Softies (1986c:466). Many Americans might think, "Thank God for Softies!," but this reference says a lot about the consumerist mindset of the Americans as opposed to the French. Simply put, this is the kind of consumerism that fuels the totalitarian economic system.

It Bowls You Over

About 10 years after *Overboard*, in 1980, Vinaver wrote *It Bowls You Over* (*A la renverse*) (1986a). According to Vinaver, this play depicts a more advanced stage of new capitalism, one where "something goes wrong with the system," and consequently, he affirms that in this second play the firm becomes "the total space of life" (1982:262). So Vinaver acknowledges his dramaturgical response to the socioeconomic shift in his society. The American multinational Sideral has already acquired a French company that makes suntan lotion, Bronzex. The play begins at the point of crisis for the French subsidiary: A famous celebrity sun-worshipper, Princess Benedict, is dying from skin cancer and she has agreed to give a series of televised interviews to deplore her irrational love affair with the sun. The media coverage will, of course, dampen the consumers' interest in tanning their skin. Bronzex goes bust. Sideral sells the company to the workers and it becomes a workers' cooperative. The sale of the company to the workers was not motivated by any corporate generosity but in order to bypass the rigid French system of workers' rights, such as their rights to indemnity payments and severance pay. But subsequently, Sideral is bought by a smaller but powerful conglomerate, headed by the former CEO of Sideral, named Siderman, "a one-of-a-kind self-made man" (1986a:112–113), who earlier in the action was fired by the Sideral board, becoming an apparent sacrifice to the capitalist system. At the play's end, we hear that Siderman, the corporate magnate rising from the ashes, is also planning to acquire the workers' cooperative for a pittance. Thus the true and ultimate victims will be the workers. Corporate capitalization will win out over the socialization of the company, which was initially family-owned — and named "Dr. Sens," which signifies "Dr. Sense" or "Dr. Meaning" in French — then corporatized by the Americans, then French-worker-owned, and ultimately will wind up in the grips of an individual corporate giant who is now in a more dictatorial position than he was as the CEO of Sideral. In this phase, it becomes quite clear that a new capitalist system is firmly in place, one which is totalitarian, and totally irrational — the irrationality facilitating its totalitarian tendencies — and one which cannot fail.

There is one primary space, center-stage, surrounded by three separate satellite spaces. In this primary space, French business executives of Bronzex discuss their professional lives. This particular French space is the only one with a live presence — with real actors representing individual characters. The other spaces, not only the sets but the characters that inhabit them as well, are constructed out of plaster casts. Satellite 1, which I will call the Americano-global space of Sideral, represents the American conglomerate's headquarters in Cincinnati, a space where anonymous American business executives discuss the fate of Bronzex, the product and the French employees who produce it. They also discuss the fate of traditional French culture, social as well as business culture. Satellite 2, is the space where a generic French family watches the nightly televised interviews with the princess, a space I will call the mediated French space. The television is real and its "real" images are also reproduced and multiplied via real television monitors positioned throughout the audience space. Satellite 3, the French-worker space, represents the packaging unit of Bronzex where three plaster-cast female workers operate the naturalistically presented machines that fill the plastic vials. Positioned around an apparently real packaging machine, through the use of a voice-over technique, the workers remark on the drudgery of their daily lives.

Though the French affiliate Bronzex occupies the center-stage, Satellite 1, the Americano-global space of Sideral, is at once the most abstract of all the spaces in this play and the most dominant and influential, the one which determines the present and the future of all others. The name "sideral" refers to astral phenomena as well as to the notion of the revolution of the sun. (Note also the association with the name Siderman.) So we are dealing with an entity of a cosmic, universal nature and reach, and one which also suggests the revolution or recycling of everyday reality. In French, the verb *sidérer* also means "to stupefy." We remember as well that, to write his book *America*, Baudrillard says he came to the U.S. "in search of astral [*sidérale*] America, not social and cultural America, but the America of the empty, absolute freedom of the freeways ... the America of the desert speed, of motels and mineral surfaces" (1988:5). Satellite 1 is the macro-cosmic origin of the ethereal yet eruptive realities that play out elsewhere on this heterotopic theatrical space. At the conclusion of his introduction to this play, Vinaver poses the artless question that ostensibly sets the dramatic tension: "What decision will be made at Cincinnati (USA) by the managers of Sideral Corporation, the multinational conglomerate of which Bronzex is one of the innumerable branches? What will happen to the workers in Bronzex's packaging unit?" (1986d:28).

The main stage represents the most direct effect of attitudes taken and decisions made in Satellite 1, or better, by standing in deference to and compliance with the visions and desires of the characters occupying Satellite 1, it represents the French reproduction of an American corporate mentality. Satellite 3 is a more obvious microcosmic space, the packaging unit, the space of the female worker-bees, where the corporate caprices that issue from Satellite 1 pass through the French executives of the main stage to locate their final victims. In Satellite 3 we hear fragments of conversations consisting of individualized, concrete details of the working class life, the cost of living, the pressures of the workplace (1986a: 135–137). The workers are, of course, nameless plaster casts whose conversation is conducted via an anonymous, disembodied, and non-individualized voice-over. In Satellite 2, the predominant action does not relate to or derive from the French family but from the images and the information which are relayed through the television set. The French household is simply the receiving end of the configuration of mediated and mediating images of the television interview; and since television sets are placed within the audience space, the space of the presumably French audience, we get the impression that we are the French household whose reality is in the process of being mediated, even concocted. Furthermore, the extended presence of these satellite spaces reinforces the physical horizontality and the impression of social extension even as it remains at counterpoint with the socioeconomic verticality of the American empire in Satellite 1.

The final lines of the play alternate between a disembodied "Voice of the Story" (that narrates background information) and the French characters who are seen changing out of costume. (At the beginning of the play they visibly change into costume.) They are in the process of transitioning from their theatrical roles to their individual, non-theatrical identities. The conversational, fragmentary "outbursts" of the characters seem ambiguous and nonsensical. But, in the context of the story and framed as they are by the narrative Voice which is in the process of revealing the story's conclusion, the lines become more insidious: "Oh it's nothing it'll be alright;" "Did they at least understand;" "So this is what became of them;" "You'd better believe that that can happen to any of us" (1986a:207–209). These utterances contribute to the magma of the play which, like the characters who are transforming back into actors, is transitioning beyond the stage into French culture at large. The magma responds to the circumstances produced by Sideral, for whom "the strategy of the conquest of the market for leisure products was a disaster." In fact, the company is taken over by the "new powerful conglomerate Solderco five times smaller than Sideral of course but much more aggressive," a conglomerate organized and headed by none other than David Siderman, the original CEO of Sideral who was earlier fired by the board. In sum, we get a good glimpse of the irrationality of the Americano-global market. "By means of a very confusing and daring operation on the Stock Exchange," Siderman "repurchased at a cheap price the majority of stock of the collapsing firm that he had created." The play concludes with the Voice telling us that Siderman is on "a world tour in search of new acquisitions" and he will be meeting Piau (the director of the workers' cooperative) in France to take a look at the new (old) company (1986a:212). So it's *déjà-vu* all over again! This is the epitome of the world turned upside down by capitalism: mergers and takeovers evidence an uncanny logic, one company can absorb another one which eventually is reabsorbed by the "prey" it once consumed, and even workers can become executives — albeit unsuccessful and hypocritical ones.

David Bradby rightly points out that in this play which "takes the capitalist process as its exclusive subject" capitalism cannot fail. The play "presents capitalism as a dynamic, self-perpetuating system that can turn its own defeat into the principle of a new advance.... Capital will flow, rapidly and flexibly.... This is the reality of the commercial world dominated as it is by the multinational conglomerates that are sufficiently diversified to be able to play off one business interest against others." And, quoting Jean-Paul Sartre: "Every catastrophe propels [capitalism] forward" (1993:86). But what is the human cost of the System's indestructibility and who pays? As French society and its dramatist spokesperson see it, capitalism's win is society's loss. The quantitative gain of the System entails qualitative sociocultural loss. Vinaver does not present an orthodox Marxist or neo-Marxist approach to the topic. No social or proletarian revolution is in the works. On the contrary, the great (non-)tragedy of this play is that there is no hope of relief by social proletarian revolution or otherwise. Vinaver's prophetic magma establishes the System as a new divinity, one which works in strange ways, producing and depicting characters and spaces which are both crushed by the System and in perfect communication with it.

High Places

In 1983, Vinaver wrote *High Places* (*Ordinaire*, literally translated as "Ordinary"), a play about the executive corps of an American multinational on a business trip to Latin America. The company manufactures trailer homes and wants to sell them to the Chilean government for use by the masses of the nation's poor. The executives' plane crashes high in the Andes mountains — at the top of the world. The surviving characters struggle to endure, and they resort to cannibalism. Vinaver's play is based on the factual news story of the Uruguayan rugby team whose plane crashed in the Andes Mountains in 1972 and whose survival depended on the practice of cannibalism by earnestly Catholic athletes. This historic event was the subject of a book (*Survival*) which was recently made into an American film (*Stranded*). Vinaver understood the ontological import of this experience and its relevance to future understandings of human nature. He transposed and transformed the universality of the athletes' dilemma from the local (the local, Catholic Uruguayan sports team) into an Americano-global one, played out by an American business elite, a small but very powerful "community" of uncultured individuals whose single-minded concern with global business controlled the lives of so many global citizens and whose own lives were consumed and controlled by the system that they fostered.

In the absence of unattributed dialogue, plaster-cast characters, and voice-overs, this play has a more conventional, less metatheatrical, and less disjointed structure than the ones that preceded it — but still no punctuation. While it recounts a more clearly delineated story, however, it is far from a naturalistic depiction of the Americano-global business world. The story conflates American business with the theme and practice of cannibalism; it is equally a study of cannibalism, social organization, and big business. The literal practice of cannibalism refracts the figurative form of self-consumption evident in the cannibalism of business and in a business-oriented society. Also new here is the presence of the Third World. The play presents and differentiates in effect the triadic referential spaces of the U.S., Europe, and Latin America: the American multinational has turned to the exploitation of the Latin American market — a market wide-open to bribery and corruption — because of its frustrations with the sociopolitical safeguards of the highly regulated European market. Moreover, for the first time in his writing about the effects of American capitalism on France and the world, Vinaver presents mimetically a distinct microcosm of an American business "family," or clan-like pseudo-family, including four female counterparts to the all-male executive corps: the CEO Bob's wife and his secretary-mistress, the girlfriend of one of his vice-presidents and the adolescent daughter of another. The story begins briefly in-flight (in the company plane flying to Chile) and, following the crash, it plays out at the highest of "high places" (the English-language title of the play) in the Chilean Andes Mountains. It does not take place on French or U.S. soil, and in many ways the "new landscape" of this play, as Vinaver puts it — vertically and environmentally distant from the urban civilizations where big business thrives — offers a new exercise in the depiction of an Americano-global non-space, a new angle on the "nowhere" of American business culture, from which and through which we can witness the System's appropriation of foreign territories, foreign politics and economies, and foreign and familiar minds. The American characters' business-oriented language and actions betray the totalitarian nature of the System. Business once again conquers all with its totalitarian one-track mind (the French refer to the *pensée unique* of new capitalist economies) and its takeover of social and cultural life. But it conquers in a new way.

As Bradby explains it, the play shows "how the most intimate details of human behavior can serve the interests of 'the system' or be conditioned by it" (1993:101). At least two important features of this play relate closely to the spatial isolation conveyed by the setting. First, the extraordinary authority of Bob the CEO (and the other characters' equally extraordinary obsession with him) personifies the totalitarian tendencies of not only this particular American business, the corporation that manufactures trailer homes, but also all Americano-global business. Throughout much of the action, Bob expresses all of his experiences from a business perspective, including the apocalyptic event of the crash and the extreme existential circumstances in which he and his vice presidents find themselves. Instead of dealing with the most obvious implications and consequences of the crisis at hand, and despite the progressive threats to life and limb and the declining possibility of rescue, he obsessively indulges in corporate executive "shop talk," speaking of hiring, firing, and replacing key company officers and making lofty pronouncements concerning the future of the company in the Latin American market. In such unusual circumstances, he talks business as usual with his subordinates. Even as the group of survivors begins to consume the bodies of their fallen associates, Bob promises to treat them to the best table in the Chilean capital of Santiago (1986b:338). In order to secure their positions and promotions within the company hierarchy, Bob's vice presidents indulge and mimic his pompous attitude and behavior as they vie for his favor. Bob and his staff remain absurdly, hyperrealistically unaware of their situation and optimistic about the future. They concentrate their attention on their survival in the business rather than in life, in the business which has become their life. Ignoring the deep reality of the situation, they act as if everything were "ordinary" (the original French title of the play) in the extraordinary new world thrust upon them.

In part owing to the businessmen's denial of tragedy, when Bob himself finally winds up in the cooking pot, not only does his death not produce any tragic effect, but it also lacks consequence. His executives do not seem to notice he is no longer physically present to socially and professionally consume them, and that they have physically and literally consumed him. But there is another more fundamental reason for this non-tragic tone. Since Bob represents the indestructible System, though his flesh winds up in the cooking pot, his socio-professional legacy lays claim to immortality. Bob's hegemonic leadership of the company exemplifies the overwhelming, totalitarian takeover of the individual and social minds of a "community" of business professionals, and consequently, it helps explain the paradoxical absence of true tragedy under such normally tragic circumstances. In essence, the play demonstrates the logical end of capitalism: no denouement (tragic knot), no true tragedy. Capitalism survives. It survives, if not in the person of the most corporate-capitalistic character who does not survive the conclusion as a whole living being, then in the person of the play's only non-corporate-/anti-corporate-minded character.

From the beginning, the character of Sue, the girlfriend of one of the vice-presidents, displays singular force and mystique. Her female identity contrasts with those of the other women. Bob's wife Bess, the Waspish, moralizing, shallow, and self-righteous CEO wife, plays the most conventional, stereotypical female role and she demonstrates a particularly acute resentment toward Sue, one which increases Sue's mystique: "Who made you come on this trip? What is your role here?/I never understood what you were doing on this plane" (1986b: 308). Sue has planned all along to break up with her boyfriend and remain in

Latin America. Thus Bradby points out that she is the only member of the group who really wants to be in Latin America (1993:97). In many ways, Sue is the antithesis of Bob, and Bradby points in this direction by noting that while "Bob is rapidly established as the authoritarian center of the group.... Sue will gradually reveal herself as the undisputed leader and the best able to adapt to the new circumstances forced on them all by the crash" (1993:92). I believe, however, that it would be more accurate to see her as an alternative CEO surrogate, as the new, hyperreal torchbearer for a system of advanced, globally-oriented corporate capitalism that, in its newly achieved totalizing mode, crushes and conditions all subjects equally, its most obstinate advocates as well as its foremost detractors.

Sue plays an emblematic role in this theatrical case study of the adaptability and indestructibility of Americano-global capitalism. She opens the play with the following line on the theme of termination and implied renewal, a line she delivers to her corporate boyfriend and ostensibly referring to their relationship: "It's over Jack/It's the end of our story" (1986b:293). Considering that the plane will shortly crash into the mountains and that all its "corporate" passengers other than Sue and the most passive executive will perish before the conclusion and that most will be cannibalized, this initial line exceeds the immediate reference to their amorous relationship. Sue begins the play and she will end it. During the course of the action, she is the one who initiates the cannibalism, in the interest of survival, and the one who decides to move the cannibalism further toward the extreme by introducing for consumption the less noble parts of the human anatomy, like the testicles and unemptied intestines: "Everything is there," including the shit (1986b:345). Toward the conclusion of the play Sue reveals her mysterious past, her non-corporate and existentially enlightening adventures with a Mexican prison, Mexican peasants, and a Mayan chief, who explained how the world was born through the asshole of a mouse (1986b:361). Despite her apparently free-spirited (rather than free-marketed) background, however, by the end of the play Sue becomes, in effect, the new Bob. Bob carried the corporate image into the story and sustained the image long after his death and after the communal digestion of his body by the disciples of his person and his faith. Sue is his anti-corporate counterpart, his Judas or Thomas, who in this case, despite her denial of Bob's totalitarian divinity, will carry the corporate image and faith through the end of the story into the afterlife of the corporate crisis.

In the short final scene of the play, Sue and one vice-president, Ed, remain. By now the audience and Ed are convinced that the surviving couple too is doomed; but Sue has been making plans for the fateful final expedition down the mountain. Over a conversation about Ed's potential ascendancy to the company throne and the phenomenal raise in income this will bring, Sue rekindles Ed's faith in survival (both corporate and personal) by convincing him of her (mostly mercenary) interest in marrying him to become an exemplary first-lady of the company. The play ends with Ed being led by Sue, both slowly disappearing into the background (1986b:371). This ending is not believable.

The play's ending culminates Vinaver's assault on verisimilitude. Following the theme of the irrational nature of capitalism, the story presents a contradictory mix of courage, corruption, pseudo-romance, pseudo-community, pseudo-tragedy, non-tragedy, and real money, all parts of a System that keeps going. Working outside all rational logic, the System is not a verisimilar process but a hyperreal one based on illusion, one whose "logic" belongs to the spectacle of the simulacrum. It is neither the community which survives, nor the couple, nor the individuals — but the System. Sue and Ed are not a couple, just as the group of stranded co-workers and families were in no sense a community. Sue has, in effect, migrated from the margins of corporatized, systematized society, to the center-stage of the company's survival — and she does it for money?

In fact, Sue's character contrasts with Bob's in all ways but the way of money — the way of all flesh in the new economy, it would seem. Only at the end of the play we realize — or Sue realizes — that money is the only route to survival. She is the true company-survivor, the one who differs from the other characters, male and female, in that her background and motives lie in a different professional, cultural, and socio-mythical dimension. But her body-mind too has been "snatched" by the System, even if she seems to be merely absurdly under its spell, or merely *playing* along with it. She is nonetheless responsible for the company's corporate survival, for the survival of the System beyond the borders of the story.

Vinaver locates/moves the space of American business in *High Places* to the summit of the western world. Yet, given the total indoctrination of the individuals who generate as well as collaborate in the Americano-global business world, this location becomes the exemplar of non-life. Despite the reality of and potential for physical, moral, psychological, and professional suffering, there is no tragedy in this play. There is no threat to either the non-existent social bonds among characters or to any individual character's existential awareness of or connection to life, i.e., no loss of happiness, of "real" life. There is no tragedy because the System and money cannot die.

King

Fifteen years later, in 1998, Vinaver wrote *King*. While the stories of the other American plays were contemporary with their dates of publication, this is Vinaver's first retrospective, which turns back the clock to the turn-of-the-century story about one of the founders of Americano-globalism: King Gillette, who pioneered the first disposable razor blades, which catapulted him to the top of the corporate world as one of the first and most powerful multinational corporate leaders. This is also Vinaver's first one-character play and we note the evolution in the scheme (in semiotic terms, the "system") of characters of the author's American plays. In *Overboard* an essential voice is given to workers and to non-corporate characters who are eventually conscripted into the company, and the American characters and American space remain in the background. In *It Bowls You Over* non-corporate characters and workers still have a place, but American corporate executives come into prominence. In *High Places* American executives become an exclusive club and they are physically and morally isolated. Finally, in *King* the focus on the power and thought processes of one American CEO is more or less absolute.

Vinaver divides the role of King among three actors, however, representing three generations — King the Younger (33–49 years old), the Mature (50–69), the Elder (70–80)—each to be played by a different actor. The "action" of the play alternates among short scenes featuring one of these voices as well as a fourth type of scene, called the Trio, in which all three generations/voices alternate together. This polylogue includes frequent flashbacks and flashforwards and moments where King speaks to himself as another character in his life, one absent from the stage, mixed with other moments in which he relates the utterances of other characters: a veritable hodgepodge of direct and indirect references to the magma of King's life and thought processes, the content of which, according to Bradby, expresses "the enigma of the duality of human existence" (2000:50).

King's life is two-sided: on the one hand, his is the story of the making of an American corporate King, on the other hand, it is the story of King's second life as a revolutionary socialist utopian, one who believes all of society's ills come from competition, and he even has written books on the topic. The conjunction of the three voices in the Trio sequences of the play primarily denounces the scourge of competition. Vinaver explains that he used the form of the Trio to express conceptions of utopia because, from the age of thirty-four until his death, "King persists in his vision both of the world transformed and the means to employ to obtain this transformation" (1998:230). The Trio enacts an enduring vision shared among generations. King does not see the fundamental contradictions to his dualistic world view — and neither does the early twentieth-century American culture within which he thrives. He and his business and national cultures are, in effect, living contradictions.

In its strange way the play reviews the strange life of this pioneer of global enterprise. Space-wise, Vinaver chooses the simplicity and abstraction of empty boards to present this American play focused on one powerful corporate persona. In the background appears a huge promotional image of Gillette Blade. At the beginning, the three actors dress on stage and they begin to resemble the portrait of the man at the center of the projected image (2005:38). Scene 1 is a "Trio" in which all the generational voices are mixed. As a young salesman on a business trip for the Crown Cork and Seal Company in 1889, in Scranton, Pennsylvania, "the crossroads of great commercial routes," King the Younger has been encouraged by his boss to seek a disposable product to invent and exploit for its guaranteed profitability. Then the text jumps to King the Elder who exclaims, "And now I'm ruined is it possible" (2005:40), referring to the company's failure during the Depression — a failure not unrelated to the fraud committed by two of King's trusted managers, and to the eventual buy-out of the company by a smaller company. So right from the beginning we get a schematic glimpse of King's corporate lifespan. As the play progresses through its 74 segments, we learn that on that Scranton business trip, stuck in his room in rainy weather, King had the intuition that all of humanity's problems have one cause: competition. Six years later, King has the vision of a disposable razor. During the rest of his life, even as he strives to create one of the first multinational corporations for products of mass consumption, King equally dedicates himself to conceptualizing and formulating a world revolution to abolish competition, replacing it with a global system of material equality. King thinks big and simplistically. His contradictions are huge, raw, and ingenuous.

The most remarkable feature of this work is that King's socialist agenda is, in the end, a veiled form of totalitarian capitalist enterprise. King envisions a socialist project which can only be realized through a ruthless, aggressive form of monopoly. In his own words, his utopian United Company will be the "greatest predator in the global economy.... A strange anomaly: the whole of the people entering into competition with each of its individual members" (2005:65). King approaches socialism from a hyper-competitive, business point of view. His hypothetical, ostensibly utopian United Company might not be exactly like the company of the same name that we see in *Overboard*— Vinaver's first Americano-global play — yet it has a similar objective, a similar drive toward monopoly and totalitarian control. Already at this early stage of advanced capitalism, in the name of the System, the United Company fabricates, projects, and fosters the ultimate illusion of a social contract and its social beneficiaries resemble what we have seen in *Overboard*: not just a company but a "family." So the way to end competition — and to end history — is through "total competition": "Don't wait for United to annihilate you" (2005:78). The war of business and the war of utopia merge in the mind of the capitalist magnate, who cannot help but wildly exaggerate the grandeur of his product and his person. Consequently, both capitalism and socialism, competition and cooperation, fail in this story even as the system of capitalist competition thrives. The "enigmatic duality of human existence" has a clear bias, as we have seen in all these Vinaver plays, a bias toward the resolution of totalitarian capitalism.

At the time I write these lines, in the midst of the most catastrophic financial crisis the U.S. and the globe have experienced since the Great Depression, I find myself wondering just how culturally and economically insightful and prophetic Vinaver's Americano-global plays might be. King, for example, recounts the fraud committed by his two most trusted managers. Having established a system of remuneration that provided them with a percentage of the annual profits, they cooked the books, so to speak, including the recording of "fictitious sales" (2005:113). This act of fraud in Gillette, one of the country's and the world's most important industries, contributed to the Wall Street crash of 1929. It is clear that the CEO King's constant pressure for increased income and growth was complicit with if not responsible for this fraud and the resulting financial meltdown. As in his other plays, Vinaver also includes in this story an episode in which one of King's smallest competitors winds up taking over his company and he suggests a mythical framework for the event: "What people could have invented for itself a story like the one in which the tiny Gaisman swallows up the giant Gillette" (2005:120). Despite what Vinaver claims of his own "neutral" portrayal of the System, all of his plays reveal the sociocultural failures of the new capitalism, failures which irrationally lead to the advance of the capitalist economy, which requires an "advanced" reconfiguration of social relationships. The plays may not represent a blatant indictment of capitalism or of American business practices, but they are a depiction of a terrifying new reality and a new false consciousness produced by a global economic revolution. Today, we are all both crushed by the system and in perfect communication with it. And, as we might realize now with the bailouts of the most powerful Americano-global companies, the System, and the companies — no matter who or how they might in the end be reappropriated or restructured — cannot lose.

UNIVERSITY OF TENNESSEE, KNOXVILLE

References Cited

Baudrillard, Jean. *America*. New York: Verso, 1988.
Bradby, David. "Parcours dans l'oeuvre." *Michel Vinaver. Théâtre Aujourd'hui 8*. Paris: CNDP, (2000):10–54.
_____. *The Theater of Michel Vinaver*. Ann Arbor: University of Michigan Press, 1993.
Debord, Guy. *The Society of the Spectacle*. New York: Zone, 1994.
Debray, Régis. "Confessions d'un antiaméricain." *L'Amérique des Français*, edited by Christine Fauré and Tom Bishop. 199–220. Paris: Editions François Bourin, 1992.
Eagleton, Terry. *The Meaning of Life*. Oxford: Oxford University Press, 2007.
Essif, Les. "Dialectical Representations of (Undialectical) American 'Unculture' in Late Twentieth-Century French Drama." *Dalhousie French Studies* 67 (Summer 2004):143–54.
_____. "The Hyperrealities of America's Vietnam War and 9/11 in the French Theatre of Armand Gatti and Michel Vinaver." *Text and Presentation, 2007*, edited by Stratos E. Constantinides. 61–76. Jefferson, NC: McFarland, 2007.
Hutton, Will. *A Declaration of Interdependence: Why America Should Join the World*. New York: W.W. Norton, 2003.
Reinelt, Janelle. "Performing Justice for the Future of Our Time." *European Studies* 17 (2001):37–51.
Vinaver, Michel. *A la renverse. Théâtre complet 2*. 107–212. Arles, France: Actes Sud, 1986 [1986a].
_____. *Ecrits sur le théâtre 1*. Lausanne: Editions de L'Aire, 1982.
_____. *Ecrits sur le théâtre 2*. Paris: L'Arche, 1998.
_____. *King. Théâtre complet 7*. 35–132. Arles: Actes Sud, 2005.
_____. *L'Ordinaire. Théâtre complet 2*. 291–372. Arles, France: Actes Sud, 1986 [1986b].
_____. *Par-dessus bord. Théâtre complet 1*. 385–506. Arles, France: Actes Sud, 1986 [1986c].
_____. "Présentation des oeuvres." *Théâtre complet 1*. 23–33. Arles, France: Actes Sud, 1986 [1986d].

Attacking the Canon through the Corpse
Cannibalism and Surrogation in *Hamletmachine*

Sonya Freeman Loftis

Abstract

This essay applies Joseph Roach's theory of surrogation to Hamletmachine, *exploring how cannibalism represents cultural surrogation in both Müller's play and its Shakespearean source text. Although the concept of surrogation has not been previously applied to Shakespearean adaptations, Roach's theory illuminates the metaphorical conflation of body and text that appears throughout Müller's work. In his writing and interviews, Müller's exploration of surrogation in theatre, culture, and literature employs metaphors of the human body as a figure for history and literary adaptation. These metaphorical bodies become central to his rewriting of* Hamlet, *as Müller's Hamlet violently attacks his father, who serves as an embodiment of patriarchal culture and a symbol of an author-centered literary canon.*

Hamletmachine memorializes the literary past by consuming the flesh of the dead. As many critics have pointed out, the cannibalization to which the play subjects its Shakespearean source is every bit as violent as the fury the play turns against the human form (Williams:188). Indeed, the cannibalization of the text and the dismemberment of the body bear a strong symbolic connection in Müller's play. Ultimately, both represent violent acts of surrogation, ways of destroying yet preserving the cultural and literary dead. While Müller's style of violent appropriation has received a great deal of critical attention, critics have yet to point out that Müller's conception of theatre and rewriting of Shakespeare's work enacts Joseph Roach's theory of surrogation. More than a mere case of literary influence, surrogation points not only to the anxieties of the appropriator as he reworks the artistic past, but also to the larger cultural process through which the dead are displaced or replaced. Roach argues that bodies and violence are central to the process of surrogation, and Müller's style of adaptation is unique in its focus on violence against the human form as a figure for literary adaptation. Applying Roach's theory of theatrical and cultural reproduction to *Hamletmachine* illuminates Müller's use of the human body as a symbol for the literary canon. *Hamlet* is a play deeply concerned with the act of cultural surrogation, and *Hamletmachine* amplifies its source play's fears of the dangers inherent in genealogies, duplications, and replacements, and projects them obsessively onto the play's tortured landscape. Throughout his writings and interviews, Müller's exploration of surrogation in theatre, culture, and literature employs metaphors of the human body as a figure for history and literary adaptation. These metaphorical bodies become central to his rewriting of *Hamlet*, as Müller's Hamlet violently attacks his father, who serves as an embodiment of patriarchal culture and a symbol of an author-centered literary canon.[1] Ultimately, the father symbolizes the past against which the young Hamlet struggles, just as Müller's text struggles against its Shakespearean source. In *Hamletmachine*, Müller's violence against his predecessor's canon and Hamlet's violence against his father's body suggest the anxieties of cultural and artistic surrogation, representing a struggle to destroy and yet to preserve the corpse/corpus of the past.

Although the concept of surrogation has not been previously applied to Shakespearean adaptations, Roach's theory illuminates the metaphorical conflation of body and text that appears throughout Müller's work.[2] In *Cities of the Dead*, Roach describes cultural and theatrical performance as a process of "surrogation," which is "the enactment of cultural memory by substitution." Roach posits that the process of displacement and replacement presented on the stage mirrors the larger cultural process through which society deals with death and loss (80). Through the act of surrogation, "repetition is change": the society uses the surrogate to embody its cultural and artistic past, while this replacement figure simultaneously leads society forward into the future (30). Both cultural and theatrical surrogation focus on bodies, especially the bodies of the dead, lending special power to "the folkloric tradition that regards with special awe and dread a corpse that has been dismembered, disturbed, or improperly laid to rest" (94). Through the process of surrogation, the human body is able to serve as a vessel for cultural and literary memory, so that the preservation or destruction of a human corpse represents the preservation or destruction of the literary canon. Specifically, the body of the famous poet or playwright can embody and contain cultural memory, serving society as an "effigy of flesh." Roach explains that "effigies — those fabricated from human bodies and the associations they evoke — provide communities with a method of perpetuating themselves through specially nominated mediums or surrogates" (36). Those who participate in the process of cultural or theatrical surrogation are usually unaware of the ongoing process of displacement and replacement: however, the modern stage and the act of Shakespearean appropriation increased Müller's awareness of the process. Müller's violence against Shakespeare's corpse and corpus shows a desire to destroy and consume Shakespeare's canon in order to replace it with his own.

"A king may go a progress through the guts of a beggar": Surrogation Is Cannibalism

Müller's writing shows a life-long engagement with theatrical, literary, and cultural surrogation. Although the playwright died shortly before theorists such as Joseph Roach and Marvin Carlson began to theorize the haunted theatre, he deliberately presented himself as a grave robber through his public persona, and he explained his approach to drama and literary adaptation through metaphors of raising the dead, cannibalism, and haunting.[3] In fact, Carlson points to Müller's drama as a place of particularly powerful ghosts. Jonathan Kalb agrees that "Every text Müller wrote was, in some fashion, dialogue with the dead" because he created "most of his texts in direct response to other literary works" (15). Müller was a writer who worked primarily in adaptation, and his method of rewriting older plays suggests the violent destruction of the old canon.

In fact, his plays, interviews, and other writings show that Müller frequently used the metaphor of the grave robber to explain modern drama's engagement with the art of the past. His language suggests an intimate connection between history, literary canon, and corpse, as he uses metaphors of the human body to explain his approach to history and adaptation. Müller conceived of theatre as an act of surrogation, a performance of the dead for the dead. The playwright repeatedly explained the nature of theatrical performance as that which empties the grave: "If we do have a theatre, it will be a theatre of resurrection ... our work is raising the dead; the theatre troupe is recruited from ghosts..." (1990:225). He goes on to say that the set is "a travel guide through the landscapes beyond death" (225). Müller's conception of theatre mirrors the work of recent performance theorists. As David Savran points out "If the playtext is indeed a kind of memorial, then theatrical performance must be akin to awakening the dead" (119). One might take Roach's ideas one step further with Müller, who claims that he writes for the dead, because "the dead ones are the majority. There are many more dead people than living ones, and you have to write for a majority" (1986:96–97). Metaphorically, a performance of the dead for the dead is cultural surrogation in its purest form. A performance that evokes ghosts to speak directly to history is a cultural ritual akin to ancestor worship: this is drama at its fullest cultural power as envisioned by Roach and Carlson. For Müller, the living performers represent ghosts who communicate with the past. Roach explains that through surrogation, "audiences may come to regard the performer as ... a medium for speaking with the dead" (78). For Müller, drama is about the dead, about preserving and speaking to history. The playwright explains, "We have to dig up the dead again and again, because only from them can we obtain a future. Necrophilia is love of the future. One has to accept the presence of the dead as dialogue partners or dialogue-disturbers — the future will emerge only out of dialogue with the dead" (qtd. in Kalb 15). Only through surrogation can "necrophilia" be the "love of the future." Müller understood the human corpse as an "effigy of flesh," that which represents the past and yet simultaneously moves the society into the future. It is impossible to move into the future without first dealing with the past, a past that for Müller was constantly cast in the language of corpses and of grave robbers — the language of surrogation. Yet for Müller the human body was a metaphor not just for theatre, but also for history itself. According to Müller, the problem with history is "that it's covered with flesh and skin, surface. The main impulse is to get through the surface in order to see the structure" (1990:57).

Throughout Müller's writing, the metaphor of the grave robber represents not only theatrical performance and history itself, but also the act of literary adaptation. Müller described the process of writing *Hamletmachine* as an act of destruction and desecration:

> The first preoccupation I have when I write drama is to destroy things. For thirty years Hamlet was a real obsession for me, so I tried to destroy him by writing a short text, *Hamletmachine*. German history was another obsession and I tried to destroy this obsession, this whole complex. I think the main impulse is to strip things to their skeleton, to rid things of their flesh and surface. Then you are finished with them [1990:55–56].

For Müller, the act of composition is one of stripping the canon of its skin, the same metaphor through which he explains theatrical performance and human history itself. The writing of *Hamletmachine* is intended to destroy both literary and cultural history, and throughout the play Müller presents both destructions as an act of violence against the human body. Through the act of surrogation, all three are connected: the human body that remembers and embodies the past, the drama that awakens motion and memory in the body of both the living and the dead, and the history that the body relives through dramatic adaptation and performance. Again, Müller explains that writing drama is the act of robbing the grave: "I believe that the function of literature at this point is something like the liberation of the dead.... I wanted to dig up things that had been covered by dirt and history and lies. Digging up the dead and showing them in the open" (1990:67). Müller's plays frequently display his attitude toward literary adaptation as the violation of a corpse. For Müller, however, robbing the grave and tearing off the surface is only the first step in surrogating the old corpse/canon.

Müller himself began the common trend in Müller criticism of referring to his works as acts of literary cannibalism. Müller once said that "To know [the dead], you have to eat them. And then you spit out the living particles ... [Reading is] an absolute luxury. Eating literature is faster" (1990:67). Again, the canon is the corpse and the corpse is the canon: both must be eaten in order to truly internalize the past and to make it a part of the future. Kirk Williams explains Müller's use of the motif of cannibalism: "Eating is a kind of memorialization, at least according to Freud, who exerts his own influence on Müller's text. To take the lost object into oneself, cannibalizing and consuming it through ritual or metaphor, is one way that the subject masters the potentially paralysing ambivalence of loss" (188–189). The process of surrogation maintains a constant tension between the desire to properly bury the past and yet keep the past alive in the bodies of the living: with this concern over bodies, both living and dead, comes attendant anxieties about cannibalism. According to Roach there is "a deeper terror that lurks at the heart of surrogation as a cultural process: the fear of being replaced, a fear that plays itself out in tropes of monstrosity and especially cannibalism" (112). In *Cities of the Dead*, Roach examines cultures in which ritual cannibalism performed the role of cultural surrogation (140). The mythology of cannibalism, which suggests that the cannibal gains the power and knowledge of the dead by consuming their bodies, also suggests the paradox central to surrogation as a cultural process: cannibalism represents destruction and yet repetition. By eating the victim, the cannibal both destroys and yet preserves, making the body of the surrogated into a literal part of the surrogate's body. Williams explains, "The dead live on, but they do not return; eating the dead, to paraphrase Müller, allows us to know them and be finished with them at the same time" (189).

In both *Hamlet* and *Hamletmachine*, cultural surrogation is equated with cannibalism, a metaphorical motif in *Hamlet* that finds fulfillment on stage in Müller's rewriting. Considering *Hamlet*'s central canonical status and its central interest in surrogation, it is not surprising that this particular play became the source of a long-lasting fixation for Müller, nor that he chose it as the source text for the most celebrated of his many theatrical works of adaptation. A failure in surrogation is central to *Hamlet*'s plot: King Hamlet's murder and Claudius's usurpation show the failure of the son to adequately replace the father. In Shakespeare's play, murder, incest, and political intrigue all represent a broken genealogy. This failure in surrogation produces a replacement King who is inadequate and leads to a duplication in father figures that requires a haunting to reestablish the past's proper hold on the present. Surrogation includes any kind of cultural reproduction, one of its most common forms being the replacement of the parent with the child. As Roach points out children are "both the auguries of surrogation and its realization in the fullness of time" (125). Although surrogation often involves parents and children, it plays a doubly powerful role when that parent is also a king. Leaders are in particular need of cultural surrogates (Roach 37). The death of a king is an important event for a community's sense of cultural stability and the disposal of the King's remains and memory can become a source of particular anxiety: "It seems that the most powerful natural symbol for the continuity of any community, large or small, simple or complex, is, by a strange and dynamic paradox, to be found in the death of its leader, and in the representation of that striking event" (Roach 37). For Hamlet, the question of how the King's body should be remembered, transformed, and preserved into the future is bound up in the continuity of a community whose genealogy of security and memory has been permanently disrupted by violence.

Throughout Shakespeare's play, the Prince is obsessed not only with dead fathers and kings, but also with images of the human body transformed in death, and with how the bodies of the past, the corpse of the father/king, can find life in new bodies. Specifically, he repeatedly suggests that the body of the dead king is a cultural effigy that the populace consumes through cannibalism, a motif that serves as a central point of inspiration for Müller's violent rewriting. The metaphor of the king's body as a source of nourishment for the people appears throughout *Hamlet*. In the graveyard, the Prince contemplates the remains of great men, and he imagines that "Imperious Caesar dead and turned to clay/ Might stop a hole to keep the wind away" (5.1.213–14, 203–204). Caesar's transformed body becomes a dwelling place for the people. Discussing the dead Polonius, the father figure mistaken for Claudius behind the arras, leads Hamlet to contemplate not just the dead body of the father figure, but surrogation as cannibalism. The text of *Hamlet*, like the text of *Hamletmachine,* presents overlapping father figures who are killed and cannibalized. As Janet Adelman explains, "The fathers Hamlet tries so strenuously to keep separated keep threatening to collapse into one another; even when he wants to kill one to avenge the other, he cannot quite tell them apart" (21). According to Hamlet, the body of Polonius, the father figure who stands in at various points in the play for both King Hamlet and Claudius, is "At supper ... Not where he eats, but where 'a is eaten; a certain convocation of politic worms are e'en at him" (4.4.19–20). This line clearly refers not just to Polonius, but also to Hamlet's father, for the Prince goes on to say that "A man may fish with the worm that hath eat of a king, and eat of the fish that hath fed of that worm" (4.4.27–28). When Claudius interrogates Hamlet, the prince claims that he speaks only to "show you how a King may go/a progress through the guts of a beggar" (4.3.27). Throughout *Hamlet,* the Prince represents his father's decaying corpse as being simultaneously a symbol of the past and yet a source of social continuity: the king/father, as consumed effigy of flesh, lives on in the bodies of his people.[4] In the case of Polonius, the cannibalized dead live on in the bodies of the living, while in the case of Caesar, the living dwell in the cannibalized body of the dead. Adelman describes Shakespeare's *Hamlet* as a "grotesquely oral world" in which "everything is ultimately meat for a single table" (1992:27). Catherine Gallagher and Stephen Greenblatt explain the cannibalistic concerns of Shakespeare's Hamlet:

> By insisting on the vulnerability of matter and its grotesque metamorphoses, by dwelling upon the transformation of the dead into endlessly recycled food, by dragging a king through the guts of a beggar, Hamlet bitterly protests against the ghostly transmission of patriarchal memory and against the whole sacrificial plot in which the son is fatally appointed to do his father's bidding [154].

Not only does Hamlet's mockery of the King's decaying body object to the imposition of patriarchal memory, but it also explores the dark implications of preserving that memory within the living, and of preserving the living through the dead whose bodies nourish them. Ultimately, Hamlet's riddles about cannibalism point to the larger breakdown in cultural surrogation and memory that lies at the center of the conflict in Denmark. Even more importantly for Müller's work, *Hamlet*'s motif of metaphorical cannibalism hints at an overturn in established hierarchies of power. As Gallagher and Greenblatt explain, in Hamlet's cannibalistic metaphors "revulsion is mingled with a sense of drastic leveling, the collapse of order and distinction into polymorphous, endlessly recycled materiality" (161).

In these lines, Hamlet represents the king as being cannibalized by the people, and on one level it is a thought of political subversion to imagine the body of the king devoured by a beggar, to claim that "your fat king and your lean beggar is but variable service, two dishes, but to one table — that's the end" (4.4. 23–25). This equation reduces the king's physical body to the status of a beggar's corpse, thus stripping him of his royal power. In Hamlet's lines the beggar appears to hold power over the body of the king because death transforms the king into the sacrificial victim that feeds the beggar. At the same time, the king maintains his power over the beggar: the death of the leader and his internalization as cannibalized effigy of flesh suggests the continuity of the consumed surrogate and his power to feed the future. As in Shakespeare's play, the cannibalized King represents multiple father figures in Müller's text: King Hamlet, Stalin, Shakespeare, and even Müller himself. The use of these overlapping father figures allows Müller to explore complex interchanges of memory and power between those who eat and those who are eaten.

"What's your corpse to me?": Dealing with the Corpse/Corpus of the Father

Through the metaphor of cannibalism, both *Hamlet* and *Hamletmachine* interrogate the cultural role of the dead and their pervasive presence in the land of the living. What is internal and metaphorical in *Hamlet*, however, becomes external and actual in *Hamletmachine*.[5] Thus, Müller's Hamlet participates in the actual cannibalization of his father: "I stopped the funeral procession, I pried open the coffin ... and I dispensed my dead procreator FLESH LIKES TO KEEP THE COMPANY OF FLESH among the bums around me. The mourning turned into rejoicing, the rejoicing into lipsmacking..." (1984:53). It is significant that the eating of the king interrupts his funeral procession, because as Roach points out, processions often represent genealogies and can function as performances that preserve cultural memory (138). Specifically, the funeral procession, that which is meant to simultaneously preserve the memory of Hamlet's father and to lay his ghost to rest, is interrupted by the act of cannibalism, which represents another way of remembering and internalizing the dead king. Hamlet's belief that "FLESH LIKES TO KEEP THE COMPANY OF FLESH" reflects the importance of keeping the father's flesh alive in the flesh of the living. As in Shakespeare's *Hamlet*, cannibalization is an act of surrogation that gives a false perception of overturned social hierarchies. At first glance, the "bums" who eat the king now appear to have power over their dead leader, but the fact remains that the hungry cannibals not only need the memory of their leader to nourish them, but they also keep the leader's flesh alive through the act of dismembering and consuming his body. This false appearance of revolutionary social action works on multiple levels, because the cannibalized body of this particular father proves to represent not just one father figure, but many.

Throughout *Hamletmachine*, Müller's text represents Shakespeare as a fallen cultural icon, a figure whose corpse/corpus is cannibalized by his offspring. As the father of drama is superimposed over the other father figures of the text, he becomes one of four patriarchs in the play (Stalin, King Hamlet, Shakespeare, and Müller) who are cannibalized by their own progeny. Critics have long concurred that King Hamlet is associated throughout the text with the dead Stalin. Arlene Teraoka recognizes the first scene of *Hamletmachine* as the state funeral of both Stalin and King Hamlet, with the bodies and identities of the two dead leaders metaphorically overlapping (97). Müller makes it clear, however, that in this multilayered and complex text, the figure of Shakespeare is equally present as literary father and dramatic forerunner. Perhaps Müller's decision to conflate Shakespeare with King Hamlet was influenced by the theatrical tradition claiming that Shakespeare played the role of the father's ghost in the original production of *Hamlet*. In any case, the king on a progress through the guts of a beggar in *Hamletmachine* turns out to be Shakespeare himself.

Again and again, Müller associates King Hamlet and Stalin with the central symbol of the suit of armor, armor that Müller would associate elsewhere in his writings with Shakespeare. This armor, which Hamlet's father wears when he appears as a ghost in Shakespeare's text, is interpreted by the men on the battlements as a sign of political unrest in the state of Denmark: "This bodes some strange eruption to our state" (1.1.68). The image of the patriarch as an armored ghost making his way among the living is one that Müller also uses to suggest the "eruption" of the state, as the appearance of the ghost precedes the Hungarian revolution alluded to later in *Hamletmachine*. As Teraoka points out, the armor also "symbolizes the traditional role prescribed for Hamlet the son" (100). Halpern agrees that the donning of the armor marks a change in Hamlet's character: "Hamlet assumes his counterrevolutionary role by donning the armor of his father" (1997:274). Although these interpretations of the armor's significance have been well documented, no one has yet noted that the armored figure of Stalin/King Hamlet is also Shakespeare. The final section of *Hamletmachine* is titled, "FIERCELY ENDURING MILLENIUMS IN THE/FEARFUL ARMOUR." In a speech delivered at the Shakespeare Festival in Weimar, "Shakespeare a Departure," Müller associates this Friedrich Hölderlin quotation with the historical Shakespeare: "A Hölderlin fragment describes the still-incarcerated Shakespeare: MADDENING ENDURANCE/IN THE DREADED ARMOUR/MILLENNIA. The Shakespeare wilderness. What is he waiting for, why inside an armor, and for how long" (1995:101). Müller thinks of Shakespeare as the figure who endures millennia trapped within the patriarchal armor. Shakespeare, imprisoned in the armor associated with Stalin and King Hamlet in the text of *Hamletmachine*, becomes yet another patriarchal figure that the play attempts to subvert but can only re-inscribe upon itself. These same anxieties are evident in the play's struggle with the Shakespearean text that gave it genesis: in rewriting the original *Hamlet*, Müller simultaneously preserves the Shakespearean past and yet creates the dramatic future.

Indeed, the text of *Hamletmachine* represents the anxieties of the adaptor through the metaphor of cannibalism (Williams 188). The act of rewriting Shakespeare both destroys the old text and yet simultaneously uses the old text as nourishment for the new. Hamlet describes the set of *Hamletmachine*, "The set is a monument. It presents a man who made history.... His name is interchangeable" (Müller 1984:56). It is not clear which history-making father figure this section of the text addresses, but Hamlet points out that their names all represent the same cultural force. Hamlet continues, "The monument is toppled into the dust, razed by those who succeeded him in power three years after the state funeral of the hated and most honored leader" (56). The reference to the fall of Stalin's statue, which was dismembered and decapitated by rioters during the failed Hungarian revolution of 1956, is unmistakable (Teraoka 98). The monument, however, simultaneously represents the other father figures in the armor: King Hamlet and Shakespeare. In this case, the toppling of the monument by "those who succeeded him in power" is the rise of other powerful dramatists (like Müller himself) who push Shakespeare's canon, and the dramatic tradition he represents, aside. After the monument falls, Hamlet tells the audience that "the stone is inhabited. In the spacy nostrils and auditory canals, in the creases of skin and uniform of the demolished monument, the poorer inhabitants of the capital are dwelling" (Müller 1984:56). The image of the people living in the body of the dead dictator is clearly inspired by Shakespeare's image of Caesar's body stopping "a hole to keep the wind away." As a form of surrogation that inverts cannibalism, the idea of the living dwelling in the body of the dead suggests the same false inversion of power dynamics implied by eating the king's body. The people destroy the statue in an act of rebellion, yet when the statue of the dead leader is destroyed, they find that they must make their homes from the remains of the old regime. As the people feed off of the dead dictator, dwelling in his body, the text of *Hamletmachine* feeds off of the body of the Shakespearean *Hamlet*, living in its text. The fallen "monument" of Shakespeare represents both the "original" text of Hamlet and the "cannibalized" literary tradition it represents. Savran points out that through the body of the actor, "the theatre sometimes becomes a site for *re-membering*, literally piecing together what has been lost" (123). In this case, the dismemberment of the father becomes a source of remembering and re-membering, a way of reconfiguring the past through the human body in performance. According to Brian Walsh, Müller "preserves and annuls Shakespeare's text in presenting us with a Hamlet play that both reiterates and remakes the classic story" (25–26). Helen Fehervary agrees that "Müller's Hamlet survives by destroying the ghosts of his political fathers, and the inspirational ghost of Shakespeare as well" (49). Yet the "inspirational ghost" of *Hamlet* can never be truly absent from Müller's work, as its dismembered parts litter the landscape of *Hamletmachine*. Through the use of the Hölderlin quotation, Müller suggests that the rioting crowds not only bring down and dismember Stalin's monument, but also the monument of Shakespeare — the very text of *Hamlet*. Like the destruction of Stalin's monument, however, the destruction/ cannibalization of *Hamlet* also suggests a false revolution, a false change in established hierarchies. The new text seems to gain power through the destruction of a symbol of power, but it is unable to fully separate itself from the old text that it has internalized. As long as *Hamletmachine* and adaptations like it continue to be performed and remembered, Shakespeare's *Hamlet* will never truly represent a "dead" literary tradition. In this way, *Hamletmachine* is indeed the theatre of raising the dead.

Yet Shakespeare is not the only dramatist who is destroyed in effigy during the course of *Hamletmachine's* performance. Hamlet's tearing of Müller's photograph is a gesture that destroys the image of the dramatist, thus depriving the text of its literary parent, an act that subjects Müller to the same metaphorical violence he has worked on his dramatic predecessor.[6] Mark Fortier explains, "White, male, European, privileged, authorial, Müller uses his talent in working toward his own expropriation" (13). In a speech on postmodernism, Müller stated:

> As long as freedom is based on brutal force and the creation of art on privileges, artistic creations will tend to be prisons and masterpieces will be the accomplices of power. The truly great texts of our century work towards the liquidation of their autonomy ... they work towards the expropriation and, finally, the disappearance of the author. Working towards the disappearance of the author means resistance against the disappearance of man [qtd. in Weber 140].

This passage reveals an author intensely aware of his own cultural and social power as an artist. Müller's postmodern philosophy recognizes the dangerous cultural power of the educationally, economically, and politically privileged author, who though he may attempt to represent the struggle of marginalized groups is doomed to failure because he will inevitably be an outsider to their discourse. When one individual attempts to speak for a large number of people, voices will inevitably be lost. In attempting to represent those voices, Müller argues, the canonized masterpiece inadvertently participates in their silencing. As Fortier points out, Müller's drama attempts to stage "a giving way of the author function before collective creation" (12). Teraoka agrees that the destruction of the author's photograph "points to the privileged author's paradoxical endeavor to eliminate all privilege in art" (102). Ironically, the destruction of the author's image is a gesture that is itself doomed to contradict the artistic statement it attempts to convey (Walsh 26). Walsh notes that through the tearing of his photograph Müller both "preserves and annuls his own authority" (26). Though the destruction of the photograph suggests Müller's attempt to eliminate his presence from his own drama, it simultaneously re-inscribes his image on the play, as productions that follow the stage directions will display his face as a part of the performance.

Ultimately, Müller's postmodern aesthetics dictate that the creation of *Hamletmachine*, an attempt to create revolutionary theatre, is doomed to produce a deformed artistic product. Williams explains Müller's aesthetic of failure: "The 'Actor playing Hamlet' destroys the image of the dramatist immediately prior to announcing his desire to become a machine, suggesting that Müller sees the 'death' of the author as the prerequisite of a true revolutionary theatre and of a structure of subjectivity that exists outside of history" (Williams 197). The displaying and tearing of the author's photograph also immediately follows a speech in which Hamlet recognizes his own culturally privileged position. The author who works toward his own disappearance resembles the divided self of Müller's Hamlet, who is tortured by the realization that his social status as prince separates him from the revolutionaries with whom he sympathizes (Halpern 270). "I am/a privileged person," Hamlet says, "My nausea/Is a privilege/Protected by torture/Barbed wire Prisons" (Müller 1984:57). The Prince is also divided in that he imagines himself on both sides of the battle that the play describes in its fourth section: Hamlet sees himself as both revolutionary and oppressor (Teraoka 107, Walsh 29). Teraoka argues that in this fourth section, "Hamlet brings to light the dilemma of the privileged intellectual who is committed to the abolition of privilege" (108). The text that attempts to be truly revolutionary is also a divided text. The text of the author, with its competing voices and allusions, is permanently bound to the literary past. In the end, the art of the future is only the art of the past, a "deeply flawed social script" from which *Hamletmachine* cannot escape (Williams 195). Williams finds that *Hamletmachine* makes a larger statement about the failure of revolutionary drama: "Since theatrical history, like old kings, will not stay buried, *Hamletmachine* concludes in the only way Müller believes an authentic, pre-revolutionary drama can, namely by thematizing its own failure to be revolutionary drama" (198). Unable to escape from the image of the father/king/author, the play fails to fulfill the revolutionary agenda it proclaims. In a play overrun with surrogates and surrogations, duplications and endlessly replicated horrors, Müller's Hamlet is in constant search of origins, a journey that proves to be about violence and erasure rather than discovery. Roach explains that within the larger historical network of ongoing surrogations, "the relentless search for ... origins is a voyage not of discovery but of erasure" (6). As both characters and text attempt to discover and destroy their own origins, Hamlet undertakes the cannibalization of the author/father, whose art/body preserves the cultural past and yet creates the artistic future.

Like the people feasting on the flesh of the dead dictator, the new author attempts to devour and destroy the old text, but the play's attempted destruction fails. Filled with a cacophony of voices and competing allusions, *Hamletmachine* can never extricate itself from the voices of past authors, anymore than Hamlet can truly separate himself from his father, or *Hamletmachine* as cultural product can disentangle itself from the legacy and reputation of its world-renowned author. As the metaphor of the monument demonstrates, *Hamletmachine* is unable to destroy or dismember its source text, as the very act of cannibalizing the old text simultaneously acknowledges the cultural primacy of *Hamlet* and calls it to the forefront of the audience's memory (Walsh 26). The past maintains its hold on the present, and the figure of Shakespeare continues to loom over modern drama. In the end, *Hamletmachine* destroys neither corpse nor corpus.

UNIVERSITY OF GEORGIA

Notes

1. It has become customary to read the father figure in *Hamletmachine* as a representative of an oppressive patriarchal culture. See for example, Teraoka, *The Silence of Entropy or Universal Discourse*.

2. W. B. Worthen comes closest to my approach by applying the conception of surrogation to Baz Luhrmann's *William Shakespeare's Romeo + Juliet*. His interest is not in a rewriting of an older play, however, but in a film that uses Shakespearean language juxtaposed with pop culture references. Worthen is interested in Luhrman's film as one more cultural "iteration" of Shakespeare's *Romeo and Juliet*, not in an appropriation of *Romeo and Juliet* that uses a completely new script. In this sense, *Hamletmachine* presents a radically different kind of surrogation, in that it is an entirely new work built on an older drama.

3. Müller's plays clearly influenced Carlson's thinking about the haunted nature of theatre, and it is possible that his work may have influenced Roach's theory of theatre as well.

4. Gallagher and Greenblatt examine Hamlet's ruminations on cannibalism in light of the Catholic Eucharist, while Williams identifies a connection between the Eucharist and *Hamletmachine*. The transubstantiation of wafer and wine into body and blood underlies the references to the King's consumed (and transformed) body in *Hamlet* and goes on to form part of the history of cannibalistic rituals informing Müller's consumption of Shakespeare.

5. See Williams, who calls *Hamletmachine* the "political and sexual unconscious of *Hamlet*" (202).

6. Thanks to an attentive audience at the Comparative Drama Conference in 2009 who pointed out to me that the author destroyed in effigy need not be Müller, since the stage direction calls for the destruction of the author's image (which could be understood to be Shakespeare or the director of the performance). Mark Fortier's discussion hints at the possibility of these images of Shakespeare and Müller as interchangeable. Whichever "author" is destroyed, the event can be interpreted as an attack against the play's "artistic father."

References Cited

Adelman, Janet. *Suffocating Mothers: Fantasies of Maternal Origin in Shakespeare's Plays, Hamlet to the Tempest*. New York: Routledge, 1992.

Carlson, Marvin. *The Haunted Stage: Theatre as Memory Machine.* Ann Arbor: University of Michigan Press, 2003.

Fehervary, Helen. "The Gender of Authorship: Heiner Müller and Christa Wolf." *Studies in Twentieth Century Literature* 5 (1980):41–58.

Fortier, Mark. "Shakespeare as 'Minor Theater': Deleuze and Guattari and the Aims of Adaptation." *Mosaic* 29 (1996):1–18.

Gallagher, Catherine and Stephen Greenblatt. *Practicing New Historicism.* Chicago: University of Chicago Press, 2000.

Halpern, Richard. *Shakespeare among the Moderns.* New York: Cornell University Press, 1997.

Kalb, Jonathan. *The Theater of Heiner Müller.* New York: Cambridge University Press, 1998.

Malkin, Jeanette. *Memory-Theater and Postmodern Drama.* Ann Arbor, MI: University of Michigan Press, 1999.

Müller, Heiner. *Germania,* translated by Bernard and Caroline Schütze, edited by Sylvere Lotringer. New York: Semiotext[e], 1990.

_____. *Hamletmachine and Other Texts for the Stage,* edited and translated by Carl Weber. New York: Performing Arts Journal Publications, 1984.

_____. Interview with Elinor Fuchs. "PAJ Casebook on *Alcestis.*" *Performing Arts Journal* 10.1 (1986):79–115.

_____. *Theatremachine.* Translated by Marc von Henning. London: Faber and Faber, 1995.

Roach, Joseph. *Cities of the Dead: Circum-Atlantic Performance.* New York: Columbia University Press, 1996.

Savran, David. "Modernity's Haunted Houses." *Modern Drama: Defining the Field,* edited by Ric Knowles, Joanne Tompkins, W.B. Worthen. 119. Toronto: Toronto Press, 2003.

Shakespeare, William. *The Riverside Shakespeare,* edited by G. Blakemore Evans, et al. 2nd ed. Boston: Houghton Mifflin, 1997.

Teraoka, Arlene Akiko. *The Silence of Entropy or Universal Discourse: The Postmodernist Poetics of Heiner Müller.* New York: Peter Lang, 1985.

Walsh, Brian. "The Rest is Violence: Müller Contra Shakespeare." *Performing Arts Journal* 23.2 (2001):24–35.

Weber, Carl. "Heiner Müller: The Despair and the Hope." *Performing Arts Journal* 4.3 (1980): 135–140.

Williams, Kirk. "The Ghost in the Machine: Heiner Müller's Devouring Melancholy." *Modern Drama* 49 (2006):188–205.

Worthen, W.B. "Drama, Performativity, Performance," *PMLA* 113.5 (1998):1093–1107.

A Liberating Cruelty
Two Adaptations of Classical Tragedy for the Mexican Stage

Francisco Barrenechea

Abstract

Two adaptations of classical tragedy for the Mexican stage, Alfonso Reyes's Cruel Iphigenia *(1923) and Ximena Escalante's* Real Andromache *(2005), are rooted in a particular way of understanding the tragic: namely, as a transformation of identity through cruelty. Cruelty here is defined as a willful repudiation of society and the self.*

Cruelty plays a pivotal role in two Mexican adaptations of classical tragedy: Alfonso Reyes's *Cruel Iphigenia* (1923), a version of Euripides's *Iphigenia among the Taurians*, and Ximena Escalante's play *Real Andromache* (2005), which is based on the Andromaches of Racine and Euripides. Reyes's *Cruel Iphigenia* is notable for being the first adaptation of Greek tragedy in Mexican literature, while Escalante's is a recent — and quite successful — example of what is being done with the genre on the Mexican stage. Despite the fact that almost eighty years stand between them, both dramas are rooted in a particular way of understanding the tragic: namely, as a transformation of identity through a process of cruelty, a cruelty that is founded on the willful repudiation of society and ultimately of the self. In the following pages, I propose to sketch out how this process manifests itself in these two plays.

Reyes's *Cruel Iphigenia* takes its general plot from Euripides, as I just mentioned. The protagonist, about to be sacrificed at the hands of her father Agamemnon at Aulis, is spirited away to Tauris by the goddess Artemis, where she becomes her priestess. Iphigenia's brother Orestes arrives in Tauris and recognizes his sister. Both then plot their escape and return to Greece. Reyes introduces two radical innovations into the story: first, Iphigenia has completely forgotten her identity and is only aware of her role as priestess. Second, her brother Orestes helps her remember who she is, but in the process makes her recall the crimes of their family. Horrified by these crimes, Iphigenia repudiates her family and refuses to return with her brother, preferring instead to continue her duty to the goddess. These two innovations define Iphigenia's cruelty, her signature trait in Reyes. But in what way can the character be said to be cruel? And why is her cruelty so significant that it deserves to be mentioned in the very title of the play?

Rodríguez Monegal (12) and Xirau (751) point out the first significant aspect of Iphigenia's cruelty: her role as priestess. When describing the process by which she regained consciousness at Tauris, she neatly sums up her realization of this role: "Born between my hands was the knife,/and I am now your butcher, oh Goddess" (Reyes 318).[1] In another marked departure from the Greek original, where she merely prepared the human victims for others to sacrifice, Reyes's Iphigenia now becomes the one who dispatches them in the manner of an Aztec priest, as the playwright observes in his notes to the play (358). Furthermore, as Iphigenia's words reveal, this religious duty is the only thing about herself that she is aware of; absent all memories of her past life, it becomes her only identity. This identity, however, is not something she chose; it was imposed by the goddess Artemis. Like the knife that appears in her hands, Iphigenia's cruelty was born along with her new role.

The chorus of the play becomes a significant foil for the cruelty of the priestess: Reyes makes them all local women, inhabitants of Tauris, who treat Iphigenia as "a sacred, ferocious thing" (320), worthy of reverent awe due to her mysterious appearance in the land. Usually in Greek tragedies, a chorus of women joins the female protagonist in shared grieving and consolation: Sophocles's *Electra* and Euripides's *Helen* come to mind. But consolation is out of the question in Reyes: since Iphigenia's life story is a mystery to the chorus as well as to herself, there is no misfortune to pity — a fact the chorus is well aware of (323–324). The women only repeatedly lament that she bristles at their attempts to offer her some company (320–324). Iphigenia does lament her incapacity to take part in the society of women (319, 322), but she retreats at the same time into her religious duty (320–321, 324–325), the only thing that gives her a sense of identity. What is more, she not only rejects the women's attentions, but also further displaces her own affections *towards* her sacrificial victims. As she herself states: "I am thirsty to tame the body of an enemy./Ah, a better love than your love, women!" (321). The priestess overtly sexualizes her duty, her only true form of human contact. In her inability to enter into a normal human relationship, she is cruel towards the empathetic chorus as well as towards herself— not to mention her victims.

Thus, Iphigenia becomes, in the words of Reyes, a "haughty and cruel" character (315). Harshness, savageness, even flintiness are all qualities frequently ascribed to her throughout the play. She is outside the circle of human experience, beyond pity and the comfort of society. In this respect, Iphigenia is cut from the same cloth of certain Sophoclean heroes like Electra and Ajax, who are also described as intractable and savage (Knox 23, 42–43). But these heroes acquire their harshness due to grudges: they behave in this manner because they have not forgotten and indeed brood excessively over their injuries. Iphigenia, however, has no memory: nothing can account for her alienation and harshness. These qualities are as natural, as just simply *there*, as a mushroom that sprouts overnight — an image that Reyes conjures to describe her sudden appearance at Tauris (318, 321).

Eventually, Iphigenia does remember her previous self, but this process, which could have served to reintegrate the character successfully into society, ends up clashing with the initial cruelty of the savage, virginal priestess. At the root of the conflict is the type of role she is about to regain — that of the marriageable daughter of a royal household — and above all, the condition under which she is meant to regain it: Orestes repeatedly portrays his attempts to make his sister recall her identity as an act of taming, binding, even enslaving. For instance, he tells her: "I'll grasp you by the navel of remembrance./I'll tie you to the center from which your soul departs./I've scarcely become your prisoner/and you're already my slave" (340). This approach is not merely a response to the intractability of Iphigenia the priestess, but it is also an act of coercion: Orestes and the god Apollo command her to marry and have children, to carry on her duty to the family (317).

In the most remarkable twist that Reyes brings to the myth, the initial cruelty of the character becomes instrumental for a radical liberation. As Reyes puts it, "We have loaded Iphigenia with a god so harsh and haughty, that the harm of her race will end with her, like an arrow bouncing off a shield." (358). Along with her recollection of her previous role comes the remembrance of the endless cycle of revenge within her family. For Iphigenia, to obey and reintegrate herself into her family as a marriageable daughter means to perpetuate their violence through new offspring (347). Thus, she retreats once again to that initial cruelty that had alienated her from the chorus: she rejects not only her brother but also the god who had commanded her return. In this manner, Iphigenia willfully and haughtily liberates herself from the vendettas of her family.

The closest Greek tragic character I can think of that matches Reyes's Iphigenia is Sophocles's Ajax, who also withdraws from his family and society in order to kill himself and end the shame caused by a fit of madness, in which he slaughtered cattle thinking he was taking revenge upon his enemies. His suicide can thus be read as an act of liberation to save his honor. Nevertheless, Sophocles still makes Ajax exclaim that he is destroyed at the hands of Menelaus and Agamemnon (838), and even his death is an occasion for him to call on the gods to punish his enemies (835–844). Ajax's suicide is also in part an act of revenge for the disrespectful treatment he received at the hands of the Greeks, and as such it is deeply enmeshed within his social group. Reyes's Iphigenia, on the other hand, does not seek honor or revenge. In her final words, before she exits into the temple, she tells Orestes: "Take in your hands, grasped with your mind,/these hollow shells of words: *I don't want to!*" (Reyes 348). Hers is a simple act of refusal; she simply opts out of it all.

For Reyes, Iphigenia's refusal is positive, liberating, and even redemptive. In his notes to the play, he celebrates it as an act of personal emancipation that radically cuts her off from family and homeland (357), and by extension, from the violence associated with them (313). Reyes, however, is surprisingly coy about the consequences of her decision. He does observe at one point that "this last extreme [i.e., her duty as priestess], no matter how abominable and harsh it may seem, [is] the only certain and practical way" (313) she can liberate herself. However, he does not elaborate on why ritualized, savage violence would be a valid choice to make in order to escape violent civilization, and what is more important, he leaves unspoken the price Iphigenia has to pay for her choice.[2]

Iphigenia's initial duty as priestess, whose defining trait had been a cruel indifference to others and herself, is what she ultimately falls back on when she refuses to return to Greece. When she *willingly* rejects her family, she *chooses* to live the rest of her life in this role; by doing so, she consigns herself to perpetual virginity, rejecting her duty to marry and have children, as well as all contact with others. There is something very unsettling and even inhuman about her decision; more so, if one considers the fact that Iphigenia, faced with the prospect of servitude to her murderous family, chooses another form of servitude, this time to the goddess Artemis, as well as another murderous duty, that of human sacrifice.

Cruelty reappears as a deliberate and problematic choice in Ximena Escalante's *Real Andromache*. This play focuses on the successive acts of cruelty, both psychological and physical, that four lovers inflict on each other: Andromache resists the advances of Pyrrhus, who despises Hermione, who rejects the love of Orestes. The latter, in despair at the pain inflicted by this chain of rejection, asks for it to be reversed. He gets his wish but it merely inverts the chain: now Hermione is disgusted by Pyrrhus, and Pyrrhus despises Andromache. Both the initial chain and its inversion lead to extreme cases of mismatched desires, which produce in the characters a deep-rooted sense of emptiness. Andromache gives voice to this feeling in her opening monologue, by stating, "I've never had anything in its totality. Things come in pieces. People come, and they are pieces" (Escalante 90). This condition motivates a constant demand among the characters for something "real" that could complete them. The situation leads to various transformations in the characters, who are moved to take harsh and even violent measures against others, as well as themselves, in order to cope with the impossibility of fulfilling their desires.

The process of cruelty in *Real Andromache* is rooted in the indifference of the beloved towards his or her lover, and in the actions the latter takes to deal with this imbalance. In Euripides's version of the myth, this indifference is present only in Pyrrhus's rejection of Hermione; Racine's *Andromache* extends it to form the chain of unrequited desire on which Escalante built her drama. Furthermore, Escalante radically distills the myth in order to focus exclusively on the chain and the fallout of what turns out to be a complex constellation of rejections.

The relationship between Andromache and Pyrrhus sets the pattern followed by the rest of the chain. Andromache, as I mentioned before, resists Pyrrhus. Of all the characters, she is the only one who fully realizes her incompleteness as well as the futility of the desire that Pyrrhus and the others display towards their beloveds. Her resistance to the advances of Pyrrhus is based on submissively bestowing her body to him, a seemingly counterintuitive action, but as she explains: "piece by piece, he believes that one day he'll have it all, my totality; he believes he's going to add it all up, and thinks that that sum will give a total. But I, who remain cold to my own life, know that totals only exists in supermarket accounts" (Escalante 90). This, as Pyrrhus reasons in a later scene, is cruel treatment (123). It manifests itself in her indifference to the pain she causes in her lover by fostering this desire for completeness, given that she is fully aware that the process is futile. However, this cruelty comes at a cost to herself: she exposes her body, the "pieces," to the brutality of her lover, who resorts to violence in order to force her to bestow herself entirely to him. This awareness and willful cruelty of Andromache makes her, in part, a passive but hostile character, cold not only to Pyrrhus but also to her own self, as she herself states; she is the first link, and indeed the origin, of the chain of incompleteness in the drama.

Andromache, as Pyrrhus eventually reveals, carries "ancestral pains," whose origins she herself does not know (137), that keep her from being able to correspond anyone's affections. The playwright has dispensed with all traces of the character's myth that might explain these pains: the loss of her husband Hector at Troy, her captivity at the hands of Pyrrhus, as well as the threats to the life of her children. As a result, Andromache is an enigma not only to the other characters in Escalante's play, but also to herself; she even goes so far as to deny that she has possession of her own self (90). In this respect, Escalante's Andromache is similar to Reyes's amnesiac Iphigenia: both characters are aware of their actions but cannot fully account for them, since they have no access to their past. This results not only in their harshness of character towards others but also in a sense of deep alienation: Andromache is, in fact, an emotional void.

The harshness displayed by the beloved fosters cruelty in the lover, as exemplified by the reactions of Pyrrhus and Hermione after being rejected. In the case of the former, this cruelty manifests itself not only in his physical violence against the unresponsive Andromache (he batters her in the first scene of the play), but also in his calculated propagation of cruelty to others, along with the realization of the impossibility of possessing someone entirely. When he confronts Hermione, for instance, he rebukes her for desiring him, since this renders her "something incomplete" (94), possessed by "emptiness" (95), and therefore, an object of contempt. Pyrrhus has learned Andromache's lesson well and passes it on to another.

What is more, Pyrrhus finds a way to rationalize this behavior: "If Andromache does not love me," he reflects later in the play, that's not only a great injustice but also a great cruelty.... It's impossible to take revenge on her, because she's a sad woman, who doesn't love. So, revenge has to be unjust. Yes, exactly. I have to contribute to the web of injustice that exists in the world. Yes. Revenge should reach another" [123–124].

His revenge is unfair because he inflicts it not on the person who hurt him but on an innocent lover; nevertheless, it is indeed an attempt at rectification, in that the spurned lover makes his undeserved treatment bearable by resorting to the same behavior. In spurning and behaving cruelly towards his beloveds, Pyrrhus thus becomes "love-normal" (124), as he puts it. He perversely believes that the cycle he is perpetrating is customary and even almost inevitable.

Hermione is the first casualty of Pyrrhus's revenge. The harsh response of her beloved likewise spurs her to come to terms with her rejection by mistreating others, but she resorts to a different strategy. When Pyrrhus first pushes her away and reminds her of her incompleteness, he compares Hermione to a dirty cloth and instructs her, "Go to a laundromat. Have them clean you thoroughly. Have them make you something ... perfumed" (96). She takes this image to heart and subsequently employs it to refer to her relationship with the various men, besides Orestes, who appear onstage to court her. "For me, to say 'I wash you' or I desire you' is the same thing," she clarifies. "Both things end up being the same: fluids that come and go" (99). Her interaction with men is portrayed as an event that, like the washing of dirty clothes, can be repeated and done in different ways; in other words, hers is a repeated (and eventually unsuccessful) attempt to alleviate that incompleteness that was pointed out by Pyrrhus.

Throughout this constant coming and going, Hermione remains detached, while at the same time toying with the feelings of the men who pursue her, leading them on, and even hurting them physically and psychologically. As one of her suitors complains: "What kind of person are you, that everything passes through you like dust on your eyelashes?" (105). There is, indeed, an element of alienation in Hermione's role as a consummate tease. When the chain of desire inverts itself, and Hermione begins to pursue her former lover Orestes, she is initially rebuffed, only to be enticed again. She reacts viscerally to this treatment, the treatment she herself reserves for others, and exclaims, "Now you do love me? Ah ... well I don't. I don't love you, I never did.... I love to play, I love to hurt, I love to make men feel unhappy, I love to seduce them and then hit them, like this: (*She strikes Orestes*) ... This is my life, a coming and going of men, of bodies. I'm like that and there's no remedy" (130–131). Hermione had taken it upon herself to show her lovers that their desires can never be truly reciprocated, but now that a beloved begins to reciprocate her feelings, she finds it impossible to believe. The cycle of cruelty has taken its toll on one more of its perpetrators.

In the degree that the characters of Escalante's *Real Andromache* are both victims and perpetrators of this perpetual cycle, they are entrapped in a web of painful social relationships. Nevertheless, even Pyrrhus and Hermione, the characters who, I believe, are most affected and transformed by the process of cruelty, seek to disentangle themselves and indeed opt out of this cycle of their own making. Hermione, for her part, finally comes to accept the impossibility of a relationship with Pyrrhus. However, when she communicates this realization to him, she compares their failed relationship to "lukewarm water" (134–135), an image that brings to mind her initial comparison of relationships with doing washing. The image is unsettling: Is she referring to her affair with Pyrrhus as just another of her many failed relationships? Does her use of the image signify that she still considers her relationships as a repetitive chore in which everything is transient and nothing is ever truly shared? She might have put Pyrrhus behind her, but has she abandoned her serial mistreatment of suitors, her incapacity to trust a lover? The playwright leaves these questions unanswered.

Pyrrhus does escape the chain, but by gradually displacing his desire onto animals and objects. Escalante does not shirk from explicitly staging the darker and dehumanizing consequences of Pyrrhus's choices. He first buys two female dogs to supplant the affections of women. But since dogs have total devotion towards their masters, they are also, in this respect, "incomplete" according to his calculations. This is the reason why Pyrrhus, after explaining why the revenge for his mistreatment has to reach others, immediately calls the pets onstage and, as Escalante indicates in her stage directions, "*beats them with tremendous cruelty, until he kills them*" (124). This is, in fact, the act that makes him call himself "love-normal"—a far cry indeed from normality. It is only at the end of the play, when he buys a bicycle, that he reaches a curious state of fulfillment: "It's better than dogs and women, it's the most real companionship I've ever felt" (136), he tells Andromache. Pyrrhus finds happiness in embracing the inanimate, whose totality he now truly, really possesses; but in doing so, he willfully rejects at the same time all possible human or even animal companionship. His choice, in a way, is parallel to that of Iphigenia, in that he also resorts to alienation in order to opt out of the cycle. In an attempt to cope with his unfulfilled passion, he liberates himself through cruelty, but at the price, once again, of his own humanity.

To conclude, both Reyes and Escalante, in their adaptations of Greek myth, choose to underscore a process of cruelty. Characters attempt to solve their conflicts by willfully (and aggressively) turning their back on society in order to inflict, or harden themselves against, suffering. As a result, they liberate themselves, but at a high cost: they create a new identity, but one that is harsh and deeply alienated.

In these pages, I have attempted to show how this process of cruelty manifests itself in *Cruel Iphigenia* and *Real Andromache*. It remains to be seen whether this understanding of the tragic is peculiar to Mexican dramatists, or if it can also be found in adaptations of classical tragedy in other parts of the world. Likewise, this reading of the tragic as a liberating cruelty needs to be situated among the other interpretations of the genre that exist in contemporary theatre. I hope to address these larger issues in a future article.

BRYN MAWR COLLEGE

Notes

Acknowledgment. I would like to express my gratitude to Ximena Escalante, who kindly made available to me the script of her play before it was published.

1. All translations in this article are my own.

2. Scholars tend to follow Reyes in celebrating the positive side of Iphigenia's redemption, but Paz (281–282), Vitier (301–302), and Rodríguez Monegal (10–11, 13, 17) do acknowledge and attempt to make sense of this problematic aspect of the character's final decision.

References Cited

Escalante, Ximena. *Tres obras de traición: antología.* Mexico City: Consejo Nacional para la Cultura y las Artes, 2008.

Knox, Bernard. *The Heroic Temper.* Berkeley: University of California Press, 1966.

Paz, Octavio. "El jinete del aire: Alfonso Reyes." *Obras completas. Vol. 3,* 278–288. Barcelona: Galaxia Gutenberg/Círculo de lectores, 1999.

Reyes, Alfonso. *Obras completas. Vol. 10: Constancia poética.* Mexico City: Fondo de Cultura Económica, 1959.

Rodríguez Monegal, Emir. "Alfonso Reyes: las máscaras trágicas." *Vuelta* 67 (1982):6–18.

Vitier, Cintio. "En torno a *Ifigenia cruel.*" *Más páginas sobre Alfonso Reyes,* edited by James W. Robb. *Vol. 4,* 288–303. Mexico City: El Colegio Nacional, 1997.

Xirau, Ramón. "Cinco vías a *Ifigenia cruel.*" *Más páginas sobre Alfonso Reyes,* edited by James W. Robb. *Vol. 3,* 744–752. Mexico City: El Colegio Nacional, 1996.

Troy, Troy ... Taiwan
Transformation from Epic to Elegy
Wen-ling Lin

Abstract

This paper first examines how the public discourses of "oceanic culture" and "ocean country" influence the reworking of an intercultural adaptation of Homer's The Iliad *into a work of national imagination, alluding to Taiwan's long history of colonization and present situation with China while simultaneously paying homage to this island. Without changing the Greek names and most of the plot, what strategies do the adapter and the director use to make this well-known story of the siege of Troy an elegy for Taiwan? The prologue establishes the link between Troy and Taiwan, which is maintained not by means of the text, but through the use of various performing elements during the production. As the director indicates, he intends to create a "virtual mythic ancient Taiwan kingdom," by using the Hoklo language, local rituals, folk songs, indigenous performing traditions and the historical performing spaces. To what degree do these combined elements succeed in creating an imagined ancient Taiwan nation?*

> I dream/our island has sunk
> On the blue sea/blood stains/float
> Across the waves/voices/call out loud/unheard
> An unidentified fleet/crosses the strait/flowing /a flock of whales
> Among the spirits slowly rising/I/gaze down/at my vanished homeland
> ["Nightmare" by Li Min-yong (2005:124)[1]]

In 1997, Golden Bough Theatre produced *Troy, Troy* (*Guguo zhishen: ji telu-oyi*, if literally translated, *God of an Ancient Kingdom: Ritual for Troy*),[2] an intercultural adaptation of Homer's *The Iliad*, in the deserted Huashan Rice Wine Distillery in Taipei. This production was significant in the history of modern theatre in Taiwan. The arrest of the director on the charge of trespassing a government-owned public space caused heated debates on the use of urban wastelands, which led to the formation of Huashan Art District, the first of many such districts to be founded. In addition, *Troy, Troy,* the first production adapted from the West by Golden Bough Theatre, marked the beginning of its experiment with environmental theatre, or more precisely, open-air performing space.[3] In October 2005, Golden Bough Theater restaged the show in Huwei Fortress, a historical site in suburban Taipei, followed by performances in another historical site, Qihou Fort, in southern Taiwan in early 2006. Entitled *Ji teloyi: wanzheng-ban* (*Ritual for Troy: The Complete Version*, if literally translated) in Chinese and *Troy, Troy ... Taiwan* in English, this production not only extended the performing time from fifty minutes to one hundred, but also differed drastically from the 1997 production in the performing style and the point of focus, with the greatest thematic shift from a universal heroic epic in 1997 to an elegy and parable for Taiwan in 2005.

When preparing for producing *Troy, Troy ... Taiwan*, director Wang Rong-yu said that he was moved to tears, reading one passage from Edith Hamilton's *Mythology: Timeless Tales of Gods and Heroes*: "about three thousand years ago, near the eastern edge of Asia Minor, there existed a big city, its prosperity unrivaled, and its fame, unparalleled; its name was Troy" (2005a:10). What came to his mind, though, was not Troy, but Taiwan, which "has suffered from Trojan-like sieges of various scales in different periods and is still faced with threat even nowadays" (2005a:11). In both the program notes and the published script, he highlights that "this production is dedicated to Taiwan, our beloved Formosa, which has always been under the shadow of wars. It is also dedicated to the Taiwanese, who have strived to survive up to now for the past four hundred years" (2005a:12). *The Iliad* is thus turned into an imagination of the long colonized past of Taiwan by various alien powers and a reflection on its present situation with China, which sees Taiwan as "a renegade province" and never renounces use of force if Taiwan officially declares independence.

Interestingly, the 1997 production does not involve any specific references to national imagination, but focuses on the universal theme of the horrors of war with an implicit criticism of contemporary Taiwanese society. If situated in the political-social contexts of Taiwan, the thematic shift should have been reversed, given the fact that the memory of a series of missile tests and military maneuvers conducted by China off the coast of Taiwan from July 1995 to March 1996 must have been fresh.[4] The heightened tension even propelled America, based on the Taiwan Relations Act, to dispatch ships to this region, and unexpectedly raised Taiwan's international profile.[5] Needless to say, the missile crisis impacted the economy in Taiwan greatly, with the stock market plummeting and foreign capital fleeing. In considering Taiwan's sovereignty issue, the threat of war has always been a concern for its people and imprinted in their psyche as the above-quoted poem, "Nightmare," vividly captures. Then, why not in 1997 but in 2005 is it that *The Iliad* was reworked as a parable for the importance of defending Taiwan and an ode exhibiting intense love for the island? What strategies do the adapter and the director use to make a well-known story of the siege of Troy simultaneously an elegy for Taiwan without changing the Greek names and most of the plot?

The article written by the adapter You Hui-fen and collected in both the fifty-two page program notes and published script provides the clue. I argue that the successful discursive construction of Taiwan as an "ocean country" in the twenty-first century has shaped the national imagination of many people in Taiwan, including that of the adapter. You Hui-fen explains that while struggling to decide on one of the many themes, such as "heroic epic, anti-war, relations between gods and humans, or fate and free will," she was most struck by one passage in *The Iliad* where Zeus says, "For of all the cities under the sun and stars, of all the cities that men inhabit, Sacred Ilion is the dearest to my soul" (You 2005a:17; Homer 1997:66). For You Hui-fen, Troy is unique because it is god's favorite city. Similarly, the formation of Taiwan from the collisions between the Eurasian Plate and the Philippine Plate about four million years ago, is also a miracle "as if held up from the palm of god if described in a mythology" (You 2005a:17).

According to You Hui-fen, Troy is not only god's favorite city, but can be said to be built by gods. Punished by Zeus, Poseidon builds fortifications around Troy while Apollo herds the cows in the valley, filling the city with delightful music, for one year. Based on this description, You Hui-fen interprets Troy as a place nurtured by the sun (Apollo) while surrounded and protected by the ocean (Poseidon). The stretching of the metaphor, interestingly, turns Troy, a legendary seaport city, into a tropical island, just like Taiwan, where people have recently referred to themselves as "children of the ocean" and started to pay great attention to its ocean policies.

Moving away from geography to history, the adapter argues that "Due to their prosperity and importance as a transport site, both [Troy and Taiwan] have been subject to various invasions in history" (2005a:18). In drawing the parallels, You Hui-fen traces the formation of the island, highlights the role of the ocean, and the history of being invaded due to its geographical importance and prosperity. All of them, reminiscent of the popular discourses of "oceanic culture" and "ocean country," illuminate why *The Iliad* became a work of national imagination in 2005.

The conceptualization of Taiwan as an ocean country and its culture as oceanic has gained great momentum in the late 1990s. Although there had been discussions of oceanic culture before the mid–1990s and establishment of such foundations as "Ocean Taiwan Foundation," it was during the first popular presidential election campaign in 1996 that the proposed policy "establishing a green technology island and ocean trade country" by the pro-independence Democratic Progressive Party candidate, Peng Ming-min, set the discourse on the stage (Wang S. 2005:1; Lin 2008:2–3). With DPP becoming the ruling party in 2000, both refashioning Taiwan as an ocean country and promoting oceanic culture have become national policies. In early 2004, the Council of Marine Affairs Advancement under the Executive Yuan (Cabinet), was set up to help develop Taiwan into "an ecological, safe, and prosperous country."[6] Among the many seminars and publications, one was written by then Vice-president Lu Xiu-lian and published in February 2004. Its title, *The Great Future of Taiwan: Becom-*

ing an Ocean-based Country and an Island of the World, sheds lights on the relations between the ocean and national development. Even in the 2008 presidential campaign, "ocean" remained a hot topic. Chinese Nationalist Party (or *Kuomingtong*, hereafter KMT) candidate Ma Ying-jeou (Ma Ying-jiu) in his campaign white paper featured ocean policies, advocating "Blue Revolution, Building an Ocean-based Prosperous Country" and the establishment of the Ministry of Ocean.[7] Similarly, discussions on the nature of an ocean country and oceanic culture in the public sphere have been as keen as official ones, covering a wide range of topics, such as art, culture, trade, folk beliefs, environmental protection, and history.

The reinvention of Taiwan as an ocean country carries multiple meanings. It can be simply a geographical fact or a catch phrase for the future development of Taiwan, but more often than not, it is expanded into a Taiwanese nationalist discourse. First and foremost, invariably, most writing on any ocean country traces its formation and the importance of its geographical location, which makes it a coveted place for both immigrants and colonizers. These are exactly the reasons why You Hui-fen sees the connection between Troy and Taiwan. It does not mean that she intentionally draws on the discourses of ocean nationhood; rather, the popularity of these discourses manifests themselves in the process of adaptation and shapes how You Hui-fen perceives Taiwan.

As a Taiwanese nationalist discourse, the concept of an "ocean country" reacts against the policies of the previous KMT totalitarian regime. During its anti-communism period, the coastline of Taiwan was heavily guarded and people did not have much free access to the ocean. The ocean was turned into a dangerous frontier, a battlefield against the Chinese communists on mainland. Up to this date, numerous new ocean policies have been enforced, aimed to liberate the inhabitants from the confinement imposed by the past party-state and restore the "oceanic nature" of their ancestors, who crossed the ocean at various time periods to settle on this island and whose life was closely related to the ocean. If the ocean during the martial law rule isolated the island from the outside world, the ocean nowadays connects it to the outside world.

Moreover, "ocean country," as the name suggests, simultaneously connotes the other, "mainland" China, which, ancient or contemporary, is constructed as a "continental" country, closed and confined. For example, historically, Manchu Qing Emperors closed the door to foreign countries and enforced strict policies to prevent Han Chinese from crossing the sea to settle on the island, for fear that they would deploy Taiwan as a base to rebel against the Manchurian dynasty. Therefore, the discourse of ocean country distinguishes Taiwan from China, and more importantly, situates Taiwan as a Subject rather than simply a remote appendage to a continent.

Finally, the discourse of oceanic culture works hand in hand with the discourse of multiculturalism to resolve ethnic tension, interpret the long colonized past, and cope with globalization. The characteristics of oceanic culture are understood invariably as being open-ended, fluid, assimilating, accommodating, free, and multi-dimensional (Zhuang 304; Huang:44–47). Therefore, oceanic culture not only helps come to terms with the colonized past but also helps to reinvent a rich, distinctive Taiwanese culture that has been constantly absorbing the cultures with which it interacts, including Chinese, European, American, and Japanese cultures.

By comparing You Hui-fen's writing on inspirations for her adaptation with the public discourses of ocean country and oceanic culture, I demonstrate that these discourses, which are continually reiterated by the government through various policies, and promoted in public spheres by intellectuals, cultural workers, and environmentalists, have played a significant role in reshaping *The Iliad* into a work of national imagination. Nothing can be more revealing than referring to *Troy, Troy ... Taiwan* as "a war epic of human civilization, an *ocean* tragedy from the past to the present" (Program Notes).

Without any attempt to reinterpret *The Iliad* or to localize the story, *Troy, Troy ... Taiwan* basically follows *The Iliad*, dramatizing its important events with some minor changes, coupled with inspirations from Aeschylus's *Agamemnon* and Euripides's *The Trojan Women*. Not making any significant changes in the plot, the adapter faces two challenges to achieve her intended goal. One is how to dramatize the story of Troy, while at the same time, signifying to the audience or the readers that Troy, invaded by the Achaeans, metaphorically represents Taiwan. The other is to make the cause of war fit modern sensibilities and the parallel between Troy and Taiwan convincing.

Triggered by Helen or the disputes of the three goddesses, the siege of Troy is in no way similar to Taiwan's long history of colonization and potential threat from China. In *Troy, Troy ... Taiwan*, Helen is completely dismissed and the role of gods greatly downplayed. Instead, the cause of war is subtly attributed to the ambition of Agamemnon, whose characterization is radically changed from a sympathetic character in the 1997 production to an imagined invader, cruel and commanding.

Immediately following the prologue, where Priam, king of Troy, and his grandson, Leos,[8] happily take a walk and watch the chorus of the Trojans dancing and singing, is the first scene in which Agamemnon mercilessly kills his own daughter. It creates the impression that one side fights to protect their family and the other side kills his own family to fight. Moreover, Agamemnon does hesitate about sacrificing Iphigenia, but he exhibits little love towards her. His lack of humanity is further demonstrated in his response to her last struggle on the altar. When she cries, "Father, your majesty" twice, Agamemnon only relentlessly demands of her to follow his order.

The ambition of Agamemnon as a cause of war is revealed in the following scene when Achilles, enraged by Agamemnon's robbery of his war prize, which is a scepter in this case, condemns him: "The Trojans haven't done us any wrong. Because of your selfish ambition, we are forced to leave our homeland for over nine years" (You 2005b:27). Moreover, replacing a woman in *The Iliad* with a scepter as a war prize seems to imply that Agamemnon has great desire for power. It follows that he covets Troy for its prosperity, as represented by wide streets in his line, "I feel sad for us Achaeans. For Troy, which has wide streets, we endure much hardship" (2005b:32). In addition, Evil Spirit, occasionally dancing on the wall or among the warriors, is seen to try to kill Hector and in one scene he gives the spear to Agamemnon. It implies either that the Trojans are fighting with some unknown but terribly evil power, or that the Achaeans are on the side of the evil. By portraying Agamemnon as an ambitious enemy and discarding gods and Helen, *Troy, Troy ... Taiwan* subtly modernizes the ancient legend and situates the war as an aggressive invasion of a prosperous kingdom, Troy/Taiwan.

In contrast to the invaders, the Trojans are forced to go to war to defend their own native land and all that is related to it, such as families, sustenance, and freedom. All the Trojans, including Leos, are aware how their survival is tied to the land and they repeat its importance again and again, while the Achaeans lament that they cannot be buried in their native land. Native land (*gu xiang*), frequently referred to by both the Trojans and the Achaeans, thus becomes an important trope in this production.

Situated in the political context of Taiwan, "native land" as a signifier is constantly being constituted and contested just as the term Taiwan is. "Native land," under the KMT totalitarian regime, refers to the imagined mainland China, "stolen" by the Chinese Communist Party (hereafter CCP). It rightly reflects the longing of the first generation mainlanders, who fled to Taiwan with Chiang Kai-shek in 1949 and thought that they would return to their homeland soon. This longing of "homecoming," of retaking mainland China, became the chief goal behind all the policies enforced in Taiwan and was turned into an ideology, violently imposed on the majority of the people. Indigenous people and native Taiwanese, whose ancestors settled in this island about six thousand years ago and three hundred years ago respectively, were not allowed to voice their longings, but taught to ache for the imagined homeland with the interpellation of state ideological apparatuses, especially the schools that devoted over 95 percent of their history, geography, and literature classes to China through standardized curricula.

With the lifting of martial law in 1987 and rapid democratization, talks on the future of Taiwan as other than reunification are no longer taboo. For the first time in history, Taiwan is treated as a subject and Subject in various ways of "writing." In the process, the myth of the imagined homeland is debunked. Taiwan is re-envisioned as a country with four hundred years of history and culture, different and distinctive from China. Ironically, "homecoming," or trips to China in the late 1980s, made possible after the lifting of martial law, also contributed to the disillusion of the myth when those who visited China experienced the huge discrepancy between reality and imagination. As Joseph Bosco concludes, for native Taiwanese, such trips also "strengthen their Taiwanese identity" (393). Officially, in 1991, the termination of "the period of mobilization for the suppression of communist rebellion," launched in 1947 when the CCP tried to seize power from the KMT in China, signified that administering Taiwan, rather than defeating the CCP and reunifying China, is the only goal. Through decades of struggle, people in Taiwan are finally allowed to explore, to recognize, and to express their love for this native land.

In addition to serving as an important trope, "native land" plays a significant role in shaping one's identity, reflected in the kinship category that motherland, fatherland, and homeland all imply. The recognition of the same native land, rather than blood lines, connects those living on the land to common ancestors and binds them together as family. In *Troy, Troy ... Taiwan,* the Trojans are seen to be bound together by such a recognition when marching to the battlefield, shouting, "For freedom! For our country, family, and offspring! For our ancestors!" (You 2005b:40).

Emphasis on native land in *Troy, Troy ... Taiwan* rather than on traditional common ancestry in imagining a Taiwanese nation corresponds to nationalist strategies arising from political realities and needs. To refute "the blood metaphor" that Chinese nationalist discourse favors and to ease ethnic tensions, Taiwanese nationalist discourse highlights commitments and loyalty to the territory and the state, and their shared destiny related to them, which in turn defines and constructs one's ethnicity, or more exactly, nationality. Native land as a trope in *Troy, Troy ... Taiwan,* is far from a simple parable for teaching the importance of defending one's country, but is intertwined with Taiwan's postcolonial history and reflects its nation-building strategy.

Subtly modernizing the ancient story by shifting the cause of war, the adapter establishes the link between Troy and Taiwan mainly in the prologue through the implication that this native land refers to Taiwan. The Taiwanese folk-style song, titled "Song of Warriors Longing for Their Native Land," opening the production, repeated again in scene five and during the curtain call, depicts the homesickness of the Achaeans who fight away from home for over nine years. However, considering that the song is sung by a singer, not a character, and also in moments not related to the plot, it seems to have taken the function of a theme song, creating meanings separate from the context of the story. The song is thus also intended to pay homage to the land that nourishes the people. As the lyrics go:

My native land is very beautiful, with high mountains and a bright moon.
Good harvests of grains, fat fish and shrimp, happy are those who live there.
My heart aches to go back to my native land and see my elders.
My native land is beautiful, with green hills and crystal rivers.
Where birds sing and roads are easily travelled, my wife and son all live there.
I long to go back and take them into my embrace [You 2005b:33].

Although this song does not include any local references to Taiwan, its folk song style combined with the Hoklo language carries a strong Taiwanese flavor, signifying what the native land represents. The first line is also telling, given the fact that Taiwan is a mountainous island with Mount Jade (*Yushan*) as one of the most popular national symbols. In addition, during the productions in both historical sites, there happened to be a full moon, which created a magical effect on some observant spectators. One reviewer commented on the moving effect of seeing a full moon appearing from the tree in the Huwei Fortress production. It might be because the full moon corresponds to the first line of the song, or because a full moon has already signified native land or homesickness in Chinese culture, as reflected in classic poetry and the Moon Festival. Without specific local references, the song can be used not only to depict the homesickness of the Trojan warriors in the context of the story but express love for one's native land in general.

Near the end of the song, Priam and Leos enter the performing space, as if taking a walk together. Their first dialogue sets the tone for the production and immediately pinpoints what the native land is through reference to silver grass:

LEOS: Grandpa, Sit here. What is the most beautiful flower, Grandpa?
PRIAM: The most beautiful flower is silver grass.
LEOS: The greatest person?
PRIAM: The greatest person is our ancestors.
LEOS: The most beautiful place, Grandpa?
PRIAM: The most beautiful place is our native soil, our homeland [2005b: 22].

In the past two decades, silver grass has emerged as a symbol for "Taiwaneseness." A sea of white full-bloomed tassels against the blue sky on the hills and near the rivers in autumn is a beautiful but somewhat desolate scene familiar to most local people. Growing in the forbidding terrain, silver grass comes to symbolize resilience and perseverance in general and is further constructed to stand for the Taiwanese spirit by nationalist cultural intellectuals. In this discourse, the long colonized history of Taiwan is compared to the harsh environment in which silver grass grows. Yet, the Taiwanese have more than survived many hardships, but established Taiwan as a vibrant democracy and the world's seventeenth leading economic entity.[9] Such strength and vitality of the Taiwanese is like silver grass in bloom. The success of this discourse makes silver grass a cultural and political symbol for Taiwaneseness. It becomes a favorite subject of many *taiyu* poems (the Taiwanese language, or Hoklo), and folk songs, and is also a common title for published collections and journals of *taiyu* poetry or organizations that promote writing in *taiyu*. Writing in *taiyu* is not only intended to preserve this language and native culture, but often reflects the enthusiastic pursuit for an independent Taiwanese nation-state.

With these local references, the prologue implies that the following story is that of Troy/Taiwan, while the epilogue also works to emphasize the parallel by making the theatrical time into real time. As if echoing the prologue, Leos asks Priam several questions. One is, "Where are we now?" Priam answers, "Our native land." This moment is simultaneously theatrical and real, since the story of the Trojan War is over. The real time aligns the Trojans with the audience members in the shared territory. The theatrical performance is further transformed into a realistic ritual with the audience members as participants when Hector's wife, Andromache, burns paper money in a stove, a common mourning ritual for the dead. In the Huwei Fortress production, the crew members even set up several sky lanterns from different places, a beautiful ritual praying for peace and a bright future. The epilogue serves well to remind the audience that the production is intended to be a reflection on past and present Taiwan.

The link between Troy and Taiwan is made obvious only in the prologue. To help retain the link throughout the production, the director resorts to various performing elements to envision a "virtual mythic ancient Taiwan kingdom." Among these elements, I consider the use of historical sites and the Hoklo language most successful, and the costume least successful.

As in postcolonial theatre, language is always a key to recuperating culture and decolonizing the mind. After decades of "promoting Mandarin movement" and monolingual policies, the consequences are that many tribal languages are extinct and that fewer of the younger generation of native Taiwanese can communicate in their native languages, such as Hoklo and Hakka. Fortunately, with the rise of Taiwanese consciousness in the post–martial law period, the negative psychological impact of monolingual policies is reduced; speaking Hoklo and Hakka or speaking Mandarin with a strong Hoklo accent is no longer associated with cultural backwardness. Director Wang Rong-yu is fully aware of the role of native languages in theatre. In "The Call of Mother Language: From Instinct to Mission" collected in the script, he writes, "Language and written words are the roots of culture," (2005b:4) reminiscent of Frantz Fanon's words: "to speak a language is to take on a world, a culture" (1986:38). For the lack of a widely-adopted writing system, even though the Hoklo language is no longer repressed, many phrases and usages have already disappeared. Consciously using Hoklo in his theatrical productions, which originates from Wang's close feelings towards his mother language, has evolved into the mission of keeping it alive. The publication of the script of *Troy, Troy ... Taiwan* also indicates such an attempt.

In addition to recuperating culture, the use of the Hoklo language and other composite elements, both visual and audio, reflects how Wang Rong-yu imagines Taiwaneseness. All the characters speak Hoklo, "translated" by Wang Wen-de from You Hui-fen's Mandarin draft script. In order to showcase the beauty of the Hoklo language and to match the epic quality of this production, Wang Wen-de paid great attention to the language's nuances in tones and rhythms and used much literary Hoklo.

However, unlike most performers in traditional theatre such as *gezaixi* (Taiwanese opera) and *budaixi* (Taiwanese glove puppetry) who speak Hoklo in their daily life and are used to literary Hoklo in performances, some of the young performers of Golden Bough Theatre cannot capture the essence of the language as naturally and express it as clearly as those in traditional theatre. One can easily detect the differences in their Hoklo proficiency by listening to some characters played by the relatively young actors and to Priam, played by Wang Rong-yu's mother, Xie Yue-xia, who used to be a renowned *gezaixi* performer. In addition, the Hoklo language used in the production is too refined to be captured easily especially when the chorus sings or speaks together. I even feel that to be poetry-like, the syntax of some lines does not sound Hoklo, but contrived. Some audience members were moved simply by the aura created through the use of Hoklo and other performing elements,[10] while some expressed difficulty following the words even though they understood Hoklo.[11]

Interestingly and ironically, in this imagined ancient Taiwanese kingdom, all people speak only one language, Hoklo, the native language of the majority of people since the seventeenth century. In the same aforementioned article, Wang Rong-yu states that, aware of Hoklo culture as being only one of the multiethnic cultures in Taiwan, he started to consciously use the denomination Hoklo, rather than *taiyu* (the Taiwanese language), to refer to his mother language. It is true that Hoklo, unlike the more common denomination *taiyu,* does not seem to subsume the other native languages, nor does it create the impression of being *the* language of Taiwan. But *Troy, Troy ... Taiwan* fails to show the diversity and multiculturalism that Wang advocates in the article. I do not have doubt over Wang's respect for multiethnic cultures. The single use of Hoklo shows how one's national imagination is deeply, and understandably, shaped by one's cultural background and affinities.

The second most prevalent performing element in helping construct this mythic Taiwan kingdom is the use of the Huwei Fortress and Qihou Fort. Both fortresses aptly bring out the epic dimension of the production and, more importantly, correspond to the theme of the importance of defending the homeland. Just as Marvin Carlson argues that the production of meanings includes "the entire theatre experience," (1990:xiii) such as "the physical appearance of the auditorium, the displays in the lobby, the information in the program, and countless other parts of the event," (1990:viii) so the moment when the audience had to make the extra effort to go to a fort rather than a theatre downtown in a city, they were already in the process of creating meanings.

The building of both fortresses occurred with the invasion of the imperialists during the Qing Empire, which by then had never taken what was considered a frontier island seriously. The Huwei Fortress was built in 1886 under the instruction of Governor Liu Ming-chuan after the Sino-French War (1884–1885). If the audience arrived before it got dark, it is unlikely that they would miss Liu Ming-chuan's inscription on the main gate leading inside the fortress, which says "The Key to Northern Gate" (*bemen suoyao*), emphasizing the importance of this site in protecting northern Taiwan. And if after passing into the gate, the audience happened to turn their heads and look up, they would see the inscription on the other side of the gate, which read, "Defend Taiwan Firmly" (*jianshou Taiwan*).[12] Similarly, the building of Qihou Fort started in 1875 after the Japanese tried to take southern Taiwan in 1874, and was completed in 1876. Only two of the four characters in the inscription remain on the gate leading into the fortress, which evokes imagination from the viewers and may actively engage them in the creation of meanings.

Walking through the gates with the inscriptions highlighting the role of the fortress in defending Taiwan may have helped shape the interpretation of the show, especially when the audience watched the Trojans fight until the last moment to defend their homeland. The passage of the gate also becomes what Victor Turner calls the liminal space transporting the audience into the ancient Taiwan kingdom that encompasses the whole fortresses. And in this world, the audience becomes a witness-participant in a ritual simultaneously mourning for the past and praying for the future, tying aptly into the Mandarin title of the play, *Ji Troy*, with *ji* meaning ritual.

In this ancient kingdom of Taiwan, the characters not only speak Hoklo but sing Taiwanese folk style songs and *gezaixi* melodies. Whether the song depicts the homesickness of the warriors or the loss of a great civilization, they are the most impressive part for many audience members. Since *Troy, Troy ... Taiwan* is intended to be an elegy, what can work better than using the tragic melodies, or crying melodies (*ku diao*) of *gezaixi,* the most characteristic melody of this performing tradition?[13] For example, in Scene 4, on hearing from Hector that both sides agree to cease fighting for one day to take away the bodies that cover the battlefield, the chorus of the Trojan women burst out crying; Priam asks them to hold back their sorrow to incinerate the bodies first. Afflicted with grief, the chorus exits singing in one tragic melody, "Parting forever in clouds and smoke; crying thousand times in tears. Vengeance and hatred will never subside; the family will never be intact" (You 2005b:31). It is with this moving melody that the suffering, pain and sadness permeate effectively.

Compared to these more successful elements, the costumes, intricately and exquisitely designed, seem to reflect how the ancient Greeks are imagined and exoticized. Matching the lavish costumes are the immense, elaborate headdresses of various designs. The major colors of the costumes for Trojans, indigo and dark green, vividly contrast with those for the Achaeans, flamingo red and golden. According to the costume designer, the design was based on *budaixi*, coupled with elements from video games.[14] As for makeup, the faces and the hands exposed are all oil painted, in the color of very light metallic blue, to make the actors look like ancient statues, especially when the makeup may slightly smudge due to the sweat of the actors in performing. However, the costume and the headdress immediately recall Contemporary Legendary Theatre's well-known 1996 production, *Lolannu (The Princess of Lolan)*, an adaptation of *Medea*. Does it mean that there is a lack of innovation in imagining Greekness in Taiwan theatre? Or is the concept of Greek tragedy so entrenched in its epic dimension so that to be Greek is to be lavish?

In addition, the Taiwaneseness of *budaixi* does not translate into the costumes on the real persons. Instead, the impressively elaborate, yet anachronistic costumes seem to overwhelm other performing elements that may in fact connote Taiwaneseness. The costumes, too outstandingly powerful to ignore, create a kind of unintended alienation effect, reminding the audience they are watching a dramatization of an imagined ancient city Troy inhabited by the imagined Greek. Occasionally, the heaviness of the costume and huge headdress may even impede the movements of the actors.[15] The beautifully designed costume turns out to be less conducive to inventing an ancient Taiwan Kingdom.

Evolving from *Troy, Troy* to *Troy, Troy ... Taiwan*, the adaptation of *The Iliad* by Golden Bough Theatre goes through a drastic transformation. Dramatizing the horrors of war, *Troy, Troy* also ambiguously criticizes some social phenomena that may cause the loss of this Taiwanese civilization. Greatly inspired by the discourses of oceanic culture and ocean country that have been widely discussed in public spheres, the adapter and the director expand *Troy, Troy ... Taiwan* into a work of national imagination in 2005. It is at once an elegy for Taiwan, lamenting its long colonized past, a parable teaching its people the importance of defending this native land, and an ode to this beloved island, as opposed to the once imagined constructed homeland.

TUFTS UNIVERSITY

Notes

Acknowledgment. I am grateful to Golden Bough Theatre for the interviews, photos, publicity materials, and recorded video tapes of the show.

1. All names and terms are transliterated using pinyin system unless the alternative spellings are internationally recognized, such as Chiang Kai-shek, or are used in the cited text. Where non-pinyin system is used, the pinyin spelling is provided in parentheses. Besides, the names of the Taiwanese are presented in the customary order, with the family name followed by the given name without a comma.

2. On the website of Golden Bough Theatre, this 1997 production is also titled *Troy, Troy ... Taiwan* in English. However, it was titled *Troy, Troy* in English in a very small size on the program notes of the 1997 production. Given the fact that Troy in the 1997 production was not intended to work as a metaphor for Taiwan as it was in the 2005 production and also for the sake of clarity in discussion, I use *Troy, Troy* to refer to the 1997 production in this paper.

3. It is important to notice that the media and many theatre practitioners in Taiwan tend to conflate open-air performances with environmental theatre which explores the spatial relations between the actors and the spectators.

4. The 1995 missile tests were intended as warnings against President Lee Teng-hui's successful visit to his alma mater, Cornell University, which was interpreted by China as Lee's moving away from one China policy and attempt to re-enter the international community as a leader of an independent country, while the 1996 tests were against the approaching first direct presidential

election in Taiwan. The number of missiles aimed at Taiwan remains increasing annually to 1500 in 2009, even after cross-straits tension eased with the election of President Ma Ying-jeou in 2008, who has taken more conciliatory approaches towards China.

5. The Taiwan Relations Act, defining relations between Taiwan and America, was passed in 1979 when America shifted its recognition from the Republic of China (Taiwan's formal name) to People's Republic of China. It stipulates that America will "consider any effort to determine the future of Taiwan by other than peaceful means, including by boycotts or embargoes, a threat to the peace and security of the Western Pacific area and of grave concern to the United States." For a detailed description of the act, see <http://www.ait.org.tw/en/about_Ait/tra> (accessed 26 February 2009).

6. Website of Council of Marine Affairs Advancement. <http://www.cmaa.nat.gov.tw/en/aio show.aspx?path=90&guid=985e0d34-4f3e-4487-be65-14c35727c41e&lang=en-us> (accessed 26 February 2009).

7. Ma Ying-jeou and Xiao Wan-chang, "Dazao Taiwan bainian jianshe de jichu" (Building the foundation for future one hundred years of Taiwan) <http://2008.ma19.net/policy4you/ oceans> (accessed 26 February 2009).

8. This is the only character whose name is changed. In *The Iliad*, his name is Astyanax.

9. From 2004 to 2008, the rankings range from 16 to 19. See the website of the World Trade Organization.

10. For an audience member's comments on the show, see <http://blog.xuite.net/anthena/my/ 4932606> (accessed 2 March 2009).

11. See scholar Wang Jing-ling's article in her website. <http://2478.wwwts.au.edu.tw/front/ bin/ptdetail.phtml?Part=PT05110028&PreView=1> (accessed 14 March 2009). Growing up speaking Hoklo, I also occasionally found it a little difficult to follow the lines when watching the video.

12. This inscription was controversial, since it was added by the mayor of Taipei County, You Ching, when the first stage of restoration was completed in 1995. Scholars considered that such an act damaged the historical site. In early February 2008, the inscription was finally taken down.

13. There are several dozens of "crying melodies" in *gezaixi*, a performing genre that developed in Japanese colonial Taiwan. Scholars attribute the popularity to either the appearance of actresses whose singing in crying melodies easily evoked the sympathy of the audience, or to the suffocating, suppressed life in the Japanese colonial period. See Lin Mao-xian, *Gezaixi biaoyan xingtai yanjiu (Research on the performing styles of* Gezaixi) (Taipei: Qianwei, 2006):158–159.

14. Wang Ling-li, "Xila diaoxiang chuanqi budaixifu: ji Troy bentuweinong (Greek statue arrayed in *budaixi* costume: strong flavor of localness in *Troy, Troy ... Taiwan*) *Liberty Times*, 22 September 2005. <http://www.libertytimes.com.tw/2005/new/sep/22/life/art-3.htm> (accessed 2 March 2009). It seems to me that the reporter wrote her report based either on publicity materials or her interview with the costume designer before the production. It is interesting to note that the reporter over-interprets or politicizes the meaning of the costume, by writing "Judging from the costume, the audience will be able to see the cross-strait relations reflected here" at the beginning of her article without further explanation.

15. One audience member wrote of being touched by the performance of Xie Yue-xia, who, playing Priam, knelt to beg Achilles for Hector's body. Yet, the audience member was immediately detached from the performance when Priam had to tilt his head due to the size of the headdress, in exiting through the aisle of the seating area. See <http://blog.xuite.net/anthena/my/ 4932606> (accessed 2 March 2009).

Works Cited

Bosco, Joseph. "The Emergence of a Taiwanese Popular Culture." *The Other Taiwan: 1945 to the Present*, edited by Murray A. Rubinstein. 392–403. New York: M. E. Sharpe, 1994.

Carlson, Marvin. *Theatre Semiotics: Signs of Life*. Bloomington: Indiana University Press, 1990.

Eriksen, Thomas Hylland. "Place, kinship and the case for non-ethnic nations." *Nations and Nationalism* 10.1–2 (2004):49–62.

Fanon, Frantz. *Black Skin, White Masks*. London: Pluto Press, 1986.

Homer. *The Iliad*, translated by Stanley Lombardo. Indianapolis: Hackett, 1997.

Huang, Shen-wei. "Renshi haiyang wenhua de tezhi" (Knowing the Qualities of Oceanic Culture). *Nongxuen journal* (*Journal of Agriculture Training and Development*) 131, (January 2001): 44–47.

Li, Min-yong. "Ermeng" (Nightmare), translated by Michelle Yeh. *Sailing to Formosa: A Poetic Companion to Taiwan* 24, edited by Michelle Yeh, N.G.D. Malmqvist, and Hu Huizhi. Seattle: University of Washington Press, 2005.

Lin, Zong-de. "Xiaomi hailu de jiexian — lun Liao Hong-ji zuoping zhong haiyang de sixiang tixi yu mexue shijian" (De-bordering Lands and Oceans: Research on the Thoughts and Aesthetics of Oceanic Culture in Liao Hong Ji's Literature). Master's Thesis, Providence University, 2008.

Wang, Rong-yu. "Muyu de huhuan: cong benneng dao shimin" (The Call of Mother Language: From Instinct to Mission). In You Hui-fen and Wang Wen-de, *Troy, Troy ... Taiwan*. 4–5 [Wang R. 2005b].

_____. "Virtual Ancient Taiwan Kingdom" in the Program Notes of *Troy, Troy ... Taiwan*. 10–12. Taipei: Golden Bough Theatre, 2005 [Wang R. 2005a].

Wang, Shao-jun. "Taiwan haiyang wenxue de fazhan yu wenhua jiangou" (The Development and Cultural Construction of Taiwan Oceanic Literature 1975–2004). Master's thesis, National Taipei Education University, 2005 [Wang S. 2005].

You, Hui-fen. "The Most Beautiful Place Is Our Native Land" in the Program Notes of *Troy, Troy ... Taiwan*: 17–18. Taipei: Golden Bough Theatre, 2005 [You 2005a].

_____, and Wang, Wen-de. *Ji Teluoyi (Troy, Troy ... Taiwan)*. Taipei: Golden Bough Theatre, 2005 [You 2005b].

Zhuang, Wan-shou. "Taiwan haiyang wenhua chutan" (Preliminary Exploration of Taiwan Oceanic Culture). *Zhongquo xueshu niandan* (*Annual Journal of Chinese Scholarship*) 181, (1997):303–316.

Peeling Empire
Yū Miri's Performance of "Resident Korean" in Japan

John D. Swain

Abstract

Yū Miri, a Korean resident in Japan, won the Kishida Drama Prize in 1993 for Festival of the Fish. *She wrote her last play,* Green Bench, *in 1995, then in 1997 won the Akutagawa Prize for fiction. Yū abandoned the stage for the page. Most critics of her prose do not consider the influence of the corporeal body on the stage. Yū's construction of indeterminate ethnic and national identity in her prose clashes with the corporeal presence of the actor's body in her theatre works. This essay focuses on the somatic ambiguities built in to Yū's plays, with emphasis on* Festival of the Fish. *Those ambiguities amplify, rather than moderate, statements of marginalized Korean identification. I show that many of the identity themes in Yū's fiction that are attributed to literary textual manipulation owe their origins to the subversive corporeality of ambiguous characters and actors on stage in her plays.*

Implicit in the theatrical art are living, corporeal bodies, the concomitant indeterminacies of what is produced by the live actors on stage, and how their performance is received by spectators at the event. Although it may seem obvious, we must remember that such indeterminacies are different from those created by prose. Author Yū Miri, a *Zainichi*-Korean[1] female, is now known mostly as a novelist in Japan; however, she started as an actor, director and playwright. As a result, Yū's formative experiences as an artist and author began with the live, performing body on stage — an influence on her later prose. Critics such as Melissa L. Wender and Lisa Yoneyama have noted the threats to social order within Yū's later prose writings, and personal choices and actions. They have written about some of her drama, however, the full impact of Yū's earlier plays on her prose is not considered. Performance of her plays includes not only literary aspects, but also corporeal actors' bodies interacting with the equally corporeal audience. The ambiguity of actors' live bodies is not in playwright Yū's, nor even the director's, control. On one hand, those bodies become more radi-

116

cal and subversive of society than Yū seems to desire, while on the other, they specify her own identity in ways she later tried to avoid. This essay will re-insert the influence of theatre on her later work by arguing that the corporeal existence of bodies on stage actually serves to clarify and specify Yū's *Zainichi*-Korean identity rather than obscure it like her prose because those bodies force audiences to confront issues of *Zainichi*-Korean existence in Japan in ways that text does not.

Wender writes that in literature by *Zainichi*-Koreans, "as early as the 1970s, and certainly in the 1980s, women authors had described their oppression as Koreans as a gendered experience. They rejected the use of the metaphor of the victimized woman's body to stand in for that of the nation" (Wender 2005:158). I agree that this is true for this body of literature in general and specifically for some dramatic literature created by *Zainichi*-Korean women, but Wender's assertion applies to only to text on the page, and does not address Yū's plays as theatrical events. Wender, like Lisa Yoneyama before her, acknowledges Yū's theatrical activities and mentions that in 1993 she won the Kishida Drama Prize for *Festival of the Fish* (*Uo no matsuri*), Japan's most prestigious award for new dramatists. Although Wender provides a critical literary analysis of Yū's life and work, including a discussion of Yū's last play, *Green Bench* (*Guriin benchi*, 1995), she analyzes the play as a piece of literature, not as live theatre with its attendant effects of actors' bodies in performance.

Wender concludes that Yū's characters, and by extension, Yū herself, have an ambiguous identity — neither Japanese nor *Zainichi*-Korean. That may be true in prose, but in live theatre the somatic ambiguities of Yū's female characters on stage actually add to the specificity of a marginalized Korean identification. These specificities influenced her later novels. Focusing on *Festival of the Fish*, I will show that in her plays, the subversive ambiguities of the live bodies Yū puts on stage *do* stand in for the nation, and that those ambiguities actually served to strengthen her *Zainichi*-Korean identity, a motivating factor in her shift from the stage to a medium over which she had more direct authorial control.

"Ordinary" Zainichi-Koreans

Many scholars of *Zainichi*-Korean creative works fail to consider the simultaneous reality and illusion of theatre. In that vein, John Lie cites Yū Miri as an example of the diversity of *Zainichi*-Koreans. She is a representative for his argument that the simple fact of being *Zainichi*-Korean does not have, "a determining impact on [their] sense of self, or personal identity" (Lie 2000:201). Lie argues that when Yū stated that, "everything is a fact, everything is a lie" (204), it proves she is not concerned about her *Zainichi*-Koreanness. In contrast to Lie's interpretation, the statement appears to be made by a playwright and actor who is acutely aware of how much *Zainichi*-Koreanness affects the performance, inscription and perception of her identity. In other words, Yū is concerned about her *Zainichi*-Koreanness. It acknowledges that both the truth and the fiction of a certain state of being are inescapable.

Yū's theatrical background makes her acutely conscious of what she is performing, and the constructed nature of the "fact" conveyed. Lie fails to note that through his example Yū has provided one succinct, albeit over-simplified, definition of the theatrical event. In this definition theatre can be viewed as an event where, "everything is a fact, and everything is a lie." Like the simplified construction of identity that Yū professes, theatre is a real event that does not perform reality. At any one moment, the performer is both exactly what he appears to be, and yet he is not. He is a live human, but also an actor, performing with complete truth a changeable fictional construct that potentially makes each succeeding moment untrue. Yū is aware that at any one moment, she is completely, and at the same time entirely not, *Zainichi*-Korean. This constructed identity is as an other, and perhaps it suits her performative purpose to have her Japanese audience/reader assume that other is Japanese.

About halfway through Yū's *Festival of the Fish*, Ruri, the younger of the two Namiyama sisters, has come home from the sea, sunburnt and brine-encrusted. Although Ruri is the last of the family to gather for the wake of the youngest son, Fuyuo, she is the first to shed tears. As the rest of the family tries to respond appropriately to Ruri's raw emotions, sexuality and almost primeval appearance, she begins peeling the dead skin off her back, saying:

> RURI: Sis will you please peel the skin off my shoulder?
> YURI: You shouldn't peel it. Why don't you put some hechima lotion on it?
> RURI: (Peeling the skin off her back.) Yes, but later ... after a shower.
> YURI: Didn't you hear me say you shouldn't peel it?
> RURI: But I can't help it, it's itchy! [Yū 1996:59].

In addition to Ruri's uninhibited sexuality, her fertile body, displayed before the audience composed of both Japanese and *Zainichi*-Koreans, is a site that threatens the status quo of both groups' constructions of nationalism and "race" in Japan. Ruri's performed actions can be both *Zainichi*-Korean and Japanese. The contest between Ruri's ambiguous self-identification and her older sister Yuri's acceptance of the status quo reflects some of the social struggles that Yū as a *Zainichi*-Korean, perceives and encounters in Japan.

Yū Miri has constantly struggled against having her ethnic and personal identity classified and absorbed into any particular literary or social category. Her name is an obvious example for speakers of Japanese. She has chosen to use the Korean pronunciation rather than assimilate. Although the characters used to write her name have a Japanese pronunciation, "Yanagi Misato," the pronunciation "Yū Miri" is distinctly non–Japanese. Yū's passport is South Korean, but she was born in Japan, and only started studying Korean as an adult. Many Japanese see it as a contradiction for her to use the Korean pronunciation for her name while at the same time living and speaking only Japanese. Yū deliberately accentuates these contradictions so that she may claim both Japaneseness and Koreanness: and neither.

It seems like an oxymoron, but Yū came to precisely control the indeterminacies in her fiction. In contrast, actors' live bodies on stage are never in her control, becoming more radical and subversive because of their independence and ambiguity. Writing and reading are private actions not usually done in a public forum where other's responses affect the outcome. A staged event must use ideas filtered through other's creative energies and bodies into a public dialogue that can be subversive and ambiguous, but also undeniable because it is witnessed together with others. The presence of the living actor is a physical reality for the audience, and the audience reads specificities into the live body and its real actions.

Yū's early plays, such as *Coffin of a Sunflower* (*Himawari no hitsugi*, 1991), were performed with unambiguous signifiers of *Zainichi*-Korean identity such as Korean words and dress. Identity became ambiguous with *Festival of the Fish* and *Green Bench*. However, Yū's ultimate desire for a sense of belonging includes place and personal relationships. Her criticism of the patriarchy, men, the family system, gender, sexuality, and unpaid female labor contrasts with her nostalgia for conservative, Confucian, and patriarchal values (Yū 2001:128). Such attitudes translate into attempts at passing as Japanese and assimilationist strategies that express her desire for static, authoritative texts — desires that live theatre does not fully support.

Theatrical Classroom

Yū's desire for ambiguity can be seen in the following scene from *Festival of the Fish*. The older son Fuyuki berates his mother, Sadako, for social improprieties. The spectator is unsure about why Sadako would make such mistakes, or Fuyuki be so angry. Is it because they are, or are not, Japanese? There is a distinct possibility that both the mistakes and the anger come from concerns about social and national identity, either Korean or Japanese.

> FUYUKI: What the hell are you talking about? (*Exploding.*) It's sushi! Sushi! Sushi! Everybody knows it's supposed to be sushi for a funeral!
> (*Without eating a bite,* FUYUKI *takes his plate of curry and places it on* [his dead brother] FUYUO's *alter.* SATŌ *and* KAWASHIMA [the undertakers] *look down, feeling a little embarrassed, and quickly finish their curry in silence.*)
> SADAKO: Would you like seconds?
> (SATŌ *and* KAWASHIMA *shake their heads no. They cannot reply because their mouths are full of curry.* SATŌ *and* KAWASHIMA *hurriedly swallow*) [Yū 1996:40].[2]

In this slightly humorous exchange among characters who are labeled audibly by the unambiguously Japanese pronunciation of their names, we can ask if any of them (son, mother, or undertakers) perform "proper" Japanese behavior. Who among the characters in this play is the most acculturated as Japanese — if indeed they are Japanese? Finally, we must ask, who — the characters, the playwright herself, or the spectator — is the final arbitrator of the accuracy of that performance, Japanese or not?

Yū wants to be that arbitrator. She relies on her authorship of a text to legitimize that claim; however, the theatrical form resists one fixed point of view. Wender re-inscribes Yū's insistence on the primacy of the authorial voice. She devotes a chapter of her book to Yū, arguing that Yū represents a generation of women who are speaking out about sexual and gender related abuse, and who have the personal strength and financial wherewithal to make lifestyle choices that seem dangerous to the status quo. Wender takes this claim Yū makes for personal lifestyle choices, and applies its implications to a literary analysis of a piece meant for theatrical performance. About half of Wender's chapter on Yū is such an analysis of *Green Bench*. Wender's close reading does justice to the text as literature and as a static sociological archive, and her analysis supports the chapter's overall conclusion, however, she ignores the ambiguities of a live production that undermine authorial control.

Wender discusses how Yū, as an "other" in Japan, wants to be the arbitrator of what constitutes assimilation. This is done through Yū's early prose, most of which came after her drama, in which *Zainichi*-Korean families are not unique, but share a dysfunctional pattern with Japanese families (Wender 160). There is also her refusal to acknowledge the label of either *Zainichi*-Korean or Japanese author. In Yū's later plays the spectator sees the characters assimilate to Japanese society, yet in the act of viewing the performance the audience must deal with the indeterminacies of those characters' ethnic identification. Ambiguity may come from the actor's choices or the actor's own identity. By insisting on authorship of her own assimilation (or lack thereof), Yū has an in-betweenness that troubles both the Japanese and *Zainichi*-Korean communities. This is more profound for spectators watching the live event, and at the moment of performance it is the actor that arbitrates, not the playwright.

Personal Choices: Passing, Assimilation, Text and Performance

Passing is a form of assimilation in which a marginalized subject not only takes on aspects of the dominant culture, but also attempts to be seen or mistaken, to "pass," as a member of that culture. Judith Butler writes that the performative acts of gender identity are, "ritualized production, a ritual reiterated under and through constraint, under and through the force of prohibition and taboo" (Butler 1993:95). Passing and assimilating are similar performative acts, similar to what Butler calls the "normative requirements" of gender (243). They are strategies reflecting surrender to the constraints and threats of the dominant culture to make those on its margins "normal." Butler's statement echoes Tsurumi Shunsuke's definition of *tenkō* (recantation) as "a conversion which occurs under the pressure of state power" (Tsurumi 12). From the point of view of others that claim a similar identity, a person that does not resist the forces of othering or co-opting by the hegemonic power has committed a form of *tenkō*. Yū has been accused of *tenkō* by both Japanese and *Zainichi*-Koreans for NOT asserting one or the other identity. It seems that she wants to avoid that accusation, but in doing so may be engaging in a more pro-active approach posited by some recent scholars of "passing." According to Andrew Radford:

> "[P]assing," far from being "a metaphor of death and desperation," can be an enabling strategy for evading the cramped enclosures of an irredeemably racist, hidebound society. [Rather than] the rigidity of boundaries that surround analytic categories of identity as race, ethnicity, gender, class and sexuality, ["passing"] stress[es] their fluidity and elasticity [Radford 2002:34].

In her theatrical works, Yū both critically addresses a range of cultural, social, and political issues related to *Zainichi*-Korean existence, and at the same time re-inscribes some of the discourse that underpins patriarchal society and the Japanese neo-colonialism she criticizes. The corporeal yet ambiguous nature of the theatrical event seems to have accentuated the contradictions in her work, but more importantly, it limits her ability to control its reception.

It is not unusual for a writer to change mediums, and Yū's explanation is that she could not express what she wanted in theatre and that filtering the work through other artists made that even more difficult (Yū 1997:52). She implies that she was troubled by her inability to resolve the disconnect between her desire for textual specificity and the potential for ambiguity in performance. Furthermore, she was unable and unwilling to fully assimilate and fulfill her desire for a sense of belonging to Japan and still address *Zainichi*-Korean problems within the context of larger Japanese social issues as Wender argues she does in prose.

In both her fiction and her plays, Yū attempts to control the terms of her identity through words on the page rather than actions (including speech) performed on stage. She seemed to acknowledge this when she still identified herself as a playwright. She wrote:

> I cannot speak or write my mother tongue (Korean), so I write plays in the words of another country. However, because of this, the words of my dramas are theatrical. However, a nation's language is necessary for contemporary theatre, so the problem of my unusual language use is because of the problem of my relation to [the nation of Japan] [Yū 2000:261].

She trusts the word to reveal only those different elements of identity she recognizes as competing within her, but she cannot trust the theatrical event or elements of identity that actors may embody, or spectators may see, in a performance.

In *Festival of the Fish*, the Namiyama family's occupations and behaviors are ones commonly associated with, although certainly not exclusive to, Japanese lower classes and *Zainichi*-Koreans. The mother, Sadako, works as a bar hostess and has a succession of lovers. The father, Takashi, works as a pinsetter at a pachinko hall but gambles away most of his money. He abused his wife until the couple split up twelve years before. Since then, the eldest son, Fuyuki, now age twenty-six, has lived with his father and teaches at a cram school. The two daughters, Yuri and Ruri, are between the sons in age and spent time with both parents after the marital split. Yuri is a writer with novelist pretensions, who writes ad copy and pornography for a living. Ruri has no identifiable occupation or means of support. Both daughters moved out of their parents' houses to live on their own as soon as they could. Fuyuo is the second son, age nineteen and the youngest child. He stayed with his mother after his parents separated and was working in construction when he died.

The family has gathered at Sadako's house for Fuyuo's wake and funeral. Fuyuo's death, later revealed almost certainly to be a suicide, precipitates a possible reconciliation between Sadako and Takashi, and a reunification of the family, now expanding in the guise of Fuyuo's infant son by his girlfriend, Kyōko, and the child in Ruri's womb. The dead Fuyuo might be considered the main character in the original production of *Festival of the Fish* because he was played by a living, actor who moved around on stage, observing and responding to the action, but was never seen or heard by the others. He is only mentioned as an unseen, inert corpse lying in a coffin in the version Yū later published. In performance, the audience was always aware of his active corporeal presence on the stage as the family moved through the grieving and burial process, conveying a greater sense of discord and indeterminacy to the troubled existence of the family.

The text of *Festival of the Fish* leaves identity indeterminate, but the performance both adds and removes ambiguity. When Yū won the Kishida Prize for the play, she was cited for her use of language. The language of her stage directions waxes poetic at times, but the audience perceives it only as character actions or images, not as literature. Wender, however, discusses stage directions from *Green Bench* as literature not as theatre. She writes, "the stage directions (or commentary?) tell us that Akira has discovered that Yōko 'only truly loves their father,' and that this fills him with sadness" (Wender 165). Wender's comments, and her parenthetical question, make it clear that the audience is not privy to the specific thoughts of either Yōko or Akira. What Wender fails to acknowledge is that spectator interpretation of stage directions such as this must be filtered through the actors, shaping and potentially altering the author's expectation. This may seem a trivial point to those accustomed to analyzing theatre performance, but by not acknowledging something as fundamental as this, Wender trivializes the importance of the live event.

As with many stage directions, we can divide Yū's images into two predominant types. One describes character actions and/or the setting. An example from *Festival of the Fish* reads, "Fuyuki drinks sake. Outside dusk settles. Inside the room is lit by the slanting sunlight of the setting sun which lights Fuyuo's coffin in red. Fuyuo's white shirt outside the window is also lit red. There is the refreshing sound of the wind chime" (Yū 1996:59). There is no guarantee that the audience will notice or remember any specifics of these transitory images written by the author. Another type of stage direction describes the character's state of mind. The mother, Sadako, tries to cope with her loss by doing mundane housekeeping tasks, but at one point in the play her grief becomes too much to bear. Yū's stage direction reads, "Sadako is hanging out the washing, wishing that there were endless washing to hang out" (1996:16). How is the audience to know this thought? This evocative prose is entirely up to the director and actor to interpret non-verbally. Like the stage directions from *Green Bench*, such character emotions are even more intangible and ephemeral than lighting or sound because they must be conveyed only by the actor's skill. Therefore, the specifics of what the spectators receive, and their interpretation may be even more vague.

For us to fully understand the impact of Yū's plays, we must consider how in performance, the written text is embodied in the presence of the spectator by images or actions. Stage directions carry much of that to the director or actor, who in turn add their own theatrical choices. Putting Fuyuo, or his spirit, as an embodied presence on the stage, was a choice of the director, a decision, furthermore, that Yū chose to repudiate and exclude from published versions. Why excise this corporeal presence from the textual archive when it was such an important part of the theatrical success of the play? Part of the answer is that Yū wants control over her text purely as literature. She herself is uncomfortable with the textual interference that live bodies on stage create. Not only is there ambiguity, as Wender rightly points out, but there may also be unexpected specificity. In the next section I will discuss how that potential specificity or ambiguity is compounded by expectations of racial markers on the corporeal actor's body.

Invisible Color

Among *Zainichi*-Koreans like Yū who grow up in Japan, things such as language, accent, or behavior do not set them apart from the Japanese. They sound and look completely Japanese. Language, accent, or behaviors are not genetically encoded, as are the bodily features that are commonly ascribed to "race." More importantly, the difference between *Zainichi*-Koreans and Japanese is not marked by optical signifiers of "race," such as skin or hair color, or facial features, a circumstance that facilitates both the silencing of their voice and the concealment of their ethnic identity. The lack of optical signifiers contributes to indeterminacy, subversion and a sense of dis-ease toward those characters in

Japan because of the overall lack of racially distinct bodies. In the United States, where "race" and racism has for decades taken the form of a black/white binary, the racial markings of skin color are as obvious on stage as off. Nevertheless, in both cultures, racial passing has often been envisioned as a social problem. In American drama, this issue has been explored at least since 1859 with *The Octoroon*, by Dion Boucicault. The play hinges on the absence of skin color as a signifier. Zoe, the Octoroon, appears white, but her one-eighth non-white ancestry classifies her as black under United States law of the time. Like Zoe, the difference between Japanese and *Zainichi*-Koreans cannot be marked by physically racialized characteristics, therefore, in Yū's plays, all or some of the characters may be racialized as either group.

The visual ambiguity of racial identities is also related to sex and gender. Judith Butler writes that "'[s]ex' is ... not simply what one has, or a static description of what one is: it will be one of the norms by which the 'one' becomes viable at all, that which qualifies a body for life within the domain of cultural intelligibility" (Butler 1993:2) This comment about sex can also apply to "race." In other words, even in the absence of racial markers, identifying someone as a particular "race" forces them into a specific category of "cultural intelligibility" that is determined by the dominant culture. If we replace "sex" in the above quote with "*Zainichi*-Korean," then we can see ambiguous signifiers of the family's identity. It is their behavior and physical surroundings, elements that may vary at the discretion of actors, directors, and designers that give them a "cultural intelligibility" in Japan that predetermines how others, including the spectator, will perceive and deal with them.

The ambiguous visual signifiers in *Festival of the Fish* combine with character actions. The two undertakers, Satō and Kawashima, exhibit disapproval and condescension toward the family's behavior and economic circumstances, but the spectator does not know the precise reason for their attitude. For example, Sadako, the mother, makes the social gaffe of being highly made up and wearing a red dress when she receives the men at her home. The father, Takashi, invites their contempt through his insistence on an expensive funeral for Fuyuo, even though the physical surroundings of the house and his employment at a pachinko hall indicate low class status. This can also be ambiguous in prose, but the corporeal presence of the characters situated in the physical surroundings of the stage scenery invites the audience to speculate about several possibilities. Do the men express contempt toward the family's social behavior and economic status because they are thoroughly assimilated *Zainichi*-Koreans? Alternatively, if the two men are Japanese, are they class snobs sneering at the combination of economic disadvantage, difference and social inferiority of fellow Japanese? Or does their Japanese sense of superiority trigger their racist attitudes about people they assume are *Zainichi*-Koreans? Yū does not try to resolve those questions; however, depending on the spectator's own perception of the world, the visible bodies may suggest some specific answers.

Indeterminate Origins

Besides the spirit of Fuyuo, the most troubling corporeal representation in *Festival of the Fish* is Ruri's natural and vital sea encrusted body. The naturalness of her body contrasts with Sadako's, which is highly made-up and carefully dressed. The stage direction for Ruri's entrance reads, "At first sight we can tell that she comes here directly from the sea. Ruri's hair is set with seawater. Her skin is sunburnt and reddish" (Yū 1996:57). Yuri immediately comments on how painful the sunburn looks:

> YURI: Isn't your back sore? It's gone deep red.
> RURI: Yes, it is. It's tingling [Yū 1996:58].

The spectator will viscerally share Ruri's response to Yuri's injury. Yuri further remarks that Ruri will not be able to sleep at night because of the pain. This, and a further exchange, implies that Ruri's body is diseased and derogated, becoming a "site on which regimes of power are played out" (Gilbert & Tompkins 1996:226).

Ruri has come in from the depredations of the sun. The Empire of the Sun? The Japanese emperor, symbol of the nation, is said to be the direct descendant of the Sun Goddess Amaterasu Ōmikami. Ruri is sunburnt, but also just come from the sea, perfumed by the ocean, and adorned with its salt and sand. The effects of the sun and the ocean are competing on her body. The sea, in Japanese creation myth is the primal soup from which the Japanese islands accreted, and from which all life arose. A nameless man, of indeterminate ethnic identity, has smeared Ruri with lotion that is ineffective in preventing the sunburn we see. She proactively begins to peel the damaged skin, site of the sun's derogation, refusing the ministrations of her sister, who is assimilated and marginalized by the patriarchal Japanese culture. The spectator sees Ruri literally peeling off from her corporeal body the damage caused by the sun. She also bears within her a child whose father seems to be the primal soup of the indeterminate, borderless ocean. We usually view the land as fixed and immobile; however, Ruri comes directly from the indeterminate and fluid sea. The ocean is open to ingress and egress from any body of land, and people of any nation-state. Someone arising from the sea, as characters in fellow *Zainichi*-Korean playwright Jeong Uishin's[3] plays often do, could potentially have come from any part of the planet. Is the enigmatic Ruri from Japan, Korea, or somewhere else? Who is the father of her child? Where is he from? There are no answers to these questions, but Ruri resists the sun while embracing her pregnancy.

Being of the sea and pregnant is a set of circumstances that runs against the general observation Gilbert and Tompkins make about postcolonial drama:

> [W]ith a few exceptions, postcolonial plays by women tend not to centralise birth, perhaps in an attempt to fracture the concept of 'Mother Earth,' an ide-

alistic notion that denies women full humanity and compromises their ability to change, to choose, and to be individuated [Gilbert & Tompkins 1996: 20].

Yū is one of those exceptions. She uses the sea, instead of the land, as an indeterminate site of fertility. There seem to be several reasons why Yū's work does not fit Gilbert and Tompkins's description of reproduction and mothering in postcolonial drama. One is the image of a fertile sea, prevalent in Japanese culture from the earliest Shinto myths to author Mishima Yukio. Yū's play "fracture[s] the concept of 'Mother Earth,'" in part, because the Japanese creation myth holds that the Japanese islands were stirred up by the gods Izanami and Izanagi out of the ocean brine. Those islands were not fertile but were filled with life by Izanami and Izanagi's rampant procreation. By continuing to draw on the imagery of the fertile sea, we could say Yū is assimilating to Japan, but she also causes the whole notion of motherhood and birth to identify her as *Zainichi*-Korean. Through the indeterminate sea, she conceives an existence in Japan that allows her the choice that comes from rejecting the concept of "Mother Earth," but accepting that of "Mother Ocean." Yū has Ruri resist the derogation caused by Japanese colonialism and deal with it and its history in an unexpected and self-affirming way. Wender argues that Yū rejects patriarchal systems in general, but the corporeality of Ruri peeling her sun burnt skin implies Yū rejects the specific Japanese hegemony and circumstances of Japanese colonialism. The idea of "Mother Ocean" shifts the benefits of fertility from males to females, but the contradictions in the two concepts do not so much make identity ambiguous as amplify the difficulties of maintaining the neutral stance that Yū attempts in her later prose.

Several references to the fertility of both sexes run through the play, but the positive aspects accrue to the matriarchy rather that the patriarchy. Sadako produced the children of the family, but she is no longer fertile. She and Takashi represent an earlier, wartime/colonial generation that has lost its creative energy. The reproductive potential for the children of the couple is indeterminate. Fuyuki, as the eldest son, should be the one to perpetuate the family line, however, his sisters doubt both his virility and sexuality. Whether or not he is sexually inhibited, impotent, or gay, Fuyuki appears to be an unlikely source of procreation:

> RURI: Fuyuki, are you, by any chance, a virgin?
> (*Fuyuki has a fit of coughing. It appears that* RURI's *guess could be right*).
> YURI: Don't be silly! Fuyuki is twenty-six now. If a man of twenty-six is a virgin, he isn't normal, not normal.
> (FUYUKI *gulps down sake*) [Yū 1996:64].

Yuri, the older sister, is fertile, but has had at least one abortion and she does not show any particular possibility for attracting a mate for future procreation. Her lack of offspring is mirrored by her lack of creativity as a writer. Her novel remains unborn and unlikely to be finished as she prostitutes herself writing for ad agencies and porno publications. The more fertile, sexual Ruri has stolen Yuri's boyfriends. In contrast to Fuyuki, Fuyuo (the "normal" man?) fathered a child by his girlfriend Kyōko before his death. As with the rest of the characters in the play, Kyōko's ethnic identity is indeterminate, so the spectator cannot pin down the child's ethnicity. Furthermore, Fuyuo and Kyōko's union has not been registered as a marriage, so there is no legal tie to the family, leaving the status of the baby's citizenship indeterminate. The spectator may wonder about the child's future legal status in the Japanese nation-state, but deliberately raising the issue challenges the Japanese ideal of a racially homogeneous culture that has excluded *Zainichi*-Koreans up to now.

Yū goes further against the general trope described by Gilbert and Tompkins who write that when there are births in postcolonial drama they "tend not to represent a bright hope for the future. Instead, they symbolise evil or a social cancer; regardless of the baby's health, pregnancy is a metaphor for dis-ease" (Gilbert & Tompkins 220). The babies in *Festival of the Fish* do not represent an "evil or a social cancer" because of the ambiguity surrounding the ethnic identities of their parents (the spectator is not *sure* Fuyuo is *Zainichi*-Korean). However, "the reproductive power of the female body can undermine [fixed social] structures by producing children who do not fit the classificatory tables" (Holledge & Tompkins 2000:119), so indeterminacy could create dis-ease for the hegemonic Japanese spectator. With indeterminate identities, it is impossible to know if the future for the family, Ruri, Kyōko, or their babies is bright or dark, Japanese, *Zainichi*-Korean or both. Yū's use of the fertile sea and motherhood undercuts the notion of the masculine, nationalized land as well as the identity of the characters. It is a critique of Japanese society that could engender both dis-ease at an indeterminate cultural future and hope for a society free of racial and ethnic divisions. Although such a critique can suggest Yū's deliberate attempt to undermine a clear identity label, the fact that the Japanese may feel threatened by such dis-ease, would tend to re-inscribe a sense of otherness, and especially a specific *Zainichi*-Koreanness in the performances of *Festival of the Fish* and *Green Bench* where the author, director, and some of the actors are known to be *Zainichi*-Korean.

Multiplying Zainichi-*Koreanness*

There were unambiguous signifiers of *Zainichi*-Korean identity in the text of Yū's plays before *Festival of the Fish*, such as Korean words and phrases or traditional Korean dress in *Coffin of a Sunflower*. However, there are none in *Festival of the Fish* and the controversial element of ethnic identity that marked Yū's earlier plays is muted. The Korean diaspora could see *Zainichi*-Korean identity, but the hegemonic Japanese would see normative subjects. This work seems to be an act of assimilation, not a deliberate attempt to obscure identity. However, the corporeal reality of witnessing Ruri physically peel the sunburnt skin from her body becomes a form of experiential knowledge for spectators that is impossible to produce by simply reading the words on the page. Ruri's female body, derogated, of indeterminate ethnicity, and pregnant, by a male of indeterminate ethnicity, but seemingly by the fecundity of the sea itself, represents an aspect of Yū's dramaturgy that at one and the same time erases and inscribes *Zainichi*-Koreanness. As noted earlier, Wender and Yoneyama state that she wants to deny specificity in her later prose. Both absence and presence of a *Zainichi*-Korean identity is obscure on the page, but is literally embodied in performance. That embodiment, created and experienced by actors and spectators, is outside the playwright's control. That lack of authorial control actually gives Yū's body of dramatic work more specifics than her prose. Along with those specificities, the true indeterminacies of Yū's work were forged by her experience as a playwright.

CALIFORNIA STATE UNIVERSITY, NORTHRIDGE

Notes

1. "*Zainichi*," literally, "resident in Japan." The hyphenated Japanese and English term is short for the Japanese legal designation, "*Tokubetsu zainichi kankoku/chôsenjin*," — that is Koreans affiliated to either side of the DMZ on the Korean peninsula. As a white male from North America, I use this contingent and hybrid Japanese/English term as a way to foreground their contested existence and ambiguous identities.
2. All translations from Japanese are by the author unless otherwise noted.
3. Also transcribed elsewhere as Chong Wishin, and Chong Wishing.

References Cited

Butler, Judith. *Bodies That Matter: On the Discursive Limits of "Sex."* New York: Routledge, 1993.
Gilbert, Helen, and Joanne Tompkins. *Post-Colonial Drama: Theory, Practice, Politics.* London and New York: Routledge, 1996.
Holledge, Julie, and Joanne Tompkins. *Women's Intercultural Performance.* London and New York: Routledge, 2000.
Lie, John. "Ordinary (Korean) Japanese." *Koreans in Japan: Critical Voices from the Margin,* edited by Sonia Ryang. New York: Routledge, 2000.
Radford, Andrew. "The Performance of Identity in Nella Larsens's *Passing*," in *The South Carolina Review* 34.2 (2002):34–42.
Tsurumi, Shunsuke. *An Intellectual History of Wartime Japan: 1931–1945.* London and New York: KPI, 1986.
Wender, Melissa L. *Lamentation as History: Narratives by Korean in Japan,* 1965–2000, Stanford, CA: Stanford University Press, 2005.
Yū Miri. *NOW and THEN: Yū Miri jishin ni yoru zensakuhin kaisetsu + 51 no shitsumon* (*NOW and THEN: Yū Miri's own commentary on her work + 51 questions*). Tokyo: Kadokawa Shōten. 1997.
_____. *Sakana ga mita yume* (*The Dream of a Fish*). Tokyo: Shinchôsha. 2000.
_____. *Sekai no hibiware to tamashii no kūhaku wo* (*Cracks in the World and Emptiness of the Soul...*). Tokyo: Shinchōsha, 2001.
_____. *Uo no matsuri* (*Festival of the Fish*). Tokyo: Hakusuisha, 1996.

Ping Chong's Postcolonial Historicism and Theatricalism
Pojagi in *The East-West Quartet*
Yuko Kurahashi

Abstract

This paper examines the last piece of Ping Chong's East-West Quartet, Pojagi, *which deals with a series of encounters between Korea and colonial powers, and the tragic results as most vividly exemplified by the division of the nation during the Korean War. I will explore in what ways Chong theatricalized and semioticized the political, social, and cultural clashes he selected from his research and how his revisionist historicism could be located within recent postcolonial studies and studies of national identity of Korea. In preparing this paper I have relied on my notes on the performance of* Pojagi *I attended in New York City in 1999; viewing the video tape of* Pojagi; *interviewing Esther K. Chae, one of the three performers in the production; and identifying, researching, and applying postcolonial, poststructural and semiotic readings to the text and the stage.*

In his works which "poetically document" the relationship between the East and West (*Deshima, Chinoiserie, Pojagi,* and *After Sorrow*), Ping Chong created each stage element in reference "to a historical event or archival document" ("Cultures in Collision"). In these pieces, historical events and accounts transform themselves into an intriguing tapestry of the history of East/West relationships that have shaped the present. The first piece *Deshima*, created in Holland in 1990, deals with Japan's relationships with the West, focusing on both Western and Japanese colonialism, and on the collision of different cultures that surround Japan from the fifteenth century through the twentieth century. After *Deshima* Chong staged three historical "poetic documentary" pieces including *Chinoiserie* (about Chinese history, 1995), *After Sorrow* (about Vietnamese history, 1997) and *Pojagi* (about Korean history, 1999). *Chinoiserie* depicts several key events "leading up to the Opium War" including the "observations of a Chinese diplomat about the peculiar habit of kissing in America, the European obsession/addiction to tea, the less told history of Chinese settlers in America, and the

129

continuing trade disputes between China and the U.S." ("Ping Chong Returns").
After Sorrow consists of four short pieces about Chinese culture as told through
dance pieces performed by Muna Tseng, a Hong Kong-born choreographer and
dancer. In *Pojagi*, the last piece of the four, Chong takes the audience to "an
impressionistic journey through Korean history" (Solomon). The four pieces are
now known as *The East-West Quartet*.¹ In an interview with Victoria Abrash,
Chong describes the Quartet as a comprehensive work that "brings a certain long
overdue justice to the experience of Asians in America and contributes to a greater
understanding of the complicated and often tragic history of competition among
Europe, America, and Asia" (Abrash xxxv).

This paper investigates how Chong's theatrical reinscription/rewriting of
history portrays the "tragic history of competition" and explores how Ping Chong
could bring an "overdue justice" to Asians in both Asia and America through his
poetic narratives about racial, cultural, economic, and aesthetic clashes between
the East and West. For this paper I will focus on the last piece of the Quartet,
Pojagi, which deals with a series of encounters between Korea and colonial powers, and the tragic results as most vividly exemplified by the division of the nation
during the Korean War. *Pojagi* was originally commissioned and developed at
Harvard University's Institute on the Arts and Civic Dialogue which produced
a work-in progress production on 31 July 1999. The complete version of *Pojagi*
was performed at the DMC Festival in South Korea on 31 December 1999,² and
then premiered in the United States at La MaMa E.T.C. in New York City in
February and March 2000. By examining spoken words, dance, gestures, lighting, sounds (scored by Brian Hallas with whom Chong had collaborated for a
number of early productions), and props, I will explore in what ways Chong
theatricalized and semioticized the political, social, and cultural clashes he
selected from his research and how his revisionist historicism could be located
within recent postcolonial studies and studies of national identity of Korea. In
preparing this paper I have relied on my notes on the performance of *Pojagi* I
attended in New York City in February 2000; viewing the video tape of *Pojagi*,
interviewing Esther K. Chae, one of the three performers in the production; and
identifying, researching, and applying postcolonial, poststructural, and semiotic readings to the text and the stage.

Chong's interest in and passion for filling the voids of underrepresented history through his plays resonates with the statement of Gabrielle Spiegel that the
historian's mission could be to fill the space of the void created by the division
of the present from the past with words by scrutinizing and investigating the
"corpse" that might have never been cut open (5). This postmodern historiograph-
ical analogy is applicable to Chong's unique way of expressing the past. In every
piece of *The East-West Quartet* Chong reveals parts of history that he believes to
"have vanished into the modern world" (167). In *Pojagi*, Chong's scrutiny of the
void brings forth narratives of and about forgotten, ostracized, and silenced people such as Korean atomic bomb victims, whom I will discuss later in this paper.

In *Pojagi* the present (the performers) joins the past (the contents of their narratives and characters) and together they provide, for the audience, the medium by which to understand what Koreans went through. Wilhelm Dilthey, a German philosopher of the late nineteenth century and early twentieth century, emphasized the importance of the "sensorially given manifestations or expressions" (Dilthey 228) as well as expressed meaning in the process of reinscribing human conditions and history. For Chong, the "sensorially given manifestations"—a series of ritualistic gestures, facial expressions of the two performers, and sign language—are all indispensable vehicles in his historical narratives. For example, in the end of this ritualistic journey, C. S. Lee and Chae, as Man and Woman, draw an imaginary line from stage left to right to signify the placement of the DMZ while Woman says: "It was around midnight on August 11, 1945, that these two young colonels, with only a map borrowed from a *National Geographic* magazine, hastily drew the line at the 38th Parallel to divide the American and Russian zones of occupation" (188).

Instead of referring to a number of encounters between Korea and foreign countries, Chong chooses to explore the diversity and plurality of Korean encounters and relations with foreign countries through its relationship with Japan and the United States. This is perhaps because Chong sees Korea's relationships with the West mainly through Japan's colonization of Korea. Chong highlights Japan's first invasion of Korea in the sixteenth century, Korea's first "modern" encounter with the West, the assassination of Queen Min by the Japanese in 1895, the subsequent annexation by Japan in 1911, and the division of the nation in 1945. The focus on the five events leaves out many major events in Korean history, such as the influence of Catholic priests on Koreans in the late eighteenth century followed by their persecution under the edict issued by King Hŏngjong at the beginning of the nineteenth century,[3] the battle with French forces on Kanghwa Island, the Russian invasions as manifested in Russian diplomat Alexis de Speyer's move of his residence from Tokyo to Seoul, and the British taking up residence at Port Hamilton on Komun Island.[4] The play also does not deal with the most famous event involving American forces, the "General Sherman incident," in which 24 American sailors on the U.S. Navy ship "General Sherman" were killed by Koreans after the ship attacked Korean forts in 1866.[5]

Historian Bruce Cumings points out this Japanese-colonization centered view of Korean history by referring to some words of the Confucian scholar Hong Chae-hak such as "Japan and the West were peas in a pod," and "they all meant affliction and ruin to Korea" (105). Viewing Korean history through the Japanese-colonization centered postcolonial lens indeed reflects Chong's subjective view of the history of foreign relations between the East and West as a first generation Chinese American who has maintained deep connection with East Asian culture and history. Specifically, how Japanese aggression toward East and South East Asian countries pertains to his own family's history.

The title of the play *Pojagi*, which has dual meanings in Korea's history of resistance to Japan, itself connotes the play's focus. "Pojagi" means a "container, or vessel, that has carried the history of the nation and people, and the traditions that "have vanished into the modern world" (167). "Pojagi" also means "square or rectangular cloths of any size traditionally brightly colored and used by all strata of society for a range of purposes, including book bags, laundry bags, purses, gift wrap, and ceremonial uses" (167). The simple cloths attain a more powerful and political meaning as the narrator explains, in the play, that during the Japanese invasion of Korea in 1592, some women "filled Pojagi" with "stones and threw them off cliffs" at the Japanese (179).

Chong's "revisionist" history functions — like that suggested by Michel de Certeau who championed the need for constant [re]writings of the past — as a catalyst to tie the present audience with the past. De Certeau argues that histories are "founded on the rupture between a past that is its object, and a present that is the place of its practice [writing and re-writing]" (36). Thus the revisions of history are the "formal prerequisite for writing history" to produce the "objects of historical knowledge, which have no existence apart from the historian's identification of them" (qtd. in Spiegel 5). In making *Pojagi,* the author and director Chong, serving as a historian in de Certeau's terms, theatricalized his own "objects of historical knowledge" through writing and re-writing the historical events by placing and replacing the information he has selected and then by transforming it into his theatrical signs. In the terms of de Certeau's, Chong found both "object and practice" in the past and present. That is probably why, contrary to Chong's usual avoidance of fixed "narratives," *Pojagi,* compared with the other three East-West Quartet pieces, maintains the traditional historical accounts of facts and numbers in a chronological order.

In the performance of *Pojagi,* two performers, C.S. Lee and Esther K. Chae, wearing white costumes that resemble the traditional *hanbok* worn by Korean peasants,[6] take the role of historians/narrators, enacting a lecture/storytelling/performance on an extremely simple set which consists of two chairs and a long transparent, rectangular, photographer's table illuminated with blue light. The two actors stand, separately, at each end of the table. The sound of waves adds an atmospheric effect, helping the "transformation" of the illuminated table, in the audience's imagination, into a symbolic site of Korea's geography and history. In the middle of the performance, the third performer Shin Young Lee appears and places, on the table, triangle (pyramidal) objects that may symbolize mountains, hills, rivers, and lands which continue, from South to North, through the man-made zone at the thirty-eighth parallel.

This abstract, minimalist stage — which Chong has used in many of his works — resonates with what Hans-Thies Lehmann calls "postdramatic theatre" in which "neither plots, nor plastically shaped dramatis personae are needed" and "either dramatic dialectical collision of values nor even identifiable figures are necessary to produce 'theatre'"(34). For example, the triangle objects placed on the table might signify Korean mountains, rivers, people, and/or perhaps time-

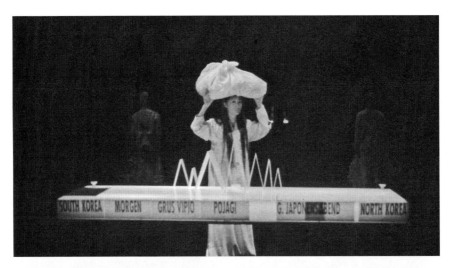

Ping Chong's *Pojagi* (photograph by Lia Chang).

less resistance against foreign power. Shamanistic dance might be interpreted as the significance of traditions or the performative ritual indispensable to bring the spirit of the past to the present. Instead of telling a story through the fixed narrative by the "plastically shaped dramatis personae," the postdramatic theatre prioritizes the creation of a new space which consists of diverse elements both on stage and in the auditorium. It maintains the power to question and destabilize the spectator's construction of identity and the "other," more so than realist mimetic drama, which remains caught in representation and thus often reproduces prevailing ideologies (5).

Chong's stage, like Lehmann's concepts of postdramatic theatre, or a "post–Brechtian" theatre (Lehmann 2006:33), refuses to be dictated by a written text and fixed characters in an attempt to "question and destabilize" the spectators' preconceptions and lack of knowledge about the subjects that they view. Chong introduces the audience to the world of his "symbols" that challenge the spectators' preconceptions of the history, people, and ideology that has been perhaps "plastically shaped" by dominant cultural information. Instead of grasping tangible meanings, the audience is, during the performance, invited to construct the meaning of history from different abstract pieces of visual and audio signs, evaluating multiple levels of signification. Chong's intention remains to encourage the audience to participate in the interpretation and creation of meanings.

Indeed this active invitation to interpretation is what Chong has demonstrated for over three decades. The multiple interpretative possibilities were particularly prominent in his early works in the 1970s and 1980s. In his article "Ping Chong's Theatre of Simultaneous Consciousness," Kent Neely argues that in many of Chong's plays, the "significance [signification] is unstable" (129) because he "eliminates the particulars of time, place, and character identity" by presenting an object that would not "maintain a continuum of time and place" (123). Chong's "multivalence," according to Neely, "contradicts a consistent or absolute significance of any one event or symbol" (129). Discussing the word games and juxtapositions in *Kind Ness* (1986), Suzanne R. Westfall argues that Chong recontextualizes the concepts, images, and ideas and makes what "we take for granted, thus moving us from the known to the unknown, from the coastline to the interior, initiating us into the idiolectic world by questioning our conventional significations and generating new associations" strange (361).

Chong's ability to recontextualize symbols is evident in his exploration of Korean national identity in *Pojagi*. The play explains Korean national identity by underscoring the "tradition" and "roots" of Korea. The performance starts with the two masked actors' synchronizing slow dance/movement. Both actors carry two white pom-pom like objects, which are modeled after the Korean traditional long sleeve *hansam* (Chae 2008). As soon as they sit on opposite sides of the table, with their backs to the audience, showing masks on the back of their heads, they start telling the creation story of Korea. According to the story, the she-bear, who was faithful to the king's instructions, became a woman while the she-tiger who was not faithful to the king's instructions, was left in darkness for a hundred days (175). Esther K. Chae enacts the she-bear's transformation into a woman exhibiting a series of different gestures and poses in blue/red lights; she becomes a bear in red light while she becomes a woman in a blue light. This section of the "metamorphosis" reflects Korea's widely popularized legend of Tan'gun's, the first Korean, who was born from "the union between Hwan'ung, the son of heaven, and a female bear" (Pai 58–60). The symbolic presentation of the popular creation story of Korea underscores its significance and value as a vehicle to express the pride and exclusiveness of Koreans as a particular, independent ethnic group.

Not only serving as an introduction to Koreans' national identity as validated and valued in the legend, this ritualistic opening also helps the audience to enter the liminal site between the present and an ancient period, allowing them to participate in Chong's "rewritings" of history. This creates what Victor Turner defines as a "liminal phase" which provides, through a series of ritual processes, "a stage for unique structures of experience, in milieus detached from mundane life and characterized by the presence of ambiguous ideas, monstrous images, sacred symbols, ordeals, humiliations" (11).

The liminal phase in *Pojagi* is not, however, a simple ritual threshold between the mundane and creative/imaginative worlds. *Pojagi* challenges the audience to enter the liminal zone, in which both historically dominant power and the dominated encounter, observe, and negotiate each other. Examining another multimedia theatre artist Robert Lepage, Jane Koustas states that Lepage's theatre challenges audiences to "experience the between zone, that liminal space between, or outside, comfortable linguistic, cultural and geographical boundaries in which the Other is frequently no longer easily identifiable" (395). In *Pojagi* and many other works, Chong, like Lepage, also blends the Other — in this case the Koreans and their history — into the centrality of theatrical discourse, encouraging the audience to see and appreciate the encounter and reencounter of different languages, exchanges between the familiar/comfortable and the Other/the uncomfortable.

The liminal site in the beginning of the play marks the onset of Chong's investigation of what it means to be Korean. The play continues to refer to distinctive Korean characteristics, in comparison to other Asiatic races, underscoring their pride in national identity. The actor explains Korean as a special ethnic group within Asia: "They are not Chinese, and still they are yellow. They are not Japanese, although their eyes are like almonds in shape. They are taller than any of the Asiatics we have in America and their faces are kinder and somewhat more solid" (186). Yet, Chong might have presented this nationalist distinction in order to provide double-interpretations. This line could be read as the ethnic traits invented by Europeans in an attempt to differentiate each ethnic group in Asia or it could be read as a Korean nationalist view of themselves as superior to any other Asian groups.

As one of the theatrical narrative tools to emphasize Korean ethnic identity, the play focuses on Japanese invasions and brutality beginning in the sixteenth century and revived in the late nineteenth century that continued to the end of World War II. One of the most dramatic examples of this brutality carried out by Japan is the murder of Queen Min in 1895 by Japanese soldiers. The play depicts Queen Min, through the story told by Esther K. Chae, as a young, innocent victim, contrary to the depictions found in many historical accounts, as a "woman of exceptional intelligence and ambition" who became the "most formidable of all the enemies of the Taewŏn'gun" (Watson 207). In *Pojagi*'s the corpse of Queen Min "looked like she must have just come out of her sleeping chamber" in "short white underwear, both top and bottom, and below the knee she was naked" (185). The queen "appeared to be twenty-five or twenty-six years old" (185). The play also provides the first-person narrative, read by Chae, of the Queen: "On October 8th 1895 at three o'clock in the morning, Japanese soldiers and Japanese thugs, dressed as Korean civilians, invaded the palace. I was stabbed to death, and my handmaidens too were put to the sword. We were dragged into the courtyard, doused with kerosene, and set on fire" (185). This portrayal of Queen Min helps the audience to see this historical moment, the assassination of Queen Min, as the permanent destruction of the long, stable regimes of Korea's kings and queens that resisted foreign invasions and influences while fighting for independence and sovereignty.

The steps taken by the Japanese government to colonize and rule Korea up to the end of World War II are enacted through a series of ritualistic citations and movements of the two actors. Lee as Man speaks the following line with occasional sign "language": "From now on you will perform *saikeirei*: a ritual bow toward the emperor in Tokyo at public assemblies. The local calendar will be changed to the Japanese. 1910 will become 2570. Japanese holidays will become your holidays. The Japanese language (*Sign 'language'*) will replace the Korean. Korean names will be changed to Japanese names" (187).

Next, Lee places the card of "annexation" into the front edge of the table. He removes the card and replaces it with another card "intervention" and then Chae replaces it with the card labeled "pojagi" and then with "time passes" and then the last card "WWII." This simple visual demonstration of major incidents is not only part of the chronological history lesson but also serves as a ritual to inform the audience of the passing of 30 years.

The actor's ethnic and cultural identity also influences Chong's narrative and theatrical signs on the stage. Originally Chong had intended to include personal accounts about medical experiments the Japanese performed on Koreans. According to Chae, it was unbearable for some performers, especially Chae, who grew up in South Korea, to deal with these accounts. As a result Chong cut and replaced them with the story of a Korean Hiroshima victim. The account of a group of Koreans who were brought to Japan as forced laborers[7] demonstrates Chong's aspiration to shed light on parts of history which "have vanished into the modern world."

The Korean forced laborer's story in Hiroshima begins as the performer, as that laborer, narrates how he finally gets to a hospital after the bombing only to discover that 'maggots had hatched on the burns' (188). This one narrative brings to light the erased or ignored realities of "tens of thousands of Korean nationals" who were "killed and injured in the cities of Hiroshima and Nagasaki during the atomic bombings of 1945," described by Kurt W. Tong, who conducted research on the state of the Korean atomic bomb victims from the 1960s to the 1980s (31).

According to Tong, many of the victims (in the case of Hiroshima, the estimates range from 48,000 to 50,000, including 30,000 who died immediately and 20,000 who survived) could not receive proper treatment in either Japan or Korea. Emergency hospitals which were set up by the Japanese after the bombing, frequently turned away Korean victims (332). For those who returned to their native country of Korea, medical treatment at the best hospitals in Seoul was too expensive. Returning to Japan in the post-war decades was also difficult because of extremely strict Japanese immigration laws (33). Korean atomic bomb victims who stayed in Japan as permanent residents also faced a layer of obstacles. For example, two laws which passed in the 1950s and 1960s established a system of registration and free treatment for atomic bomb victims in Japan. They could receive free treatment if they were identified by two independent witnesses (not relatives) as having been at a certain distance from the hypocenter at the time of the explosions. It was extremely difficult for Korean victims to find two reliable witnesses since the majority of Koreans in Japan had returned to the Korean peninsula after 1945 (33).

"The Man" in *Pojagi* represents these nameless and forgotten victims. Through the first-person narrative, the man brings the past to the present, giving a new meaning to the conventional East-West relationship in which all of the victims of the atomic bombs in 1945 were Japanese. "The Man" in *Pojagi* survives the attack of the bomb but died from a residual disorder in 1972.[8] He explains hardships after the war; he was ostracized both in Korea and Japan, his son was born deformed and he refused to eat after his father's death. The Man also expresses his isolation as a victim, which reflects the reality in which many victims were ostracized whether they stayed or left Japan: "No one wants to remember people like me. The new government in South Korea was ashamed of us, so we were better forgotten. In Tokyo we had been written off as racially inferior, so no tears were ever shed on our behalf" (188).

Reinscribing Korean history in relation to Japanese invasions and occupation is one of the important processes for Koreans in understanding themselves in relation to both the East and West. The play's focus on Japanese invasions and crimes, along with the creation legend, reflects the popular, nationalist view of Korea and its identity in the post Korean war era, yet with Chong's intellectual twist. In her analysis of the intersection of the history of Japanese imperialism and neocolonial discourses of modernization and development, Jini Kim Watson argues that mainstream postcolonial Korean studies fail to recognize Japan as one of the many colonizing countries and question the "Eurocentric notions of progress and race that Japanese imperialism relied on" (172). Instead, Kim Watson argues, because of the over-privileged "modernization studies," Korea has seen Japan merely as a wartime aggressor. Kim Watson emphasizes the importance of viewing Japanese invasions and occupation of Korea as an act of "colonial mimicry," to use Homi K. Bhabha's words, that reflects Japan's desire to be "elevated to the ranks of the great Western imperial powers, and regarded its first colony in Korea as a 'symbol of the nation's equality with the West'" (qtd. in Watson 173).

In spite of the apparent focus on Japanese invasions, the play also points to the relationship between Western colonialism and Japanese colonialism by including references to European colonial powers such as the 1882 "Imperial Decree of Commodore Shufeldt, United States Navy Special Envoy with Full Power" (183) that forced Korea to open its doors through politics and economy. In *Pojagi*, Western colonization is represented by this major event between Korea and the United States, which the narration succinctly describes as aggression against not only Korea but also many Asian countries. This criticism is vividly manifested in the following metonymical phrases in the play: "The Pacific is the ocean bride of America. China and Japan and Korea — with their innumerable islands, hanging like necklaces about them — are the bridesmaids. California is the nuptial couch, the bridal chamber, where all the wealth of the Orient will be brought to celebrate the wedding" (184).

Toward the end of the play, the play changes its focus from the history of Japanese invasions to the division of Korea in 1945 by two U.S. colonels "Charles Bonesteel and Dean Rusk without consulting Korean leaders"(188). Chae, as "Mr. Park," tells a story of a woman who loses her sister during the Korean War: "She came home one afternoon, and she packed a few things in pojagi and left. That was the last time I saw her. She went to North Korea during the Korean War, and since then we haven't seen each other" (191). Thirty four years later, they meet at the airport but neither of them recognized the other: "That was a painful moment not to recognize one's own family!" (192). Chong's limited use of narrative about post-war Korea signals the piece's focus on the voices of the people who survived World War II.

Pojagi functions as an important history lesson about Korea, highlighting the foreign invasions and control, with the two performers as lecturers. In spite of the text's complexity of postcoloniality and the semiotic stage, the play became a rather straightforward, non-interactive classroom history lecture. As Anita Gates mentioned in her *New York Times* review, "[Chong's] failure so far" was not to be able to "find the right way to blend his visual talents into his verbal ones." (E38) Yet, even this uneven "blending" of different theatrical languages invited the audience to enter and stay — for over an hour — in his highly historicized, politicized, and semioticized liminal space. Beneath the seemingly simple history lecture, the audience begins to see multilayered images of "otherness" not only through verbal but also visual languages including the actors' physicality as well. For example, Chae's presence as a Korean growing up in Korea itself functioned as a physiological site thus helping the audience feel the pain of the people through the "sensorially given manifestations or expressions." The theatrical space provides both "present problems of the living present" and "rich ethnic past," to quote Victor Turner, to "create a new cultural meaning that describes the community," in this case, Korea as manifested in Chong's theatrical narrative and presentation.[9] In making *Pojagi*, Chong, as a historian in de Certeau's terms, theatricalized his own "objects of historical knowledge" through writing and re-writing the historical events — from his subject position as a first generation of Chinese American — by placing and replacing the information he has selected and then by transforming it into his theatrical signs on the stage.

KENT STATE UNIVERSITY

Notes

1. In 2004 Chong published a collection of *Deshima, Chinoiserie, After Sorrow,* and *Pojagi* as *The East/West Quartet* from Theatre Communications Group.

2. The DMZ Millennium festival for peace and reunification, celebrated 1999–2000 New Year's eve. Esther K. Chae, 17 May 2009.

3. In spite of the official ban of Christianity, under the tolerant rule of King Chŏngjo (1776–1800), the people in Korea enjoyed relative freedom. A Chinese Roman Catholic priest smuggled himself into Korea in 1795, contributing to the growth of Catholicism in Korea. However, soon after the change of the reign, the prosecution of Catholic priests and converts began. The most pivotal incident was the 1839 massacre of 76 Catholic converts, including three French priests. See Cumings 96; Watson 34–36.

4. Cumings (114) details these historical events.

5. About the General Sherman incident of 1866, see Cumings 96–97.

6. The costume designer Stefani Mar modeled the costume after the *hanbok*. Chae, email interview, 16 May 2009.

7. Research on Korean laborers, including the victims of the atomic bombs, has been rarely conducted. One of the major investigations was done by peace activist and *tanka* poet Fukagawa Munetoshi who investigated the disappearance of 246 Koreans. See Palmer 335.

8. The circumstance of The Man in *Pojagi* resembles Ryu Choon Seung, a Korean victim of the Hiroshima atomic bomb, who is remembered in a short essay by Kuak Kwi Hoon, a doctor who helped many Korean survivors who returned to Korea after the war. See Hoon 1989:200–204.

9. See Turner 9. In this postcolonial piece, the theatrical space is both semiotic and political, constantly asking the audience to question their own understanding and knowledge of the subject of the narrative. This new cultural meaning created in the performance is interpreted differently depending on the place of the performance. For example Esther K. Chae describes the audience response at the DMZ festival: "There were huge cheering and roaring when I (female) portrayed Admiral Yi (male) shooting arrows and defeated the Japanese attacks" (Chae, email interview, 17 May 2009).

References Cited

Abrash, Victoria. "An Interview with Ping Chong." In *The East-West Quartet* by Ping Chong, xv–xxxv. New York: Theatre Communications Group, 2004.

Bhabha, Homi K. *The Location of Culture.* London; New York: Routledge, 1994.

Certeau, Michel de. *The Writing of History,* translated by Tom Conley. New York: Columbia University Press, 1988.

Chae, Esther K. Email Interview. 15 May 2009.

_____. Email Interview. 16 May 2009.
_____. Email Interview. 17 May 2009.
_____. Personal interview. Los Angeles, 28 November 2008.
Chong, Ping. *The East-West Quartet*. New York: Theatre Communications Group, 2004.
_____. *Pojagi,* directed by Ping Chong, 2000. New York: Ping Chong & Company, 2008. DVD.
Connor, Mary E., and ABC-Clio Information Services, eds. *The Koreas : A Global Studies Handbook*. Santa Barbara, CA: ABC CLIO, 2002.
"Cultures in Collision." *Asian American Arts.* November 1995.
Cumings, Bruce. *Korea's Place in the Sun : A Modern History.* New York: Norton, 2005.
Dilthey, Wilhelm. *The Formation of the Historical World in the Human Sciences,* edited and translated by Rudolf A. Makkreel and Frithjof Rodi. Princeton, NJ: Princeton University Press, 2002.
Gates, Anita. "Casting Light Bright and Dark, On a Nation's Historic Journey." *New York Times,* 3 March 2000:E38.
Hoon, Kuak Kwi. "Father and Son Robbed of Body and Soul: A Record of Ryu Choon Seung and His Son." In *The Atomic Bomb: Voices from Hiroshima and Nagasaki,* edited by Kyoko and Mark Selden, 200–204. Armonk, NY: M.E. Sharp, 1989.
Koustas, Jane. "Staging the/an Other: *The Dragons' Trilogy* Take II." *International Journal of Francophone Studies* 9.3 (2006):395–414.
Lehmann, Hans-Thies. *Postdramatic Theatre,* translated by Krena Jürs-Munby. New York: Routledge, 2006.
Neely, Kent. "Ping Chong's Theatre of Simultaneous Consciousness." *Journal of Dramatic Theory and Criticism* 6.2 (1992):121–135.
Pai, Hyung Il. *Constructing "Korean" Origins : A Critical Review of Archaeology, Historiography, and Racial Myth in Korean State-Formation Theories.* Cambridge, MA: Harvard University Asia Center, 2000.
Palmer, David. "The Straits of Dead Souls: One Man's Investigation into the Disappearance of Mitsubishi Hiroshima's Korean Forced Labourers." *Japanese Studies* 26.3 (2006):335–51.
"Ping Chong Returns." *Focus Point* 1–7 (November 1995).
Pojagi. By Ping Chong. Dir. by Ping Chong. La MaMa E.T.C., New York. 27 February 2000. Performance.
Solomon, Alicia. "The Poetry of the DMZ." *Village Voice,* 7 March 2000.
Spiegel, Gabrielle M. "Revising the Past/Revisiting the Present: How Change Happens in Historiography." *History & Theory* 46.4 (2007):1–19.
Tong, Kurt W. "Korea's Forgotten Atomic Bomb Victims." *Bulletin of Concerned Asian Scholars* 23.1 (1991):31–37.
Turner, Victor. "Are There Universals in Performance in Myth, Ritual, and Drama?" In *By Means of Performance: Intercultural Studies of Theatre and Ritual,* edited by Richard Schechner and Willa Appel. 8–18. New York: Cambridge University Press, 1990.
Watson, Jini Kim. "Imperial Mimicry, Modernisation Theory and the Contradictions of Postcolonial South Korea." *Postcolonial Studies* 10.2 (2007):171–190.
Westfall, Suzanne R. "Ping Chong's Terra In/Cognita: Monsters on Stage" In *Reading the Literature of Asian America,* edited by Shirley Geok-lin Lim & Amy Ling, 359–373. Philadelphia: Temple University Press, 1992.

Great Souls, Big Wheels, and Other Words
Experiments with Truth and Representation in Verbatim Theatre

Donald McManus

Abstract

Verbatim theatre has roots reaching back to the early twentieth century and a longer tradition of documentary and historical drama, but the form has enjoyed an extraordinary amount of interest and production since 2001. Many dynamic works have been created in a variety of styles, but with interest in this documentary approach to text comes renewed interest in theoretical questions about how drama best reflects reality on stage.

Verbatim theatre is a genre of drama that uses pre-existing words as text. The form has gained currency over the past decade. A much-publicized recent example is the opera *Doctor Atomic* by John Adams and Peter Sellars, but Anna Deavere Smith, Simon Levy, Alan Rickman, and David Hare have all had success creating performance pieces almost entirely dependent on the words of other people. There are many more examples too numerous to explore in one essay. Most of these plays have been controversial for political reasons. Utterances used out of context can be effective but also leave the author vulnerable to critics who are unsympathetic with the political argument. The specific texts discussed in this essay are united by a self-conscious political lineage and theatrical heritage, while differing in formal and aesthetic rhetoric.

Almost all drama borrows words, quotes recognizable sources, and functions on an inter-textual level, but clearly verbatim theatre is somehow less authored than documentary drama that uses invented dialogue in a more traditional manner. Who is the author of Simon Levy's *What I Heard About Iraq*? Does verbatim theatre alter the actor's function? Should the actress in *My Name is Rachel Corrie* pretend to be Rachel Corrie? Or would that play be more effective if the performer reading her diaries asserted his or her own identity?

In an effort to explore some of these questions and work out in my own mind what the theoretical implications of this form are, I created a text using the words of Mohandas Gandhi, Rabindranath Tagore, Malcolm X, Martin Luther King, and others. The end result was a play with music entitled *Great Souls, Big Wheels and Other Beats* that was performed at Theatre Emory as part of the Brave New Works series in 2009. The play quoted directly from historical figures debating such topics as religion, colonialism, democracy, capitalism, segregation and caste. I chose a subject that had historical and political importance because verbatim theatre seems to deal with issues that are pressing and tend to burst the bounds of normal dramaturgical devices, or as British playwright Robin Soans has said: "The audience for a verbatim play will expect the play to be political" (2008:19). I used this as a starting point but the identities of the speakers were purposely obfuscated to challenge the audience's conditioned sympathies with the historical figures. My purpose was to explore to what extent quotation could maintain dramatic interest if divorced from its specific historical context. Many of the statements were indisputably interesting and historically important, but I wanted to create a play that explored the way we interpret the truth in a dramatic text, and the relationship of words to our understanding of historical reality and the characters that have shaped that reality. Drama has always raised questions about truth and our perception of reality, but verbatim theatre has brought some of these old theoretical issues back into focus. Most verbatim plays re-frame truth in a self-conscious way, even if the creators purport to be simply reporting the facts. The body of this essay surveys some of the issues that verbatim plays have raised and how the authors have responded to them.

My approach in creating *Great Souls*, which I will discuss at length at the end of this essay, differed greatly from the style that has become associated with verbatim theatre in the past few years, particularly in Britain. Robin Soans, Max Stafford-Clark, David Hare, and others have interviewed subjects, as a journalist might, and extracted a documentary play based on this found material. There is a tendency to champion verbatim theatre as art that is closer to the reality of life and history than traditional theatre. This sentiment is expressed in this advertisement for a collection of essays by authors who have created dramatic texts from the words of others:

> Verbatim Theatre is the surprise success story of the modern stage. As the name suggests, verbatim plays are written using only the precise words spoken by people interviewed about a particular event or topic. The plays are constructed by the playwright from the testimony of witnesses or those close to an event in order to lend the play an authority that shifts the theatre from mere entertainment to a form of reportage, politicizing the audience [Oberon Books 2008].

If we examine this quotation a little more closely I think it is clear that there is an implicit anti-theatrical bias in the rhetoric. Why make a play based on testimony of witnesses or those close to an event? "In order to lend the play an authority that shifts the theatre from mere entertainment to a form of reportage." Why is it necessary to create this opposition between reportage and mere entertainment? Do *The Persians, Mother Courage, Major Barbara, Angels in America,* and *Uncle Tom's Cabin*, each fall under the category of mere entertainment? Does a comedy club that presents improvisations based on daily news articles carry more authority than a dramatic author's original conception simply because the "text" is prompted from "reportage?" Consider as a specific example Aeschylus's messenger speech from *The Persians*. In that play Aeschylus refers to events in the not so distant past of the city, yet tells them from the point of view of the enemy. When the messenger enters to tell the Queen of Persia the news of their loss to the Athenians, he describes the battle at Salamis in the kind of detail that only a first-hand witness could relate. The original audience would have had untold veterans from the actual battle, including Aeschylus himself, and still more who would have heard the story a dozen times. The retelling of the event invites the audience to compare the effectiveness and veracity of the story with what they already may have heard. The messenger concludes his story by saying:

> Truthful I have been, but omit many
> Of the woes a God has hurled against
> The Persians [Aeschylus *The Persians* 514–516].

Is the legend that Aeschylus was present at the battle the reason why this *tour de force* of dramatic creation is so powerful? I suggest that it is not. Indeed the argument that Aeschylus was a witness in real life is only of importance because his drama is compelling. Theatre communicates truth on many levels, and eye-witness truth is only one ingredient. If scholars unearth evidence that Aeschylus was never actually at Salamis, will we think any less of the play or his artistry? The truth of the details of the battle as told by the messenger is beyond the scope of historical reality. The play speaks to the Greek understanding of the battle in history and their ability to empathize with the enemy rather than the facts of what occurred in the waters outside of the city.

Since so many intelligent and creative people have invested their energies into making verbatim theatre a vital contemporary genre, it is not surprising that the authors, or compilers, have asked themselves how verbatim theatre reflects truth differently from other forms of drama. The conclusions that these artists have drawn are inconsistent. British playwright Robin Soans has said: "People tend to think verbatim theatre should be strictly regulated, but it's not a restricted form, it's malleable" (Soans 2007). Here Soans puts the theoretical contradiction of verbatim theatre into focus. Either direct quotation is somehow more authentic than "mere entertainment" or it is not. You cannot promote a genre as deserving to exist because it is "reportage" and then balk at the idea of being held to account by falling back on artistic license.

Manchester Guardian theatre critic, Lyn Gardner used her praise of *What I Heard About Iraq* to raise doubts about verbatim theatre as a legitimate genre. "The strength of a piece such as *What I Heard About Iraq* lies not in its staging, but in the way it presents its material in a fashion that makes the audience question every single word it hears. That's very different from a great deal of verbatim theatre which functions in a way that cajoles you into accepting that piece's particular bias as the truth and nothing but the truth" (2007). So is verbatim theatre at its best when it gets closer to reflecting, representing and presenting the truth, or when it makes us all more critical of what we accept as the truth, as Gardner suggests the strategy in *What I Heard About Iraq* promotes? It might seem that these two modes work logically in tandem, but I think that they oppose each other both logically and artistically. In one case a statement is presented as more true than invented dialogue because it was actually said by someone in a non-theatrical, non-artistic context. In another case the theatrical event is meant to challenge the reception of these actual statements. In other words the use of actual statements in some verbatim theatre is meant to focus our attention on how little truth exists in non-theatrical statements. It is interesting to read Simon Levy's introduction to *What I Heard About Iraq* because he is so self-conscious about verbatim theatre having a legacy.

> This is a cry. A clarion call. A tone poem for 5 voices. A gift for history. This is my desire as an artist/activist to respond to the most important historical event of this generation. This is also about truth, about facts, about quotes. This is not about opinions or fiction. This is about what was said and is being said. This is beyond rhetoric and about human beings [Levy 3].

I am puzzled by the last line in particular. Surely *What I Heard About Iraq* is mostly about rhetoric. I can well imagine that Levy's hope is that the play goes beyond the theatre and that it engenders political activism, but most authors of plays with some kind of valid and important content hope their work engages the audience, yet they don't all resort to so much literal quotation of rhetoric in the process. Later in his introduction he draws attention to theatrical devices such as transformation and emotional connection.

> This is also about the challenge of making polemics emotional. This should not be a diatribe of Us vs. Them. This is about theatre as Community. The power of theatre is its ability to affect people. Although this is fact-based theatre, documentary theatre, verbatim theatre — in the tradition of *Laramie Project* or *The Exonerated* or *Guantanamo* or *Execution of Justice* or *Are You Now or Have You Ever Been* and many such plays — it must also be theatre that emotionally engages and galvanizes each audience member to take action in her/his way. It's also meant to stir debate. And, this is about the art of the actor — the magic of imagination and transformation [Levy 3].

Levy implies that an artist — activist who quotes sources directly is: a) morally superior to, and b) more honest and true than a regular playwright who invents original stories and dialogue. And yet he also wants to tap into "emotion, and the actor's magical ability to transform." I found *What I Heard About Iraq* frustrating because it made little distinction between what was a rumor and what was a verifiable statement. I would have preferred a play entitled "What was said about Iraq." Yes, let us judge for ourselves how much we believe about the statements we hear, but what is stirring in *What I Heard About Iraq* is the verifiable fact that the statements were made, not whether they were true or untrue. Mixing the statements of Rumsfeld, Cheney, or Bush with less verifiable, less public utterances weakened the impact of the staging of the statements by the politicians. The first lines in the play are: "In 1992, a year after the first Gulf War, I heard Dick Cheney, then Secretary of Defense, say that the U.S. had been wise not to invade Baghdad and get bogged down in the problems of trying to take over and govern Iraq" (Levy 4). Having actors remind us of these ironic words that Cheney actually said is a very powerful way to start a play. But as the play develops the quotations take on a less cogent irony with subjective statements such as: "I heard Kassem Muhammad Ahmed say: I watched them roll over wounded people in the streets with tanks. This happened so many times" (Levy 49). However valid this utterance may be or effective as pathos, it pales next to catching the U.S. leadership in a public lie.

My Name is Rachel Corrie presents an even more problematic case. Every word from that play is from the private journal of a young woman who died trying to prevent the destruction of a home in Palestine by the Israeli Army. The problem with the play is that while she wrote all the words, she didn't say them. Her private journal was never intended to be read aloud or performed. Hiring an actress and asking her to pretend to be Rachel Corrie and act out words she wrote, but didn't say, is a logical-representation problem that I find difficult to reconcile. I'm not suggesting that it is unfair to perform Rachel Corrie's journal, but that the play that results should not claim to be closer to the truth because of its source, than a similar play created entirely from the imagination. Can a more "true" or "authoritative" form of theatre be built on a misapplication of unoriginal words?

The core of the problem in each of these cases revolves around an age-old obsession with reflecting reality or truth in theatre. Plato referred to the "ancient struggle" between philosophy and theatre in the *Republic*. All criticism positive and negative has taken its cue from there.

> Plato takes the theatre to be the antagonist of the emerging discipline of philosophy, a discipline that apparently needs to prove its dignity by distancing itself from everything associated with theatrical spectacles. This gesture of distancing remains the predominant mode in which philosophers from Plato through St. Augustine to Jean-Jacques Rousseau relate to the theatre, giving

expression to what Jonas Barish has called the anti-theatrical prejudice [Puchner 521].

Most theorists since Plato have been interested in how theatre reflects truth, but few agree on how this is best achieved or indeed where the truth lies. Playwrights have struggled with the issue of representation for generations, but they were never active partners with hostile theorists until the twentieth century.

In 1958 Harold Pinter (1930–2008) said: "There are no hard distinctions between what is real and what is unreal, nor between what is true and what is false. A thing is not necessarily either true or false; it can be both true and false" (Pinter 2005a). In his Nobel Lecture, "Art, Truth & Politics" he quoted this very line and stood by the assertion as far as it pertains to art, but said as a citizen he must ask: "What is true? What is false?" (2005b). He referred to the diminishing returns of dramaturgical devices such as comedy. His lecture provides a striking explanation of why he stopped writing bleak yet comic abstractions that implied much, but made little clear. He stopped writing "Pinter plays" because America was so "witty." The American government had co-opted Pinter's dramaturgical devices, so he stopped using them. The Nobel speech was built around this theme because Pinter wanted to use the Nobel award as a platform to speak against the U.S. war in Iraq:

> America has exercised a quite clinical manipulation of power worldwide while masquerading as a force for universal good. It's a brilliant, even witty, highly successful act of hypnosis. I put it to you that the United States is without doubt the greatest show on the road [Pinter 2005b].

Pinter's artistic strategy as he became more and more of an overtly political artist was to withdraw from the theatrical techniques that made him famous in favor of emphatic statements that employed few poetic devices. Consider this example from one of his late poems, *American Football: A Reflection on the Gulf War*:

> Hallelujah!
> It Works.
> We blew the shit out of them!
> We blew the shit right back up their own ass
> And out their fucking ears [Pinter 2005a:77].

Faced with the "wit" of the "greatest show on the road" as competition he withdrew his own skill as a writer. Somehow the techniques that made Pinter's dramaturgy so effective seemed false when he wanted to engage with important political issues. Pinter's friend and fellow dramatist David Hare has used a different dramaturgical strategy, turning to verbatim theatre as a primary device. When major playwrights like David Hare stop inventing characters and constructing original words for them to say, perhaps the old question of the death of the author has finally been answered. So what accounts for this phenomenon? As Pinter suggests in his Nobel lecture, it has something to do with the old, tortured relationship between theatre and truth. Perhaps Pinter was affected by Marxist literary theorists such as Georg Lukács (1885–1971) who argued that: "The more 'artless' a work of art, the more it gives the effect of life and nature, the more clearly it exemplifies an actual concentrated reflection of its times and the more clearly it demonstrates that the only function of its form is the expression of this objectivity, this reflection of life in the greatest concreteness and clarity and with all its motivating contradictions" (Lukács 804). The impulse to withdraw from art as if from sinful lies may account for Pinter's withdrawal from creating theatre.

In the introduction to *What I Heard About Iraq* Simon Levy refers to Eric Bentley's *Are You Now or Have You Ever Been: The Investigations of Show-Business by the Un-American Activities Committee 1947–1958*. Bentley, like Levy, wrote a preface to his 1972 play on the McCarthy-era communist witch hunts in Hollywood.

> The dialogue of *Are You Now or Have You Ever Been* is taken from hearings before the House Un-American Activities Committee. Hence no resemblance between the witness and the actual person is coincidental. These characters wrote their own lines into the pages of history. Such is the transaction — the drama — known as Investigation. The investigation of show business is presented here in the testimony of a small minority of those actually investigated, and this testimony has been abridged, edited, and arranged. All these processes — choice of witnesses, abridgment, editing, arrangement — bring into play the personal judgment, not to mention talent, of the writer responsible. To the extent that he is either a knave or a fool, the result will reflect his knavery or folly. I can only say I am aware of this, and I invite the skeptical or suspicious reader to check out his doubts and suspicions [Bentley Preface].

Bentley is arguing that his play is a justified selection of previously spoken words because the committee's "investigation" presented itself as theatre to begin with. Bentley seems to anticipate contemporary performance theory in this introduction, narrowing the area differentiating theatre as an art form and performance in the "real world." Bentley's experiment did not spark a host of similar plays based on other peoples' words. As a genre, verbatim theatre only became a commonly used technique in the early twenty-first century, but the first phase of verbatim theatre came in the early twentieth century with experiments by Irwin Piscator (1893–1966) and Bertolt Brecht (1898–1956) in Germany during the 20s and 30s. Piscator's interest in documentary theatre persisted throughout his career and he directed the original German production of *Der Stellvertreter (The Deputy)* by Rolf Hochhuth (1931-) in 1963. *The Deputy* caused an international sensation by implicating Pope Pius XII in the Nazi Holocaust. Hochhuth's dramaturgy relied on documentary evidence but verbatim accounts were not used extensively.

The way that Bentley stresses the expression "investigation" in his introduction leads me to think that, being a Teutonophile, he had Peter Weiss's *Die Ermittlung (The Investigation),* written in 1965, in mind at least in the writing of his preface to *Are You Now or Have You Ever Been,* if not in the conceptual stage and creation of the play itself. The very notion of a prose prelude to a piece of "investigation theatre" has its inception with *The Investigation. The Investigation* was based on transcripts from war crimes tribunals investigating the holocaust after World War II. Weiss's introduction is fascinating in the light of the rhetoric surrounding the verbatim theatre phenomenon of the early twenty-first century.

> In the presentation of this play no attempt should be made to reconstruct the courtroom before which the proceedings of the camp trial took place. Any such reconstruction would in the opinion of the author be as impossible as trying to present the camp itself on the stage. Hundreds of witnesses appeared before the court. The confrontations of witnesses and the accused, as well as the addresses to the court by the prosecution and the replies by the counsel for the defense, were overcharged with emotion. Only a condensation of the evidence can remain on the stage. This condensation should contain nothing but the facts [Weiss ix].

Weiss seems to be saying that if the actual emotional intensity of these events were portrayed in the repetition of the words, then the veracity of the event would be obscured. So a performance of the words that were spoken at the trials should be less real than the original trial. Verbatim theatre is not about truth in the sense of the most accurate imitation of real utterances according to this way of thinking, but rather, it is about the truth revealed in the words themselves, which have validity because somebody really said them. Clearly the Weiss concept of theatrical truth is at odds with the arguments of Levy and Soans. Simon Levy stated categorically in his introduction that passion should be engaged in performances of *What I Heard About Iraq*: "This is also about the challenge of making polemics emotional" (Levy 3). These contradictory notions of the relationship of truth to theatrical representation seem to reflect Pinter's personal journey and perhaps his passing of the mantle to David Hare.

In his play *Stuff Happens,* Hare interpolated imagined dialogues between George W. Bush, Condoleeza Rice, Rumsfeld, et al., with direct address quotations of statements by these historical figures. He explains his dramaturgical strategy in yet another preface:

> *Stuff Happens* is a history play, which happens to center on very recent history. The events within it have been authenticated from multiple sources, both private and public. What happened happened. Nothing in the narrative is know-

ingly untrue. Scenes of direct address quote people verbatim. When the doors close on the world's leaders and on their entourages, then I have used my imagination. This is surely a play, not a documentary and driven, I hope, by its themes as much as by its story and characters [Hare 2006:2].

Hare, like Levy and Soans, tries to claim truthfulness and dramatic license at the same time. Nothing in the narrative is knowingly untrue, he says, but surely the direct quotation is a different kind of truth from the invented dialogue. The ultimate effect of Hare's presentational/representational modal shift was to echo Shakespeare, with soliloquy standing in for indisputable utterance, and the core scenes representing Hare's imagined versions of dialogues that were never recorded. The result was that the imagined dialogues seem more false because of the occasional direct quotations, given in a presentational style. Presentational style functions as reporting, and representation functions as fantasy. In a play that was supposed to bring historical events into focus, the combination works more as a critique of representational style than as an exposé of the U.S. administration leading to the invasion of Iraq.

All of these examples prompt us to ask ourselves; to what extent is theatre meant to reflect reality? Is a reflection of reality ever true, or always a tainted, less pure shadow? Is truth best reflected in a cracked mirror or via pristine reportage? Do the traditional devices of theatre, engagement, humor, empathy, dramatic structure, surprise, etc. enhance or detract from theatre's efficacy as a truth telling medium, and in the case of most verbatim theatre, an agent of political action? According to David Hare, theatre enhances truth. Hare makes the bold claim that "the truth of what goes on is revealed in performance, whereas the truth of what goes on is not so clearly revealed by being written down on the page" (Hare 2008:71). Hare is going against the trend of thought on representation when he suggests that a mediated utterance, that is to say a statement interpreted by a third party, i.e., an actor, is closer to the truth than an unmediated utterance. Is an utterance that was actually spoken more true even if it was false? And is an emotional utterance less true than an eloquent speech?

Verbatim plays are usually about something important. The implication is that when the content of a play is actually important to us then we shouldn't rely on fiction. Are we compelled to use a form that is less "false" than drama? How do we do this? As Weiss suggests, you can't "play" the holocaust. Angry reaction to such films as *The Pawn Broker* and *Life Is Beautiful* remind us that some audiences continue to feel that the big issues need to be addressed in documentary form or not at all. So what does this say about drama and the playwright's role, let alone the actor's license to pretend to be somebody else?

Reading transcripts of divorce trials in turn of the century Europe might be interesting and even performable, but Ibsen's *A Doll's House* will remain an important play that does something else, frames the issues in a different way. Despite the problems of the style and the tendency of authors to overstate the case, I think that verbatim theatre can actually make us reconsider where the truth lies in the actual words we have become used to hearing and images that have been connected to those words. It is the artist's job to reframe reality so that we can see more clearly and hear more acutely.

In an effort to explore some of the theoretical problems and potential delights of verbatim theatre I devised a production of my own based on the words of Mohandas Gandhi, Rabindranath Tagore, Dr. Ambedkar, Nehru, Martin Luther King, George Wallace, Malcolm X and others. I opened the play with a mélange of voices, sounds and music in the style of contemporary hip-hop, but foregrounding the voice of Gandhi. I assumed that Gandhi's voice would be familiar enough that the audience would recognize it (or at least Ben Kingsley's impersonation of it).

While the audience listened to Gandhi's voice, an actor gave short historical biographies of the various characters whose words made up the script. A minimum of text was used to make connections between the voices. The speaker allowed pauses to let Gandhi's voice fill the room and be heard more or less alone before moving on to another biographical reference. The content of the words Gandhi was speaking in the opening sequence was primarily spiritual. I wanted the audience to contemplate Gandhi as a "great soul" before considering his other identities as politician, social critic, activist etc. It was also important to establish Gandhi's voice playing through speakers as a reminder of what we understand to be the historical reality of the man whose memoirs were entitled *My Experiments with Truth*. I wanted to test David Hare's bold statement that performance revealed truth better than the un-mediated written word. Having the audience hear the actual voice of Gandhi (or later Malcolm X) was part of a strategy to acknowledge and embrace the falseness of the actors. It became irrelevant that all the words were actual utterances. The "truth" revealed by the actors in performance was an artistic, or aesthetic truth of juxtaposition that relied on theatrical elements such as rhythm and music.

Once the rest of the actors entered (there were four actors, one musician and a narrator), no clear sign was given as to the identity of the original historical speaker. The action was arbitrary and sometimes comic. In some places the identity of the speaker was self evident such as the following longish quotation from Martin Luther King:

> I remember when Mrs. King and I were in India, we journeyed down one afternoon to the southernmost part of India. That afternoon I was to speak at a school, what would be the equivalent of what we call a high school in America. This particular school was attended by and large by students who were the children of former "untouchables." The principal of the school introduced me and then as he came to the conclusion of his introduction, he said: "Young people, I would like to present to you a fellow untouchable from the United States of America." And for a moment, I was a bit shocked and even peeved that I would be referred to as an untouchable. I started thinking about the fact

that twenty million of my brothers and sisters were still smothering in an air-tight cage of poverty in an affluent society. As I thought about this, I finally said to myself, "Yes, I am an untouchable, and every Negro in the United States is an untouchable" [King].

This quotation helped to make parallels between American racism and Indian caste prejudice a thematic thread in the first part of the play. But in most cases the audience had little guide to help them know whether Gandhi, Churchill or George Wallace made a disturbing statement about race. Frequently the audience was forced to realize that a statement that made them uncomfortable was actually a quotation from Gandhi. Gandhi's statements on caste frequently accord with those of segregationist rhetoric such as: "I believe that if Hindu society has been able to stand, it is because it is founded on the caste system. A community which can create the caste system must be said to possess a unique power of organization" (Gandhi 275). At several points in *Great Souls* segregationist Governor George Wallace was quoted to draw connections between his rhetoric and that of rivals King and Malcolm X. At the end of his career Wallace seemed to quote the final public speech of his old nemesis Martin Luther King when he said: "I feel that I must say that I've climbed my last political mountain. But there's still some personal hills that I must climb. But for now, I must pass the rope and the pick to another climber and say, 'Climb on. Climb on to higher heights. Climb on till you reach the very peak.' Then look back and wave at me, for I, too, will still be climbing" (Wallace).

Casting further complicated the audience's ability to place the speakers. There were two Asian actors and two African-American actors. One of the Asian men spoke almost all of the lines of Malcolm X while one of the African American actors spoke 80 percent of Gandhi's text. The casting disrupted the audience's preconceptions regarding the ethnicity of the voices.

Despite these cogent connections between unlikely speakers, ninety percent of the text was abstract. The most dynamic sections of the play came when the speakers switched voices quickly and distorted the syntax of famous statements. Intense repetition of key phrases such as "chickens have come home to roost," "lipstick on a pig," and the "mountain top" metaphor were used to create abstract musicality that was never entirely divorced from the characters, but functioned to keep the audience engaged with the words themselves in a dizzying array of contexts. Other aesthetic choices, such as bridging American blues and gospel music with Indian modes, were as important as drawing thematic threads or driving home an unambiguous, didactic message. Where Simon Levy's stated goal was to go beyond rhetoric to get to human beings, *Great Souls* was calculated to make the audience hear the words as words.

The famous people who are the characters of history are mostly made up of words. I was trying to disembody the utterances from the historical baggage of the "Great Men" who spoke the words. In Atlanta there is a national park where Martin Luther King's home stands. Americans take their "great souls" and put them on stamps, turn their birthdays into holidays and revere their martyrdom, but this adulation process usually diminishes their words and deeds. The leader of the untouchables in India, and author of the first constitution of independent India, Dr. Ambedkar once said:

> Heroes and hero-worship is a hard fact in India's political life. For in these days with the Press in hand it is easy to manufacture Great Men. In this country we have arrived at such a stage when alongside the notice boards saying "Beware of pickpockets," we need to have notice boards saying "Beware of Great Men" [Ambedkar 1943: 21].

The purpose of the *Great Souls* project was not to get closer to the truth of the lives of Gandhi, Malcolm, King, and the other speakers, but to examine how our reception of these figures is dependent on the myths that have been handed down to us through their words. Our understanding of the historical reality is dependent on our interpretation of the words they spoke or words that relate the deeds they did. Gandhi's status in our collective consciousness as a "great soul" is not lessened by acknowledging that he had to alter his own world view over time to come to grips with the realities of caste. His lifelong search for truth, transforming in nature, is analogous to theatrical expression. Its significance can only be understood by embracing the contradictory quality of his statements, rather than attempting to extract a single truth from a vast number of utterances.

David Hare's contentious assertion that performed words "reveal truth" better than written words cannot be defended. Similarly, Pinter's opposition between the "artist" who need not consider truth and the "citizen" who feels an obligation to the truth is, in my opinion, a false opposition. There is no hierarchy of arts or modes of communication with regard to the truth. The "great souls" project also challenged the idea that "artlessness in art," as promoted by Lukács, actually creates a more truthful form. The presentation of Gandhi's words stressed the artistic devices over the historical context. Our production was entirely about the artfulness of the words and the potential other meanings they might imply. I don't pretend that the resulting presentation was truer than another production might have been, but I can say that we were honest with the audience about the artistic devices that were used. This honesty is the most useful ingredient artists can bring to the debate of any given subject. Honesty and truth are not the same thing, but posing as truth tellers who eschew artistic principles can lead to a kind of hypocrisy.

Verbatim theatre is a fascinating phenomenon and deserves to be taken seriously as a legitimate genre. Its greatest strength is the array of styles that it encompasses. I envision verbatim theatre surviving well into the century with an expanded approach to quotation including poetic, comic and aesthetic experimentation alongside of politically committed agit-prop theatre. But the rhetoric that many of the playwrights have used to champion the form as more true than other dramatic texts, or modes of performance, actually undermines the claims they make for purer representational veracity. Honest theatrical expression is not less valid than quotation, and when creators of verbatim plays acknowledge that their approach is an addition to, but not a substitute for, the representation of truth on stage, the style will have reached its maturity and we can look forward to even more exciting works.

EMORY UNIVERSITY

References Cited

Ambedkar, Dr. B. R. *Address Delivered on the 101st Birthday Celebration of Mahadev Govind Ranade.* Bombay: Thacker & Co, Ltd., 1943.

Artaud, Antonin. *The Theatre and Its Double,* translated by Mary Caroline Richards. New York: Grove Weidenfeld, 1958.

Bentley, Eric. *Are You Now or Have You Ever Been: The Investigations of Show Business by the Un-American Activities Committee 1947–1958.* New York: Harper, 1972.

Gandhi, Mahatma. *The Collected Works of Mahatma Gandhi. New Delhi*: Publications Division, Ministry of Information and Broadcasting, Govt. of India, *1958–94.*

Gardner, Lyn. "Does Verbatim Theatre Still Talk the Talk?" *Manchester Guardian,* 7 May 2007.

Garner, Stanton B. "Artaud, Germ Theory, and the Theatre of Contagion," *Theatre Journal* 58.1 (2006):1–15.

Hare, David. "David Hare & Max Stafford-Clarke." *Verbatim: Contemporary Documentary Theatre,* edited by Will Hammond. 45–75. London: Oberon Books, 2008.

_____. *Stuff Happens.* London: Faber & Faber, 2006.

Hirschhorn, Joel. "Review of *What I Heard About Iraq.*" *Variety,* 13 September 2005, <http://www.variety.com/review/VE1117928172.html>

King, Martin Luther, Jr. Sermon at Ebenezer Baptist Church, July 4, 1965. Research and Education Institute, Stanford. <http://mlkkpp01.stanford.edu/index.php/kingpapers/article/chapter_13_pilgrimage_to_nonviolence>

Levy, Simon. *What I Heard About Iraq.* Unpublished manuscript, 2005. <www.fountaintheatre.org>

Lukács, Georg. "Art and Objective Truth." *Writer and Critic and Other Essays,* edited and translated by Arthur D. Kahn, 25–61. New York: Grosset and Dunlap, 1971.

Oberon Books. Press release. 2008. <http://www.oberonbooks.com/frameset.htm>

Pinter, Harold. "American Football: A Reflection on the Gulf War" in *Death etc.,*77. New York: Grove Press, 2005. [2005a]

_____. *Art, Truth & Politics, Nobel Lecture,* <http://nobelprize.org/nobel_prizes/literature/laureates/2005/pinter-lecture-e.html> [2005b].

Puchner, Martin. "The Theater in Modernist Thought." *New Literary History* 33.3 (2002):521–532.

Soans, Robin. Interview with Philip Fisher. Theatrevoice.com, 19 September 2007. <http://www.theatrevoice.com/listen_now/player/?audioID=506>

_____. "Robin Soans," in *Verbatim: Contemporary Documentary Theatre,* edited by Will Hammond. 15–45. London: Oberon Books, 2008.

Wallace, George. Retirement Speech. Montgomery, Alabama. April 2, 1986. <http://www.pbs.org/wgbh/amex/wallace/filmmore/reference/primary/86retire.html>

Weiss, Peter. *The Investigation,* translated by Swan & Grosbard. New York: Pocket Books, 1966.

"Sounds Indistinguishable from Sights"

Staging Subjectivity in Katie Mitchell's *Waves*

Sharon Friedman

Abstract

Experimental theatre has become a virtual laboratory for inventive stagings of myths, classical and modern drama, the novel, the poem, and even the personal and philosophical essay. As a case in point, critic Ben Brantley noted the visionary "morphings" of Virginia Woolf's novel in Katie Mitchell's Waves, *first produced at the National Theatre in London in 2006 and later presented in Lincoln Center's "The Literary Muse" series. Mitchell's multi-media ensemble production is a semiotic transposition of Virginia Woolf's 1931 novel that on its own terms sought to transcend the generic boundaries of the novel, the poem, and the play in what she called a "play-poem." This essay focuses on Mitchell's staged interpretation of Woolf's rendering of subjectivity in the interrelated monologues of six friends over the course of their lives. Through the incorporation of video and sound technology into live performance, Mitchell and company render interior lives, the characters' sensuous and symbol making apprehension of the world and each other.*

Re-visioning classic texts has developed into its own theatrical genre in recent years, and experimental theatre has become a virtual laboratory for inventive stagings of myths, classical and modern drama, the novel, the poem, and even the personal and philosophical essay. Despite the skepticism of critics who maintain that "pages ... weren't meant for stages" (Isherwood B6), *New York Times* critic Ben Brantley observed that "genre-bending, time-straddling adaptation had become an exceptionally lively art on London's stages," and that "reconfigurations of classics are testing and stretching the traditional limits of theater in the age of cross-pollination" (2007:B9). Encounter and reconfiguration are key words in contemporary adaptations that connote a dialogue with source texts that emerge in entirely new forms. Citing several productions, Brantley noted the visionary "morphings" of Virginia Woolf's poetic novel *The Waves*, devised by director Katie Mitchell and company and performed in 2006 at the National Theatre in London. In 2008, it was produced in New York as part of Lincoln Center's "The Literary Muse" series, which celebrated the "power of words to manifest meaning through different artistic forms" (Program Notes 2008).[1]

Mitchell's multi-media, ensemble production entitled *Waves* is a semiotic transposition of Woolf's 1931 experimental novel that on its own terms sought to transcend the generic boundaries of the novel, the poem, and the play. In her diaries Woolf records her intentions as she imagines what *The Waves* will become: "...prose yet poetry; a novel and a play"— in other words, what she calls a "play-poem." Three years later she reflects that its structure was "resolving itself ... into a series of soliloquies" (Woolf, L. 103, 134). However, critics have noted its affinity to the prose poem (Cohn 264), the lyric, and the imagist poem (Kronenberger 5) in its use of figurative language to express states of mind, impressions of scenes or objects, and the process of perception.[2]

This essay focuses on Mitchell's staged interpretation of Woolf's rendering of subjectivity in the interrelated monologues of six friends over the course of their lives. The monologues are grouped episodically according to stages in the life cycle, and introduced by nine italicized pastoral "interludes" that trace the progress of the sun across a seascape and landscape over the course of one day. Described by an anonymous third-person narrator, the interludes serve metaphorically to link the stages of the characters' lives to phases in a day (e.g., dawn, high noon, sunset). Mitchell's script pares down the 228 page novel to 40 pages, comprised almost entirely of extracts from the novel interspersed with additional passages from Woolf's autobiographical writing published posthumously as *Moments of Being* in which she reflects on her own moments of discovery or revelation of "some real thing" behind the "cotton wool" of appearances (1985:72). Woolf scholars have commented on the paradox of the immediate and yet abstract dimensions of the monologues conveyed through formal prose when describing the ordinary. The style is uniform and does not vary according to character or give us a realistic reproduction of speech (Cohn 264–265). George T. Wright describes the tense as "lyric present" ("I dance," I fall"), which he argues contributes to both a "timeless dimension" associated with poetry as well as to a self-conscious tone.[3]

For the purposes of this discussion, I define subjectivity as the process of the self as it experiences itself and its surroundings, and as it reflects on that experience. The self or "subject" is theorized by many postmodern thinkers to be unstable and fragmented, constituted by the unconscious as well as the conscious mind. At the same time, it is conceived of as "an embodied being in a spatio-temporal structure of things and events" (Mulhausler and Harre 88), a being whose identity is constructed through language and discourse and subject to the determination of material circumstances, social structures, the laws of the physical world, and to developmental processes of the psyche and specific family dynamics (Green and LeBihan 140–142).[4]

The characters in the novel (*The Waves*) and the theatrical production (*Waves*)[5] intermittently allude to these determinants (rural and urban environments, schools, canonical poets, the workplace, commerce, social class, parents and lovers) and situate themselves in the material and physical world. However, they are preoccupied, together and apart, with articulating and making sense of their shifting perceptions, desires, and anxieties in the flux of time. They resemble the "partially 'knowing subjects'" that anthropologist Sherry Ortner argues have "some degree of reflexivity about themselves and their desires..." (111). At the same time, the imagistic rather than narrative prose of their monologues represents a conscious thought process informed by symbols and phrases associated with dream states and the "bubbling up" of the subconscious as much as they are by cultural discourses and expectations. The lyricism of the text resonates with Julia Kristeva's conception of poetic language — to disturb "identity, system and order. What does not respect borders, positions, rules..." (Kristeva qtd. in Monson 177).[6]

Mitchell's mixed-media production represents these interior lives, or what Dorit Cohn calls "transparent minds," through the incorporation of video and sound technology into live performance to render the characters' sensuous and symbol making apprehension of the world and each other. Working in collaboration with video artist Leo Warner, Mitchell and company share Woolf's attempt to represent visual and aural impressions simultaneously, and, in the process, evoke a sense of immediacy in the viewer that is integral to subjective experience. The production engages spectators in contemplating the mind thinking, the formation of the illusory self-image from multiple subjectivities, and the sharing of subjective states by individuals in their interactions with each other. As the actors recite the monologues we see mediatized bodies on a large screen and close-ups of facial expressions and manipulated objects to which they refer; we hear amplified utterances and simulated sounds that evoke an almost tactile response. Words, pictures, and sounds settle momentarily into images and metaphors associated with the characters. These motifs recur and develop into a skeletal narrative as the characters move through their fictionalized lives. Gradually developing distinct identities, they define themselves by difference, their desires for connection, and their fears of dissolution. They become "intersubjective[s]," as John Lutterbie defines the term in *Hearing Voices*, dependent upon "the exchange of reflections for self-imaging" (2).

What is most striking in this production is the performance of a dialogic and relational subjectivity that Woolf critics have observed in the novel (Little; Fand). Judy Little, for example, has discerned a relational subjectivity in Woolf's innovative structure of alternating and interrelated monologues:

> The formal and ideological modus of this experimental novel is the device of the six voices, talking and developing in relation to each other. It is as though

the friends belong to a sort of primal alumni group, the six graduating into discourse at about the same age and then continuing their relational phrases and friendship for the rest of their shared and dialogic lives [74].

Little's description of the novel's characters resembles the actors' ensemble in their production of *Waves*: they "cooperate in creating a text that the entire small community has produced," and "construct and reconstruct illusion, phrases, their lives" (35, 68). In Mitchell's *Waves* actors visibly work together to produce a theatrical illusion of individual subjects in relation to other subjects across porous boundaries. The production process might be seen as a theatrical metaphor for relational subjectivity. In addition to "acting" a monologue, each actor performs the roles of narrator, camera operator, sound effects technician, dresser, and stage hand — plucking props from shelves on either side of the stage as needed to represent a persona or scene. When one actor speaks into a microphone while another's face or body is projected onto a large screen, they appear to share this internal monologue and together construct the identity to which it is attached. Their performance becomes performative as they bring into existence the complex and reciprocal relationship of self and other that emerges in Woolf's imagistic prose.

Mitchell adopts the basic structure of Woolf's novel as well as her poetic language in the monologues (some as brief as a sentence) of these six friends — three females (Susan, Jinny, and Rhoda) and three males (Bernard, Louis, and Neville) — whose lives intersect from childhood through middle age, roughly corresponding to the years 1893 to 1933. As children, they bring a Wordsworthian mind's eye to investigating insects in grass, picking up fallen petals, playing in the tool-house, and sitting lonely in classrooms fathoming numbers and shapes. Away at school they respond to the authority of headmasters and teachers, their socialization to church and state, and the regimentation required of them for social cohesion. Bernard observes the visage of "'old Crane, the Headmaster [who] has a nose like a mountain at sunset ... mouthing out tremendous and sonorous words ... too hearty to be true;'" Susan notes that Rhoda and Jinny "'sit far off in brown serge and look at Miss Lambert who sits under a picture of Queen Alexandra reading from a book before her.'" Susan hates the school day — "'whiny and orderly, with gongs, with lessons, with orders to wash, to change, to work, to eat,'" and wishes to bury the "'oily portraits of old men — benefactors, founders of schools.'" Only Louis, the T. S. Eliot–like character, says that he likes the "'dimness that falls as we enter the sacred building [chapel]" and "'march, two by two ... orderly, processional...'" (*Waves* 28–34). As adults in the hub of London, the sounds and sights of eating-shops, train stations, offices, and museum queues weave through and around them. The specter of Empire looms in the distance in references to colonial ventures and Louis's trade maps showing how "'the different parts of the world are laced together'" (*Waves* 70).

The seventh friend, Percival, does not speak, and thus we are not given access to his thoughts. Seen from the others' perspectives, he appears as an attractive lad at school — conventional, athletic, noble in bearing — who inspires love, lust, and sometimes envy. Neville, in particular, yearns for his presence and leans sideways in the rear of the classroom to catch "'the flick of his hand to the back of his neck. For such gestures,'" Neville says, "'one falls hopelessly in love for a lifetime'" (*Waves* 29). The video projections show a sequence of close-ups alternating between Neville's perception of Percival from the back and Percival looking forward — displayed naked from the shoulders up — in a somewhat relaxed pose resembling a nude statue, in Neville's words, "'remote from us in a pagan universe'" (29). We learn later that as a colonial administrator in India, Percival dies in the prime of life in a mundane accident while riding his horse. In Jane Marcus's reading of *The Waves* as a novel about imperialism, Percival signifies "the violent last of the British imperialists" elegized by Bernard and the others. In his "quixotic ride" we might interpret "England's fall from imperial glory and the upper-class *angst* of the intellectuals..." (66). However, he also serves as a focal point for the characters' communion with each other, their projections and reminiscences. Frozen in time, he embodies their youthful passions as well as their fear of death and dissolution.

Two pivotal dinners structure the friends' collectivity even as they develop along separate paths. As young men and women, they gather in a restaurant to bid Percival farewell before he leaves for India. The actors are seated next to each other on stage at a long table set with china and goblets. However, the placement of the video projectors gives them the appearance of facing each other in a series of images, in some scenes looking attentive and congenial, and in others, distracted or withdrawn. As the audience hears the clinking of glasses and silver upon porcelain, the scene exudes conviviality and anticipation, but the images suggest difference and potential alienation in the midst of community. In middle age, the group reunites for a dinner at Hampton Court and reflects on the passage of time and the significance of existence (88–94). For Neville, Percival, long gone, continues to serve as a touchstone for his hopes and disappointments: "'the door will not open; he will not come'" (94). As the "blackness on the beach deepen[s]" they draw nearer to each other seeking communion as they struggle against aging and confront extinction (86).

Mitchell's production renders the passage of time through several forms of media ranging from writing, to film, to the most sophisticated video and sound technology. The interludes identifying the phase of day are marked by an actor writing on a chalk board and then immediately erasing the phrase as if to signal the ephemeral nature of time as one moment disappears into the next. However, the unifying device of the diurnal movement of the waves is represented by previously filmed images of the seashore accompanied by sound. In contrast to the chalk board and the shifting images produced in simulcast video in conjunction with the monologues, the pre-recorded video of the seashore suggests a kind of permanence, the existence of an eternal "impersonal world" to which the characters respond and that shapes their perceptions at different points in their lives. Writing about the novel, Molly Hite compares the sound of the waves to "a continuous bass line underlying a piece of music: fundamental, repetitive, and suggesting eternity" (xl). In the first interlude, they rise, heap themselves and break upon the shore; they pause and then draw out again, "sighing like a sleeper whose breath comes and goes unconsciously" (*Waves* 7).

Critics have noted that the movement of the waves also functions as a metaphor for the formation of identity in chronological and psychic time. As the characters struggle, alone or with the others, to achieve an integrated self, a distinct identity, a shared cognition if not consensus about their ideas and relationships, their fragile constructs of self and identity fracture and dissolve much like the waves. Tamlyn Monson argues that the central metaphors of the novel — the wave and the drop — suggest a "cyclical model of subjectivity":

> ... a process of self-constitution and dissolution represented by the image of a wave rising and then crashing, only to be drawn back into the sea where it rises once more; of a drop forming, becoming heavy, tapering to a point, and then falling, followed by the next drop. Each wave, each drop, embodies a stage in the individual's life; each stage is precipitated by a loss of self preceding the formation of another reconfigured self [Monson 173].

In Marcus's discussion of *The Waves* as a text that "revels in oscillation," she perceives a kind of "'quantum text' presenting the relativity of time in a doubled temporal structure." Readers of Woolf's novel and viewers of Mitchell's theatrical production (which adheres to the novel's structure) must "collate" the simultaneous cycle of the sun and waves in one day with their "experience of 'listening in' on several minds thinking at once and over a life time in the text itself" (63).

Woolf actually claimed to write *The Waves* to a rhythm rather than a plot, and a rhythm "in harmony with the painters" (Bell 316). And in a letter to Ethyl Smith on August 28, 1930, Woolf anticipates the difficulties that readers might encounter in attempting to grab hold of a linear narrative in a form that is "completely opposed to the tradition of fiction" (Woolf qtd. in Beer 84). However, the critic Gillian Beer, in discussing the aptness of the novel's form for expressing "at once" chronological and psychic time, allays the reader's anxiety and inadvertently gives us a cue for how a theatre artist might perform this text:

> Certainly, the reader of *The Waves* needs to swim, to trust to the buoyancy of the eye and the suppleness of the understanding. It is no good panicking when sequence seems lost or persons are hard to pick out. The rhythms of the work will sustain us comfortably as long as we do not flounder about trying to catch hold of events. The events are there, sure enough, but they are not sundered from the flow. This is to say that the form of the waves is acted out in the

actual reading experience, and the reader must trust the medium. The rhythmic patterns of the book, this "play-poem," provide the clues for performance [Beer 89].

Katie Mitchell's inventive staging resonates with Beer's reading of the novel. Mitchell captures this flow through the production of continuous and simultaneous sights and sounds that envelop spectators, especially in a small and intimate theatre. The performance of actors reading from the script as they manipulate video, film, sound, light, stage props, and bits of costumes produces a flow of visual images and sounds associated with the characters and the accumulated and shared perceptions among them. The images are created in the moment on stage beneath a projection screen, as the actors create the sound effects of people moving through their daily lives, "running for trains, doors opening or closing, the movement of clothing, the noise of eating." These sounds are "laid over sections of the text or synchronized with specific movements in the video pictures" (Mitchell 2008: Foreword), and, as noted above, the actor reciting the text does not always correspond to the actor projected onto the screen. At times, the characters seem almost interchangeable in the flow of perceptions. Even Mitchell's omission of the article "the" in her title *Waves* suggests an unending cycle beyond a specific time and place.

Reviewer Neil Blackadder brought a close observation to a scene that clearly delineates Mitchell's process. As one actor spoke, another used props to simulate the sounds she described, a third embodied the character, and a fourth shone a light on her face, held up a sheet of Plexiglas, and sprayed it with water. A fifth actor shot the live-video footage, and it appeared as if the woman was looking out of a window on a rainy day. Blackadder interprets the composition of these images as "prompt[ing] the audience to ponder how we see, how we experience, and how we remember" (140). This process, visible to the audience, might also suggest metaphorically that how we make meaning is integral to the meanings that we make in life and in art.

Woolf, of course, understands that she needs to "throw her readers a rope," (Woolf qtd. in Beer 84)[7] and therefore gives each speaker motifs, recurrent images, and allusions that appear throughout the episodes. Mitchell incorporates many of these recurrent phrases, which do not "fix" the characters so much as they serve to focalize them, that is to identify them with a particular way of seeing or being in the world. Louis is an outsider who speaks English with an Australian accent, "'his father a banker in Brisbane.'" Although successful in commerce ("'Mr. Prentice at four; Mr. Eyres sharp at four-thirty'"), he is steeped in the classics, a poet who imagines that his roots "'go down to the depths of the world'" (*Waves* 70, 9). Bernard, a would-be writer, makes phrases and invents stories for every observation ("'the story of the boot-boy,'" "'the story of the man with one eye'") and sees himself in Byron; yet he struggles to finish a letter to a young woman, inserting a carefully placed "'careless blot'" to suggest that he is casual and profound, slap-dash, intimate and still respectful (*Waves* 30, 42). On screen we see a coffee cup with the smudged beginnings of a letter on a pale blue flowered tablecloth. Jinny revels in her body as she feels it rub against surfaces, sparkle, shimmer, and always call forth men: "'The door opens. O come, I say to this one, rippling gold from head to heels'" (48). Rhoda, alienated, outside the circle, struggles with intimacy as she finds herself "'turning back to stand burning in this clumsy, this ill-fitting body to receive the shafts of his indifference and his scorn.'" Detached from what she senses is the "'real world,'" feeling that she lacks substance ("'I have no face ... I shift and change and am seen through in a second'"), she yearns for escape in the recurrent image of the pools lying on the other side of the world, reflecting marble columns. Always, the "'swallow dips her wing in dark pools'" (32, 48). In many instances a character will assume a conflicted attitude toward all that has concerned her, but continues to use the images with which she identifies herself. Susan is aligned with nature, childbearing, agriculture, the seasons. Yet, she says "'sometimes I am sick of natural happiness, and fruit growing, and children scattering the house with oars, guns, skulls, books won for prizes and other trophies. I am fenced in, planted here like one of my own trees. I think sometimes of Percival who loved me'" (74–75). More than once, she cries out: "'I love, I hate.'"

Factual information about their lives is presented in simple sentences embedded in the stream of self-reflections or lyrical descriptions of the common place. We learn almost inadvertently that characters attend school together, take lovers, marry, have children, separate, achieve success in one or another endeavor, die, or commit suicide. In his elegy to the beloved Percival, Neville says: "'He is dead. He fell. His horse tripped. He was thrown. The sails of the world have swung round and caught me on the head. All is over'" (*Waves* 63).

In addition to these verbal cues, Katie Mitchell offers her audience what she calls "footholds" (akin to Woolf's "rope") in the form of "trigger images" as if on a flashcard that "lie[s] at the heart of memory" (Mitchell 2006). Her close-ups on screen are like those flash images that retrieve a memory — wild roses and ivy serpentine, a bowl of water with floating petals. In the production, a close-up of Rhoda's shoes, one gently touching the other toe as if to hold its owner back, hovers near a puddle mentioned many times in the text — the "'cadaverous, awful grey puddle in the courtyard,'" that Rhoda cannot cross. "'Identity,'" she says "'failed me'" (*Waves* 38). In addition to Rhoda's prophetic declaration: "'I launch out now over the precipice.... Everything falls in a tremendous shower, dissolving me'" (85), Mitchell's production reveals Rhoda's suicide in the video image of an outstretched hand, palm-side up, the wrist slit and bleeding in a bowl of water.

The play-script devised from the much longer novel foregrounds not only the imagery associated with each character but also the repetition of phrases shared by characters that point up their profound intersubjectivity. They seem able to share perceptions, experience each other as subjects — to experience themselves as seen by another subject — and most poignantly to express empathy as well as need. Mitchell's production highlights those moments when, as Roxanne J. Fand observes in the novel, "individual motifs are sensed intuitively by the other characters and picked up by them in their soliloquies like a reflected bit of colored glass in a kaleidoscopic pattern" (54). For example, in the production, Susan, as a child, expresses shock when "'through the chink in the hedge'" she sees Jinny kissing Louis. "'I saw her kiss him.... Now I will wrap my agony inside my pocket-handkerchief. It shall be screwed tight into a ball.... I will take my anguish and lay it upon the roots under the beech trees'" (*Waves* 10). A series of on-screen images focus on Susan's stricken eyes peering through the brambles (the projection of a leafy branch on stage). The camera then refocuses on her hands burying dirt — "'the agony'" — in a crisp white handkerchief. Later in time, at the farewell dinner for Percival, after she remarks "'it is hate, it is love,'" presumably her thought on what brings them together, she remembers that "'through the chink in the hedge I saw her kiss him.'" Jinny's monologue picks up Susan's phrases, as if in dialogue but uttered independently; "'it is love,'" said Jinny, "'it is hate, such as Susan feels for me because I kissed Louis once in the garden.... But our hatred is almost indistinguishable from our love'" (57–58).

In the childhood scene, the characters respond to the event and to each other through a series of observations and images inflected with desire and anxiety. When Susan experiences hurt, Bernard, alongside Neville in the tool-house, observes that "'Susan has passed us.... She has passed the tool-house door with her handkerchief screwed in a ball.... I shall follow her, Neville, to comfort her when she bursts out in a rage and thinks, 'I am alone'"" (*Waves* 11). Bernard, in this moment of intersubjectivity, attempts to feel what Susan feels, and take ups her reference to her handkerchief screwed into a ball. However, the viewer is also presented with the unavoidable "lapses in understanding" when, as Tomlyn Monson observes in the novel, the characters' narratives are juxtaposed, "revealing each self in its own terms" and "exposing the violence of subjectivity as, under the power of a new voice, the self who was 'I' is displaced as the first person and becomes reduced to the other determined by the primacy of an alternative totality" (179). Mitchell's text omits Neville's account of feeling abandoned by Bernard, but it includes Neville's hurt and profound need for one person expressed in his perception of Bernard. We see a close up of Neville, identifiable by his large glasses peering through the leaves, like Susan before him; and we hear his disappointment in Bernard's sudden and seemingly random attachment to Susan: "'Where is Bernard?'" says Neville; "'he has my knife. He is like a dangling wire, a broken bell-pull, always twangling. I hate dangling things: I hate wondering and mixing things together'" (*Waves* 14). And it is Neville who later becomes most fixated on Percival, the departed.

Bernard, the maker of stories, who only feels alive when he engages the lives around him, comforts Susan by inviting her to "'explore'" the "'white house lying among the trees'" — a place he calls Elvedon. Here, "'the Lady sits between the two long windows, writing. The gardeners sweep the lawn with giant brooms. We are the discoverers of an unknown land'" (*Waves* 12). In both the novel and Mitchell's production, Elvedon, the lady writing, and the gardeners sweeping form a recurrent image of escape, discovery, and perhaps constancy for Bernard and Susan throughout their lives.[8] The characters come together and they take leave of each other, distinct and yet part of a whole, as Bernard observes later at the dinner for "'love of Percival'": "'There is a red carnation in that vase. A single flower as we sat here waiting [for him to enter the door], but now a seven-sided flower, many-petalled, red — a whole flower to which every eye brings its own contribution'" (*Waves* 54). What is this seven-petalled flower? Who is this woman writing? Is she the narrator of the interludes? Is she Woolf? Is she an androgynous Bernard who imposes meaning on his perceptions of himself and others by linking phrases, constructing sequences, making disparate "events and sensations" coherent? (Monson 178).[9]

In a pointed departure from Woolf's text, however, Mitchell does not conclude her production with Bernard's extended, chapter length, soliloquy in which he sums up the lives of his friends and struggles to keep hold of himself in his fight against death. Instead, Mitchell ends with Woolf's penultimate chapter, the scene of the reunion dinner where the characters, at first tentative about their connection, ultimately share their desolation in middle age. For Mitchell, the multiplicity of selves and shared impressions seems paramount to her theatrical interpretation of subjectivity in the novel as relational rather than autonomous. In their final monologues, the characters incorporate recurrent phrases shared among them, such as "'abysses of infinite space'" and the "'silence'" that falls "'drop by drop'" (*Waves* 88–93). Louis notes that they "'advance down this avenue, I leaning slightly upon Jinny, Bernard arm-in arm with Neville, and Susan with her hand in mind.... It is sweet to sing together, clasping hands, afraid of the dark'" (89). A match is lit on a darkened stage, the gilded heel of a shoe steps on autumn leaves, and a hand wraps purple flowers in a handker-chief — all projected on the large screen.

Perhaps anticipating a sense of unease in theatre-goers expecting a linear plot and more clearly defined characters, the company has created a paratext that can be purchased to review the performance — a beautiful book that includes the script and carefully selected and placed photographs of the images. Once again artistic invention and the construction of meaning are foregrounded in ways that resonate with Woolf's record of her own process expressed in her diaries, essays, and letters. In the production text Mitchell inserts the passage from Woolf's reverie on composition drawn from "Sketch of the Past" after the first interlude, and this passage seems to comment on both the novel and the production: "If I were a painter I should paint these first impressions of childhood in pale yellow, silver, and green ... and what was seen would at the same time be heard ... sounds indistinguishable from sights" (*Waves* 7).[10]

In this theatrical moment of intermedia, rendering minds transparent on stage still relies on "direct aural and visual performance experienced in real time," but with complex "intersemiotic transpositions from one sign system to another" (Hutcheon 13, 16). This mode of production requires as active a viewer as Woolf's text demands active readers. Philip Auslander argues in his book *Liveness* that in our televisual world, live and mediatized forms do not necessarily compete, but rather fuse. The instant replay, the "'simulcast,'" and the close-up, which had been considered "secondary elaborations" of what was at inception a live event, are now "constitutive of the live event itself," and produce the "'intimacy and immediacy'" associated with theatre (25, 32). In addition to creating this new form of immediacy in *Waves*, Mitchell may have found an intriguing strategy for rendering the conscious and unconscious mind simultaneously. Auslander cites actor Robert Blossom's speculation that film in live performance functions as "'repressed consciousness,'" and that live actors represent "'corporality, physical existence'" (Blossom qtd. in Auslander 37). Mitchell's actors in dialogue with Woolf's text manage to convey an intense bodily presence as they project onto the screen expressions and images that seem to emanate from the unconscious. As the characters respond to their environment, the audience, individually and collectively, responds to the performance — a multiplicity of subjects struggling to capture impressions in the flow of words and images, sounds and sights. In that "moment of being" Woolf's "play-poem" becomes a poetic performance of sensibilities shared by actors and audiences.

NEW YORK UNIVERSITY

Notes

1. *Waves*. Devised by Katie Mitchell and company from the text of Virginia Woolf's novel *The Waves*. Director: Katie Mitchell. Performers: Kate Duchene, Anastasia Hille, Kristin Hutchinson, Sean Jackson, Stephen Kennedy, Liz Kettle, Paul Ready, Jonah Russell. *Waves* opened at the National Theatre's Cottesloe Theatre on 18 November 2006; the production was revived in the Cottesloe on 20 August 2008 before touring nationally and internationally. It was produced at the Duke Theatre, New York in November 2008.

2. Dorit Cohn gives special attention to *The Waves* in his discussion of the relations between the dramatic monologue, the prose poem, and the interior monologue in fiction. He says: "There is at least one major novelist who has dwelt at (and on) this generic crossing-point at length: Virginia Woolf, while writing *The Waves*" (263).

3. Wright qtd. in Cohn. 264. Molly Hite suggests that the utterance of psychological and metaphysical events implicitly invites readers to universalize as well as sympathize with the speaker (Hite xlii).

4. In their extended definition of subjectivity, Green and LeBihan cite Kaja Silverman's discussion of the unconscious in the constitution of subjectivity in *The Subject of Semiotics*, (Oxford: Oxford University Press, 1983):126–130; they also cite Chris Weedon's focus on the role of language in the construction of identity in *Feminist Practice and Poststructuralist Theory* (Oxford: Blackwell, 1987):34–35. See also Paul Smith's book length study of subjectivity in *Discerning the Subject* (Minneapolis: University of Minnesota Press, 1988) in which he distinguishes between the terms individual and subject.

5. Except as noted, all subsequent references to the monologues in this text refer to Katie Mitchell, *Waves: A Record of the Multimedia Work Devised by Katie Mitchell and the Company*

from the Text of Virginia Woolf's Novel The Waves (London: Oberon Books, 2008). Mitchell's text is made up almost entirely of extracts from Virginia Woolf, *The Waves* (New York: Harcourt, Inc., 1931, renewed 1958 by Leonard Woolf), and extracts from Virginia Woolf, *Moments of Being*, edited by Quentin Bell and Angelica Garnett (New York: Random House, 1985).

6. Tamlyn Monson draws on Julia Kristeva's analysis of the "subject-in-process" (*Powers of Horror: An Essay on Abjection*, New York: Columbia University Press, 1982, 4, 2) to examine the metaphor of subjectivity in *The Waves* and explore its relation to "language, history, and social convention." Monson argues that Woolf's rejection of realist style as well as her use of stream of-consciousness juxtaposition attempts a "complicit interrogation of language and, with it, meaning and subjectivity" (177).

7. Gillian Beer is quoting from Woolf's letter to Ethyl Smith, 28 August, 1930.

8. Susan looks to Elvedon when she expresses her dissatisfaction with home life.

9. Monson is not the only critic to give special attention to Bernard who, as she says, is the character "most seduced by language," and "harnesses the power of language" to cover his vulnerability. See also Cohn's reference to critics who perceive the monologues and interludes as emanating from the same mind "incarnated" in the person of Bernard. Cohn argues that Bernard "recapitulates all the preceding sections in a soliloquy that takes the precise form of an autobiographical monologue" (263). Jane Goldman refers to Bernard's androgyny in his statement: "Nor do I always know if I am man or woman." Goldman, *The Cambridge Introduction to Virginia Woolf* (Cambridge: Cambridge University Press, 2006):74.

10. Virginia Woolf, "Sketch of the Past," 66.

References Cited

Auslander, Philip. *Liveness*. New York: Routledge, 1999.

Beer, Gillian. "*The Waves*: 'The Life of Anybody.'" *Virginia Woolf: The Common Ground*. 74–91. Ann Arbor: University of Michigan Press, 1996.

Bell, Anne Olivier, ed. (Assisted by Andrew McNeillie) *The Diary of Virginia Woolf*, Volume Three. New York: Harcourt Brace Jovanovich, 1980.

Blackadder, Neil. "*Waves* and *Attempts on Her Life*" (Review). *Theatre Journal*, 60.1 (March 2008): 139–141.

Brantley, Ben. "When Adaptation is Bold Invention." *New York Times*, 18 February 2007: B9.

Cohn, Dorit. *Transparent Minds*. Princeton: Princeton University Press, 1978.

Fand, Roxanne J. *The Dialogic Self: Reconstructing Subjectivity in Woolf, Lessing, and Atwood*. Selinsgrove: Susquehanna University Press, 1999.

Goldman, Jane, ed. *The Cambridge Introduction to Virginia Woolf*. Cambridge, U.K.: Cambridge University Press, 2006.

Green, Keith and Jill LeBihan. *Critical Theory and Practice*. New York: Routledge, 1996.

Hite, Molly. "Introduction." Virginia Woolf, *The Waves*, edited by Mark Hussey. xxxv–lxvii. New York: Harcourt, Inc., 2006.

Hutcheon, Linda. *A Theory of Adaptation*. New York: Routledge, 2006.

Isherwood, Charles. "Pages That Weren't Meant for Stages," *New York Times*, 23 November 2008: Arts, 6.

Kronenberger, Louis. "Book Review: *The Waves*." *New York Times*, 25 October 1931:5.

Little, Judy. *The Experimental Self: Dialogic Subjectivity in Woolf, Pym, and Brooke-Rose*. Carbondale: Southern University Press, 1996.

Lutterbie, John H. *Hearing Voices: Modern Drama and the Problem of Subjectivity*. Ann Arbor: University of Michigan Press, 1997.

Marcus, Jane. "Britannia Rules *The Waves*." In *Decolonizing Tradition: New Views of Twentieth-Century British Canons*, ed. Karen R. Lawrence, 136–162. Urbana: University of Illinois Press, 1992.

Mitchell, Katie. "Breaking the *Waves*." *The Guardian*, 11 November 2006.

_____. *Waves: A Record of the multimedia work devised by Katie Mitchell and the company from the text of Virginia Woolf's novel* The Waves. London: Oberon, 2008.

Monson, Tamlyn. "'A Trick of the Mind': Alterity, Onotology, and Representation in Virginia Woolf's *The Waves*." *Modern Fiction Studies* 50.1 (Spring 2004):173–196.

Muhlhausler, Peter and Rom Harre. *Pronouns and People: The Linguistic Construction of Social and Personal Identity*. Cambridge, Mass.: Basil Blackwell, 1996.

Ortner, Sherry. *Anthropology and Social Theory: Culture, Power and the Acting Subject*. Durham and London: Duke University Press, 2006.

Woolf, Leonard, ed. *A Writer's Diary*. New York: Harcourt, Brace and Company, 1954.

Woolf, Virginia. "A Sketch of the Past." *Moments of Being*, edited by Jeanne Schulkind, 64–159. San Diego: Harcourt Brace Jovanovich, 1985.

Down with Plot
Eisenstein, the Tramp, and the Subversiveness of "Montage of Attraction"

Sascha Just

Abstract

What are the parallels between Sergei Eisenstein's theatre work and Charlie Chaplin's films? Both artists applied montage techniques in their productions to challenge authoritarian power structures. Sergei Eisenstein is best known as a film director, yet he developed montage of attraction for his stage productions in the early twenties. Montage of attraction is based on the juxtaposing of conflicting fragments in order to create a specific reaction in the audience. No wonder, the technique has been criticized as a means to control the audience. However, Eisenstein staged his productions as series of attractions privileging effect over narrative. Ideologies depend on narratives, and rendering narrative secondary undermines the power of ideology. Chaplin enjoyed immense popularity as a hero of rebellion with the Russian and early Soviet avant-garde. His mask and persona of the Tramp was built of contradicting features that ultimately represent a montage. While Chaplin, a former music hall performer, always tells a story, he, too, favors effect over plot, dazzling his audience with a string of comical acrobatic tricks. A close comparison of Eisenstein's theatre productions The Mexican *(1922) and* The Wiseman *(1923) with Chaplin's film* The Adventurer *(1917) will highlight the connections between the two artists, and emphasize the scope of the subversive quality of montage.*

A gentleman sits down to eat. He wears baggy black pants, a tight frock coat with holes, and worn shoes a couple of sizes too big. The dining room is a wooden shack through which the Alaskan winter wind blows mercilessly. The gentleman takes silver ware from his pocket, wipes it clean on his coat, and proceeds to eat his shoe. With the grace and expertise of a true signore, he wraps a shoelace around the fork and chews it with delight. The gentleman, of course, is Charlie Chaplin as the Tramp in a scene from his film *The Goldrush*. This scene encapsulates the impossibility of man's struggle to survive at all costs, while at the same maintaining his dignity, also at all costs. And it epitomizes Chaplin's key technique: a montage of contradicting features that in communication with each other create a complex unit; here a deeply moving mixture of laughter and tears.

Cut to Sergei Eisenstein, the artist most frequently associated with montage technique. Eisenstein gained international fame as a film director; however, by the time he directed his first feature film, *Strike,* in 1925, he had already established himself as a scene designer and theatre director with a series of influential stage productions, for which he developed the concept of montage of attraction. Like Chaplin, Eisenstein used the device as an expression to subvert and defy authority. It is obviously appropriate to attribute Eisenstein's innovations to his talent and intense passion for the performing arts; however, it is equally important to position his artistic contributions in the context of the period in Russia. The beginning of the twentieth century experienced an upsurge of new styles, often as a response to political and social changes. This is particularly true for Russia, because the country experienced World War I, two revolutions (one failed, one successful), followed by a civil war and the restructuring of the entire political and bureaucratic system from absolute monarchy to, at least nominally, an egalitarian Soviet Republic. Artists and artistic movements reflected those developments. Montage is one of the styles that coincided with these upheavals. The principle exists in the juxtaposed forms of abstract painting or in the seemingly clashing chords of modern music; poetry or the modern novel offers countless examples of opposing images, narrative strings, and voices.

Eisenstein's concept of montage differs from other versions — for example filmmaker Lev Kuleshov's — that use the technique of arranging fragments to drive a narrative forward. As Eisenstein explains in his first essay "Montage of Attraction," published in 1923 when he was preparing for his stage production *The Wiseman*, montage of attraction consists of the juxtaposition of conflicting or opposing elements out of which grows a third element, a specific audience reaction. Eisenstein derived this notion from a Marxist and/or Hegelian dialectic, which supposes that the confrontation of a thesis with an antithesis would create a synthesis. Eisenstein's concept emphasizes the moment and the effect, and renders plot secondary, as expressed in his anti–Aristotelian claim "Down with Plot." Eisenstein went as far as mathematically calculating emotions he aimed to elicit in his audience through the juxtaposition of moments of excitement. The juxtaposition of moments of aggression or excitement primarily serve to elicit specific preconceived emotions in the spectator, and only secondarily (if at all) to propel the plot to a climax or conclusion. From the primacy accorded to the director, it follows that the role of the actor was diminished. Actors were treated as elements to design an effect to control the audience. This intended control is one of the key points for which the principle has been criticized. However, due to Eisenstein's reputation as the most renowned Soviet filmmaker, the subversive components of montage that earned the device the label "formalism" during the Stalin era, are frequently overlooked. Some of the components, treatment of plot and of perspective in particular, that were threatening to the dominant ideology of Stalinism are apparent already in his theatre productions *The Mexican* and *The Wiseman*.

Eisenstein, like so many avant-garde artists, was fascinated by theatrical traditions that privilege moments or attractions over plot, such as *commedia dell'arte*, and the *balagan*. The influences can be detected in all of his productions. Interest by avant-garde artists in those popular theatre traditions was part of an effort to re-theatricalize theatre and thereby to overcome naturalism as practiced for example by Stanislavsky's Moscow Art Theatre. This movement was spearheaded by Eisenstein's mentor, Vsevolod Meyerhold. Not unlike *commedia dell'arte* shows, that typically consist of a mixture of improvised plot and acrobatic acts, or *lazzi,* the *balagan*, a specific Russian form of fairground entertainment, was appealing for similar reasons. The *balagan* offered simultaneously a myriad of attractions such as acrobatics, wild animals, harlequinade, pantomime, puppet, and magic shows. At the *balagan,* as Douglas J. Clayton describes in *Pierrot in Petrograd*, performers often mocked authority and expressed the needs of the lower classes. The satirical quality of the performances and the various booths, where spectators could choose the attractions they were interested in, made the *balagan* an anti-authoritarian, if not egalitarian form of entertainment.

The circus was another theatrical tradition that Eisenstein and many avant-garde artists cherished as a plotless spectacle. In fact, the young avant-garde considered the circus, as Daniel Gerould points out in "Eisenstein's Wiseman," "the highest and most difficult of all the arts because of its precision, discipline, and daring" (Gerould 1974:72). The trend to integrate circus elements in other forms of theatre productions, which grew out of this popularity, is called Eccentricism or circusisation. Eccentric in Russian is one name for clown, and the term Eccentricism, itself derived, according to Robert Leach, "from the Auguste of the circus and from the solo music-hall comedian" (1994:50). The clown held a particular political relevance for the pre-revolutionary and the Soviet avant-garde. It is the interplay between the White clown and the Red clown — the Auguste — that gave the circus such political meaning. The way the White clown sadistically subjugates the Red often mirrors oppression in experiences of everyday life. Charlie Chaplin famously embodies both the qualities of the Auguste and of the White Clown. In his films, Chaplin alternately experiences oppression or subjugation by representatives of authority, and glee at hitting and kicking his opponents. Before his film career, a music hall performer, Chaplin combines aspects of the aggressive Harlequin and the peaceful and poetic Pierrot of the *commedia*. In his acting he unites the physicality and often sentimentality of both circus and *commedia*. While Chaplin always tells a story, (very simple and formulaic) he repeatedly interrupts the narrative with comic acrobatic feats, similar to the acrobatic tricks or *lazzi* that are interjected in the plot of *commedia* performances. Ultimately, these "interruptions" outweigh the importance of the plot in Chaplin's productions.

Chaplin's first films came to Russia in 1918, and during the 1920s Chaplin's films were distributed widely in the Soviet Union and enjoyed immense popularity. Until 1930 Soviet authorities welcomed the Tramp as a working class hero, but to the avant-garde he was an underdog of any established society, or even an outcast. Chaplin to them represented personal freedom from materialistic as well as societal restrictions, yet also individual alienation from the mechanized industrial order of modern life. The Tramp, a character without a personal biography, eternally positioned in the present time, is a carefully constructed mask: immutable, ageless appearance juxtaposed with equally consistent dignified posture. Clad in a worn black tail coat equipped with matching black hat and walking stick, the persona of Chaplin's Tramp consists of opposing fragments, and consequently represents a living montage of contradictions — and a profound comment on modern man's struggle to establish or even maintain the sense of a complete identity in an increasingly fragmented world. Chaplin, who did not perform live in Russia, but was only known through his films, became a vital part of Eccentricism.

In 1921 Eisenstein directed his first play, *The Mexican*, at the Proletkult Theatre in Moscow, in which he experimented with assembling fragments of *mise-en-scène*. This was one of the many highlights in his fast-paced career. Only three years earlier, Eisenstein had joined the Red Army, and during the Civil War he was assigned as a scene designer and painter to Proletkult. This alignment proved positive for Eisenstein, as after the war, he continued to work for Proletkult and quickly moved up in the ranks of the scene department, designing several productions, for example *Precipice* by Valeri Pletnyov (1922), and *The Garter of Columbine* (1922), based on the *commedia*-inspired play by Aleksandr Blok. Together with his collaborator Sergei Yutkevich, Eisenstein dedicated *The Garter of Columbine* to his master Meyerhold, with whom they both studied directing, composition, and biomechanics — a highly physical acting technique that Meyerhold in part developed from his studies of *commedia*. Yutkevich remembers in an interview that the term montage of attraction grew out of the term "scenic attractions" that they used to describe their plans for *The Garter of Columbine* (Yutkevich 1973:32). They took the label directly from Yutkevich's experience of riding his favorite attraction at the fairground.

Officially Eisenstein was only hired to design *The Mexican*, but he advanced to co-directing together with Valeri Smishlayev. *The Mexican* is an adaptation by B. Arvatov of a short story by Jack London about a boy who trains as a boxer, wins the championship, and uses the prize money to support the revolutionary cause. The production was designed and directed in the eccentric manners: actors in clowns' suits performed in cubist settings. The scene, for which Eisenstein was responsible, presented the opposite from this non-naturalistic *mise-en-scène*. Eisenstein juxtaposed the pivotal moment of the play, a boxing match, with the realistic set. The boxing match took place in a ring surrounded by clowns. The boxing ring was placed center stage, occupying a large part of the rectangular open platform, and making the theatre audience spectators in a sports event. Behind the ring, stage back right and left were actors reminiscent of circus clowns and *commedia* performers, responding with large gestures and movements to the action in the ring. These two worlds clashed and interacted at the same time. The clown-like characters constituted the stage audience of the boxing match. By juxtaposing two completely different styles Eisenstein created a montage of *mise-en-scène*s that represents worlds, and even worldviews. Presenting two worlds simultaneously, not unlike the structure of the circus or the *balagan*, offers the audience the choice of where to focus. Essentially this eliminates a dominant perspective. Rejection of one dominant perspective is a chief criterion that upsets the status quo and makes montage anti-authoritarian.

Eisenstein had at this time already studied biomechanics with Meyerhold — a technique that remained important throughout his career — and it seems fairly safe to assume that these studies had an impact on his work with actors in this highly physical scene. In the ring two men are seen at the end of their fight, one knocked apparently unconscious to the floor. The action in the ring is calculated to have a specific effect on the theatre audience, as Eisenstein remembers in "Through Theatre to Cinema": "While the other scenes influenced the audience through intonation, gestures, and mimicry, our scene employed realistic, even textual means — real fighting, bodies crashing to the ring floor, panting, the shine of sweat on torsos, and finally, the unforgettable smacking of gloves against taut skin and strained muscles" (Eisenstein 1947:7).

This quote brings to life the visceral effect that caused an enormous stir in the audience. The sensual and physical aspect of the boxing Eisenstein describes stands in sharpest contrast to the abstraction and deliberate non-realness of the *mise-en-scène* surrounding the boxing ring. Eisenstein aimed at the appearance of real boxing, not actual boxing, creating the appearance of realism on stage, and asking the audience to suspend their disbelief. Encapsulating Eisenstein's notion that the meaning of action lies in the action itself instead of in the reflection of the action, the reason why these characters are boxing is less important than the appearance of a fist in a glove actually hitting a face. In short, the effect outweighs the narrative or the plot.

Privileging the immediacy of an effect, of an attraction, over plot, relegates narrative to secondary role. Ideology depends on a narrative that, no matter how incredible, must be accepted by everyone. Treating narrative as secondary undermines the power and relevance of any ideology. Any narrative can now be replaced by another. Perhaps more dangerous, by favoring an effect, montage of attraction challenges the time continuum of past, present, and future. In *The Mexican*, when a boxer's fist hits the chin of his opponent, for a very engaged spectator, the time continuum is momentarily interrupted. Before the invention of slow motion, Eisenstein achieves this through focusing attention on a highly intensified physical and emotional moment. He thereby unsettles the reliability of the continuum. Since we perceive ourselves, as individuals and as a group, going forward in time, this continuum functions as the foundation for our sense of existence. It is often experienced as progress, a positive development; and ideologies depend on this vision of progress. Montage of attraction upsets the perception of chronology. As a result, stories and history can be viewed in a "disordered" manner that violates the function and definition of any ideology.

Similar patterns of montage can be found in Chaplin's film *The Adventurer*. The film, set by the sea, tells a David-and-Goliath story typical of Chaplin. The Tramp faces numerous obstacles that give Chaplin the chance to string together a series of acts like a series of *lazzi* from *commedia*. The film is a variation of a story Chaplin keeps telling. This time the Tramp escapes from prison. Policemen chase him, and after an acrobatic obstacle run, the Tramp swims to freedom. *The Adventurer* works with obvious contrasts, beginning with Charlie's black-and-white prison suit that makes him look less a criminal than a toddler in pajamas. Yet, Chaplin aptly demonstrates that he does not need the Tramp-costume to embody his famous archetype. As so often, the Tramp is much smaller than his opponents. The policemen who chase him are big, well fed, and armed. Nevertheless, due to his acrobatic expertise and childlike spontaneity, he is able to outwit them, making the representatives of authority look inept and ridiculous.

As Eisenstein mentions in his essay "Charlie the Kid" (Eisenstein 1970:113), Bergson observed that everything that makes a human being appear mechanical is funny to us. Chaplin's angular, jerky movements,— his feet turned outside as if stuck in an uncomfortable ballet pose — are reminiscent of a marionette. What is a marionette but a person whose devices, to use Victor Shklovsky's words, lie bare (Shklovsky 1990:147)? A marionette is a painted wooden skeleton on strings, a person literally stripped to the bones. The Tramp moves like a marionette on invisible strings, making us laugh at ourselves as we laugh with him, because he embodies the endlessly repeated and repetitive efforts at attaining liberty from the invisible puppet master. It is this broken marionette-like body language that maintains the Tramp's montage quality in any costume or setting. In "Montage of Attractions" (1923), Eisenstein takes notice that "the lyric effect of certain Chaplin scenes does not in the least detract from the attractions communicated by the specific mechanics of his movement" (Eisenstein 1942:231). The little marionette-man's child-like nature, that Eisenstein admired as "infantilism" (Eisenstein 1970:110), give him the power to win against authority: shot in the heart, just as he admires the sunset, he drops dramatically to the ground, only to toss the police man off the mountain with one surprising, swift kick from behind.

Eisenstein reportedly attended a stage-screen experiment of the artists collective The Factory of the Eccentric Actor (short FEKS), founded in 1922 in Petrograd. The production, a free interpretation of Nicolai Gogol's play *The Wedding* integrated a screening of a scene from one of Chaplin's short films. While this scene was playing, actors on stage, dressed in police uniforms, acted in synchronicity with the actors on screen. The audience here was challenged to select which part of the production to pay attention to, stage or screen; thus, the two media entered a new and symbiotic relationship. In 1923 Eisenstein directed his best-known production, *Enough Simplicity in Every Wise Man*, at the Proletkult Theatre in Moscow. It has entered theatre history simply as *The Wiseman*. *The Wiseman* is a very lose adaptation of a play by Aleksandr Ostrovsky, a nineteenth century satire on mores and manners in mid-level aristocratic Russian society, an environment governed by flattery and hypocrisy. The main character, a young man named Glumov, pursues his goals, to marry a wealthy girl and to live comfortably ever after, through expression of false adulation and outright lies to people from whom he can benefit. Glumov's external life is contrasted by his internal one: he obsessively writes the truth about the socialites he meets in his diary. At the end of the play, his diary is discovered, but Glumov manages to turn all accusation of betrayal against his accusers and defend his actions as the only way to expose society's dishonesty.

Eisenstein used Ostrovsky's play as a skeleton for his eccentric production. He rewrote the text, reconceived the characters, and finally transformed the drama into a circus-like spectacle with trapeze artists, acrobats, and clowns. According to Eisenstein's own description, the stage was modeled after a circus arena framed by a red barrier. The audience was seated around three-quarters of the stage; a raised platform was placed at the back of the stage. When the main character moved from the rink to the platform it indicated a change of scene, as Eisenstein recalls: "Instead of changing scenes, Glumov [Yezikanov] ran from one scene to the other and back — taking a fragment of dialogue from one scene, interrupting it with a fragment from the other scene — the dialogue thus colliding, creating new meanings and sometimes wordplays" (Eisenstein 1949:10). The careful blocking displays Glumov's hectic attempts at joining the fragments of his lies to a sensible unity. Constant costume changes into roles that could please the character from whom he wants to benefit further symbolized Glumov's fragmented personality.

The acrobatic tricks like jumping down on stage in parachutes, or walking on high wires over the audience were performed by regular actors from the Proletkult ensemble who underwent special training for the production. The physical acting followed a specific concept, as Eisenstein explains in "Through Theater to Cinema": "Rage is expressed through a somersault, exaltation through a salto-mortale, lyricism on 'the mast of death'" (1949:7). The idea "that images and actions express what otherwise would have been in the dialogue" (1949:7), aligns Eisenstein closely with Chaplin.

The humor of the production did not grow out of witty dialogue, but out of physical comedy, a skill in which Chaplin excelled. Every moment of this entertaining production was filled with stunning attractions. Since Eisenstein was much more interested in these attractions, the satiric twists and turns of the original storyline were mostly lost, and meaning had to be found in each moment of the performance. Eisenstein here undermined the relevance of the plot, and of course was criticized for it, because the audience was unable to understand the narrative. Obviously, if spectators are accustomed to primarily experiencing theatre as a storytelling format, their enjoyment suffers when a production renders the plot insignificant. After all, storytelling and listening to stories are vital human desires. The extent, to which the plot disappeared in *The Wiseman* was probably not entirely intentional. Eisenstein was still experimenting and soon accommodated the audience with plot summaries in the program and even with introductions before the show.

Nevertheless, interpreting a (famous) dramatic play as a string of circus attractions constitutes a further development in montage of attraction. While in the production of *The Mexican*, Eisenstein interrupts the narrative, in *The Wiseman* he practically abandons narrative in favor of emotional impact, excitement and, last but not least, fun. Narratives written by ideologies cast citizens and rulers in roles. In the case of the Soviet Union, the narrative demanded that Stalin played the role of the benevolent sovereign, while the citizens enjoyed their parts as happy subjects. Rendering narrative insignificant also makes these roles insignificant. Rejecting narrative was one of the steps in Eisenstein's artistic evolution, the attempt at throwing patriarchal standards and philosophies, which he considered dated, overboard.

The production culminated in a film Eisenstein shot as a visual interpretation of Glumov's diary. Through editing, in the film, aptly titled *Glumov's Diary*, Glumov transforms himself into exactly the object or creature that suits the situation. He changes into a machine gun, a clown, and a donkey, always precisely what his scene partner wishes to see in him. Similar to the work of the FEKS, the juxtaposition between film and theatre comprises a montage of attraction. The interactive film projection as part of a live show was on the one hand a break with traditional performance codes, yet, on the other, created new ones. While theatricality calls attention to its vehicle, it serves as a tool in creating metadrama, defined by Tracy Davis as "a play, which comments on conventions of its genre" (Davis/Postlewait 2003:14). Metadrama in turn provides a platform (literally a stage) for elements of theatricality (theatrical devices). In *The Mexican*, the eccentric *mise-en-scène* and the boxing ring constitute the different worlds. In *The Wiseman*, stage and screen represent distinct spheres, between which actors move back and forth.

The film *Glumov's Diary* ends with a chase scene in which an actor jumps from an airplane into a moving car. The theatre audience watched on screen as the car drove through the city and pulled up in front of the theatre. The actor ran into the theatre, onto the stage in front of the screen with the film roll under his arm, just as Eisenstein's face with a cheeky smile on his lips appeared on screen. The merging and contrasting of cinema and theatre were still a novelty at the time and caused great excitement. What is more, Eisenstein in this instance plays with the audience's sense of time and space. By presenting the content of a previously completed film as present in the moment, Eisenstein changes the order of the time continuum around, creating a montage not only of media and spaces, but also of time frames. The close-up of his winking face indicates the glee he felt at tricking his audience.

Both Eisenstein and Chaplin were certainly tricksters of "the great mute," as early Russian filmmakers liked to call their muse. Eisenstein watched many of Chaplin's films when he lived in Mexico and Hollywood during the 1930s, and wrote admiringly of Chaplin. Yet, the parallels between these two renowned and controversial artists of the twentieth century began earlier, with their roots in theatre. It is not surprising that both encountered problems of varying degrees with authorities. Stalin praised and at the same time oppressed Eisenstein, and Chaplin felt forced to leave the U.S. during the McCarthy era. The similarities in their early work point to parallels of their later productions, to a state of mind, even to a philosophy: the continuous joy in challenging the dominant cultural order — with a kick in the knee or a stunning montage of images.

CITY UNIVERSITY OF NEW YORK, THE GRADUATE CENTER

Notes

List of Terms

Lazzi: physical acts that interrupt the (improvised) plot of a *commedia dell' arte* performance.
Montage of attraction: juxtaposition of theatrical elements to elicit a specific reaction in the audience.
Balagan: Russian fairground offering a wide variety of attractions and performances.

References Cited

Clayton, Douglas J. *Pierrot in Petrograd: The Commedia dell'Arte/Balagan in Twentieth-Century Russian Theatre and Drama*. Montreal: McGill-Queen's University Press, 1993.
Davis, Tracy, and Thomas Postlewait, eds. *Theatricality*. Cambridge: Cambridge University Press, 2003.
Eisenstein, Sergei. *Film Essays and a Lecture*, edited and translated by Jay Leyda, New York: Praeger Publishers, 1970.
_____. *Film Form: Essays in Film Theory*, edited and translated by Jay Leyda, New York: Harcourt, 1949.
_____. *The Film Sens*, edited and translated by Jay Leyda, New York: Harcourt, 1942.
Gerould, Daniel. "Eisenstein's Wiseman." *The Drama Review: TDR* 18.1 (1974):71–76.
Leach, Robert. *Revolutionary Theatre*. London: Routledge, 1994.
Shklovsky, Viktor. *Theory of Prose*. Elmwood Park, Ill: Dalkey Archive Press, 1990.

14

Rita Felski's
Rethinking Tragedy
A Review Essay

Helen Moritz

Rita Felski, ed. *Rethinking Tragedy.* Baltimore: The Johns Hopkins University Press, 2008. Pp. 368. Paperback $24.95.

Reading this wide-ranging collection of essays is like virtually attending a topics session at an academic conference. The moderator (editor Rita Felski) sets the theme in its scholarly context and briefly anticipates the participants (Introduction). A scholar who is something of a lion in the field (George Steiner, author of *The Death of Tragedy*) sagely intones a keynote address. Fourteen other scholars make their presentations from a variety of perspectives. Cross-references to each other's papers approximate some discussion among the participants. The event concludes with a balanced but entertaining response (Commentary) by another eminent scholar whose views are highly distinct from those of the key-noter and who appears to have something of an animus concerning him (Terry Eagleton).

Felski's "Introduction" provides an excellent contextualization for the volume (and, *en passant*, some excellent bibliography). She identifies three referents for the word "tragic"—literary genre, philosophical world view, or, in the "vernacular," a "very sad" or disastrous event—all of which will be tapped in the essays to follow (2–3). She notes that interest in tragedy has waned in English departments along with deference to any canon, but not so in comparative literature or continental philosophy (1)—or, one hastens to add, in classics. Quoting Edith Hall that "More Greek tragedy has been performed in the last thirty years than at any point in history since Greco-Roman antiquity," she observes that tragic art itself is more alive than tragic theory, and that the time is thus ripe for a reconsideration of the latter (5).

For George Steiner, "Rethinking Tragedy" involves rethinking Steiner. Reviewing the concepts of his *Death of Tragedy* (now translated into 17 languages, as he boasts [44] and for which Eagleton teases him [344]), he finds them ultimately sound (44). Steiner acknowledges that a cryptic remark of Plato in *Laws* 7.817b, that the "polity," as a "dramatization of a noble and perfect life," is "the most real of tragedies," shows that "we do not know, at some elemental level, what it is we are talking about" (29–30). (Steiner's "polity" represents the Greek *politeia*, usually translated as "constitution"; his "dramatization" translates *mimesis*; in citing the same passage Goldhill gets the Greek right but surprisingly misattributes the passage to the *Republic* [44]). Steiner also says that Aristotle's *Poetics* "raises far more problems than it solves" (30). Hence, Steiner prefers his own "indispensable core" of tragedy: "the axiomatic constant in tragedy is that of ontological homelessness" (30); "high tragedy engages the (mis)fortunes of the privileged" (37); hence, lofty language is "primary" (39); hence again, "absolute or high tragedy ... is rare" (39). Finally, Christianity, which looks forward to salvation, "made total tragedy implausible" (41). Though Steiner says that the survival of only one trilogy and the "absence ... of satyr plays" makes the evaluation of Greek tragedies hazardous, he is content, at least on a provisional basis, to restrict the notion of high tragedy to a few plays (40). As Eagleton later observes, "such a dogmatic stance constrains one to dismiss as nontragic a ridiculously large sector of distinguished tragic art, not least the *Oresteia* (344). Steiner also ignores the *Cyclops*, the one satyr drama we do have.

For Simon Goldhill and Page du Bois, "Rethinking Tragedy" means rethinking Aristotle. Goldhill observes that, in making little mention of the *polis*, or of "the chorus as a collective or as a different authoritative voice," Aristotle reduced "the impact of the civic frame" (54). This in turn influenced German Romanticism and its failure "to appreciate how, for example, tragedies address and engage with ancient democratic values" (60). In the teleological orientation that put *Oedipus* at the apex of the genre, Aristotle indirectly facilitated the formation of a narrow "canon within a canon" that "distorts perceptions of the genre," which was, in truth, "highly experimental" and concerned with the "complex interaction ... between the general and the messy particular" (60). Hence, it is ironic but salutary that "the most significant critical turn in the last thirty years ... has been precisely the relocation of tragedies within a ... socio-political context" (54).

Page du Bois also addresses the (il)legitimacy of Aristotle as its authoritative spokesman, in order "to return us to a less partial and reductive view of Greek tragedy" (129). As a non-citizen remote in time from the "rich moment" of Athens' production of tragedy (129), Aristotle was critical of democracy and "distant ... from the fervent participation of citizens in the tragic celebrations of Dionysus" (132), whom he does not even mention. Like Goldhill, du Bois notes that later readers — here Hegel and Freud — looked only to Oedipus, "in a metonymy that ignores other characters, the chorus, the language, and other myths that serve as the matrix for the very many Athenian tragedies that fall out of the tradition" (134). By way of corrective du Bois points to three ways in which Greek tragedy "exceeds ... the tragic hero": the ubiquitous presence of slaves, the constancy of mourning which otherwise (*qua* Nicole Loraux, cited 139–140) the city seeks to limit, and the choral song that is "necessarily collective, diverse, and heterogeneous" (136)— not only citizens, but often "foreign, inassimilable persons, slaves, barbarians, or ecstatic maenads" (141).

Wae Chi Dimock resonates with du Bois in insisting upon the need to attend to the tragic chorus and its composition. She pays particular attention to Euripides's plays dealing with the aftermath of the *Iliad* from the side of the losers, including the *Hecuba* and *Trojan Women*, in which the chorus are "in the thick of it" with the protagonists, suffering the same "breakdown of immunity" (78). This "redundancy" of the chorus, at odds with Aristotle's dictum that the chorus should be treated as one of the actors, "suggests that the scope of tragedy is an open question from the very first, as is the localizability or containability of harm" (78–79). But Dimock's starting point is Hurricane Katrina and the vernacular use of the term "tragedy." She is most interested in disproportionate destruction, undeserved, that "extends across the biosphere" and "would even apply to global warming" (67–69). This scope is also found in the prose works of W.G. Sebald treated by Stanley Corngold. A "challenging modern" who always writes of ruin, including the massive destruction and loss of life in World War II, Sebald is concerned with "suffering that is drastic or disproportionate to common sense as it now affects entire genera, ontological orders of creatures" (234). In this regard, while we heed Eagleton who "takes pains not to dismiss ... everyday usage [of "tragic"] as misguided" (cited p. 3), it is also true, as Felski says, that a category made infinitely elastic ... will soon be depleted of effectiveness as an analytical tool" (10). To be fair, on the basis of Sebald's work Corngold does offer "ten items toward a revised thesis on modern tragedy," including the incorporation of many voices, inexorable attention to detail, and melancholy mood (234–237), but it is difficult to see why Sebald, however tragic his subjects in at least the vernacular sense, should be privileged as the basis for a new conception of tragedy.

Martha Nussbaum's essay is something of an outlier in this collection. Using Sophocles's *Philoctetes* as a touchstone for four critiques of pity deriving ultimately from Plato and the Stoics, she concludes that pity is a legitimate response to the loss of fundamental human needs (158–161) and that it can, in fact, motivate right action (161–162). While the play "shows compassion in league with hierarchies of heroism and birth" and so reflects tragedy as "aristocratic art form" (165), *we* need a "world that is fair to the sufferings and the strivings of all" (166). In the end, "Pity is needed to prompt the creation of good institutions and ... to sustain them" (167). Nussbaum's essay is at once narrower than others in this collection, in considering a tragic emotion but not the nature of tragedy per se, and broader, in addressing general political and ethical imperatives rather than tragedy as an artistic genre or world view.

Other contributors address the relationship between optimism (and its opposite) and tragedy. Kathleen Sands agrees with George Steiner that tragedy is ultimately incompatible with Christianity, since for Christians tragedy is a "subspecies of the problem of evil," so that "[t]heistic faith is ... the conviction that tragedy is only apparent, ... not really ultimate" (89). But she herself still finds room for tragedy: "[I]f we place value on humanity as it exists in the world and in history, tragedy is the price of the ticket" (89). Critical of feminism's "antitragic dream of social perfectibility" (96), Sands argues that "[t]o uncover tragedy is ... to confront the crushing limitations of humanity and to reignite the desire for lives and selves that are better" (100).

Joshua Foa Dienstag traces the "death of tragedy" to a much more ancient "optimism," the influence of Socrates and Plato, who "destroyed the pre-existing cultural grounds for Greek tragedy" (107) by holding that virtue can be taught, so happiness lies within the grasp of all (110). Dienstag seeks to restore Nietzsche's notion of "Dionysian pessimism" with respect to tragedy, the (pre-Socratic) idea that human existence is subject to the vicissitudes of time and so lacks permanent features (106–107), as well as his "Dionysian wisdom," learning to hope in the absence of an expectation of progress (114). This concept of pessimism "has ... appealed to the contemporary democratic political theorists" in that it discounts perfectibility but does not deflate political energies (118–119). Eagleton later pronounces Dienstag's notion of pessimism "well-nigh indistinguishable from optimism" (342).

Two contributors address modern re-workings of ancient tragedies. Simon Critchley investigates Racine's *Phèdre*, drawing on Heidegger's notions of *Geworfenheit* and *Faktizität* (183–184). Phaedra's "rent subjectivity" is imposed by the influence of two ancestors, the Sun and Venus, conscience and desire, a situation from which she cannot escape (177–178). Positing that "tragedy is tragic because someone dies" (189; he apparently forgets Oedipus), Critchley argues that, uniquely, Phaedra's life cannot be escaped in death because her father Minos is a judge in Hades (179); hence, perhaps "more tragic than tragedy" (189), this play inspires not pity and terror but rather horror (181). Critchley offers an interesting reading of Racine's play but is less reliable with its ancient original *Hippolytus*, in which Critchley calls the forgiveness of Theseus the "central theme of the drama" while he consistently misspells Euripides (192). Perhaps most intriguing is Critchley's question — prompted by the Wooster Group's comic production of *Phèdre* and by Sarah Kane's play *Phaedra's Love* — whether, in contemporary times, "the tragic is only tragic as the comic" (190).

In a dense essay Olga Taxidou reads Brecht/Berlau's *Antigone-Model 1948* in light of Brecht's *A Short Organon for the Theatre* and finds Brecht's relationship with tragedy "complicated, fraught, but potentially promising in the way it experiments with the possibility of modern tragedy" (241). It is ironic that the playwright who wanted to create an epic theatre as against Greek tragic theatre should start with a story that was part of the (narrow) canon and crucial to German Romanticism (244–245). But Brecht's model, photographed through the female gaze of Ruth Berlau (254), did challenge ancient, especially Platonic, strictures by emphasizing spectacle, mourning, and the centrality of gender for tragic form (242). Taxidou concludes that in challenging the "impossibility of modern tragedy" the Brecht/Berlau experiment "inevitably fails, but it *fails spectacularly...*" (259).

Timothy Reiss and David Scott investigate the applicability of tragedy outside the West. Reiss discusses the Greek-based works of playwrights Wole Soyinka, Ola Rotini, Efna Sutherland, and others, finding in West Africa since the 1960s a climate of social turmoil, political challenge, and new beginnings, as well as a deep and multi-faceted social "embeddedness" of the individual, not dissimilar to the situation in fifth-century Athens. Thus, as ancient tragedy "became a way to create and understand the life of the *polis*," so African "reworkings of or intertextual references to Greek tragedy give ways to think about social conditions and renew society, echoing the goals and power of ancient tragedy in new ways and with new applications" (272). Reiss argues that what these African playwrights advance "is to re-establish not an autonomous 'authentic realm' fixed in static atemporality, an Other of Western history, but traditions that are *part* of African modernity — more precisely, of African and other modernities" (279). Overall, Reiss's article is highly informative and satisfying. However, his off-hand assertion, "Inasmuch as the Greeks ... always acknowledged their debt to African culture, there may be deeper historical reasons for these proximities..." (264–265), seems uncharacteristically injudicious, ancient Greek contact with Africa being chiefly with Egypt.

David Scott discovers that, by the addition of six paragraphs at the beginning of its final chapter (which, oddly, Scott never quotes), the 1963 edition of C.L.R. James's *The Black Jacobins*, a tale of Toussaint Louverture and the Haitian revolution first published in 1938 (203), was transformed from a Romance of slavery giving way to emancipation (202) to a tragic dilemma in which Toussaint was confronted with alternatives both absolute and impossible (213), either "a return to a past of slavery ... or a future for Haiti without France and the enlightenment she represented" (210). Scott sees the character Toussaint, as Reiss sees the West African playwrights (and, in effect, as they see themselves), as "paradigmatic of a certain kind of encounter with the modern," "so transformed by modern power" that he "can neither return to the past nor face the future outside the conceptual languages bequeathed by colonial enlightenment" (213).

Two contributors explore the possibility of the tragic in modern film. Elizabeth Bronfen looks at *Double Indemnity*, a *film noir*, a genre "usually ignored by tragic theorists" (288), and finds the *femme fatale*, Phyllis, an example of tragic sensibility (289) in that she comes to an *anagnorisis* that her longed-for independence is a delusion (290) and enacts the taking of responsibility, including the responsibility for her fate (296). However, if Phyllis "accepts the tragic consequences of her action" (300) of conspiring to kill her husband, her death would nonetheless not be tragic by Aristotelian canons since the *peripeteia* from good to bad fortune of an evil person is productive of moral satisfaction, not of the tragic emotions of pity and fear.

Heather Love turns to what she calls the tragedy of social types, specifically the lesbian (304–305), in an investigation of the film *Mulholland Drive*. The film deals with "the disastrous consequences of fixing on an object that is by definition lost" (311), to wit, the suicide of the character Diane, who is rejected by the bi- (hetero-?) sexual Camilla. Love finds the film "remarkable because it takes Diane's tragedy seriously" (315), for, as Love argues, "Given that homosexuality is considered a tragic state of being, it is difficult for any individual homosexual life story to signify as tragic" (314). Difficult in this case, indeed. While Diane's story is "very sad" and exemplifies one of the "tragic others that modernity produces with such alarming regularity" (316), the character appears to lack any sense of agency in her downfall that separates tragedy from victimization. One thinks of Felski's caution about a category being "made infinitely elastic because of nervousness about exclusion" (10).

The final entry is a translation from the French scholar Michel Maffesoli. Maffesoli shares Dienstag/Nietzsche's unstable — and cyclical — view of time as well as the pervasive view that modernity's confidence in progress, perfectibility, and the individual's control of destiny has given way to a postmodern sense of the vanity of human action and a yielding to fate. But, uniquely, he finds a participation in the "tragic sense of life" (319) in the Dionysian tribalism of youth, whether it takes the form of identifying with rock stars or New Age religious practices (*passim*). Even the fascination with television news he finds to be a confrontation with and embrace of Destiny (335). Eagleton judges that "one might charitably remark that something has no doubt been lost in the translation" (338).

In his closing Commentary Eagleton is mostly appreciative ("these deft, suggestive pieces," 341), but introduces some counter perspectives. Against the postmodernists he argues that for many modernity has been an emancipation (338), but he notes that "[t]he tragic hubris of a capitalism which acknowledges no bounds" does not much appear in the volume (341). The particularism of some contributors glosses over the radical Enlightenment insight that anyone has a claim on us in light of raw humanity (341). Against Steiner's claim that tragedy "must be immune to hope," Eagleton urges that, "What makes for tragedy, often enough, is exactly the fact that we can indeed conceive of a more humane condition" (344).

The essays in this volume cover a lot of ground and not all will appeal to everyone. But virtually all are solidly grounded in philosophical and/or literary scholarship hardly even adumbrated in this review. Collectively, they offer important insights or reminders: how the focus of Aristotle's *Poetics* is itself an impediment to a genuine understanding of the full corpus of extant Greek tragedy; how modern thought based on Aristotle contributed to the further contraction of the "canon" of Greek tragedy to little more than *Oedipus* and *Antigone*; how postmodernism, with its rejection of utopianism and acknowledgment of the fallibility of self-agency, is once again open to tragedy; how, as in ancient times,

Greek tragedy is finding itself highly exportable, in and beyond the West, in innovative productions that reflect and interrogate social and political realities and
in applications of the concept of tragedy, some successful, some less so, to more
contemporary art forms. *Rethinking Tragedy* merits a place in one's library.

SANTA CLARA UNIVERSITY

Review of Literature:
Selected Books

Bernard Freydberg. *Philosophy and Comedy: Aristophanes, Logos, and Eros.* Bloomington & Indianapolis: Indiana University Press, 2008. Pp. 235. Hardcover $65. Paperback $24.95.

In introducing this new study of the Athenian comic master Aristophanes (c. 448–c. 386 B.C.), Bernard Freydberg draws attention to the deficit of a "book … that presents a systematic *philosophical* treatment" of the Aristophanic oeuvre (1). In response, Freydberg offers a unique exploration of the "philosophical yield" of four seminal comedies — *Clouds, Wasps, Assemblywomen,* and *Lysistrata* — and seeks to disclose Aristophanes's "contribution to thought" (7).

The scope of *Philosophy and Comedy* is both ambitious and ambiguous, and the result is a book that could benefit from a sharper circumscription of its goals. The "philosophy" implied in the title is not clearly defined until the conclusion, where Freydberg explains that he has sought "to connect [Aristophanes's] comic image-making with the kind of philosophical questioning and image-making that takes place in the dialogues of Plato" (197). Indeed, *Philosophy and Comedy* might best be described as an intertextual exploration of two key themes — *logos* (speech, reason) and *erôs* (libido, love) — across four Aristophanic comedies and several Platonic dialogues.

The first part of the book centers on the examination of *logos* (Chapter 1 on *Clouds*; Chapter 2 on *Wasps*), while the second part explores *erôs* (Chapter 3 on *Assemblywomen*; Chapter 4 on *Lysistrata*). Throughout these four chapters, Freydberg mines the Aristophanic text for passages where "one cannot help but think" of Plato (22, of *Clouds* and *Republic* VII) or where "Platonic themes echo" (84, of *Wasps, Apology* and *Phaedrus*). He draws attention to the manner in which these themes might resonate with an audience "on the page or on the stage" (54). Aristophanes and Plato, in Freydberg's view, share a motivation for their craft: to change minds and improve souls. For instance, the "coarseness and stupidity" of the comic protagonist Strepsiades serves the same function as the "irony" of Plato's Socrates (24), namely, to disclose "genuine *logos*" and to induce a state of "self-aware ignorance" (54). More broadly, Freydberg concludes that Aristophanes and Plato encourage their audiences to discover "proper measure" in all things, including *logos* and *erôs*, and to conduct themselves accordingly (200).

But the methodological foundations of this approach, however fruitful, are never explained. Freydberg often writes as if Aristophanes responds consciously to the Platonic text: thus the titular chorus of *Clouds* "mock" the Platonic dialogues and "obscure [their] clear distinctions" (25); *Wasps* "echoes" *Republic* VI (79) while *Ly-*

sistrata "echoes" *Republic* II–IV (187); Diotima's speech in *Symposium* "resonates throughout *Lysistrata*" (163); and in general Aristophanes is made to "enhance" (190) and "mimic" (197) Platonic dialogue. A non-specialist reader could easily infer from such language that the Platonic dialogues predate and influence the comedies of Aristophanes — but chronologically, critics almost always maintain the reverse, as Freydberg himself seems well aware (42).

The root of this difficulty is not chronological confusion, but Freydberg's somewhat uncritical reliance on the assumption that Plato portrays the "genuine" (27) or historical Socrates, to whom Aristophanes may be read as responding. For instance, Freydberg compares the *Clouds*' famous debate of the "Stronger" and "Weaker" Argument with passages in the *Apology* of Plato, and concludes on the basis of certain similarities that "Aristophanes was acutely aware of contemporary Socratic practice" (42). That connection might be defensible, but is certainly contentious, and the reader at least deserves some notice of the sprawling literature on the historical Socrates, and the reliability of Plato as a witness to a "contemporary Socratic practice" that might have influenced Aristophanes. Instead, we are left to guess at Freydberg's own views on the prickly "Socratic problem."

This is not to detract from the potential interest of Freydberg's general conclusions. Nonetheless, the book's argument would be much stronger, and its readership of "philosophers, classicists, [and] literary scholars" (2) better served, if its methodology were spelled out and defended from the outset. Undoubtedly there are legitimate cases where the Platonic and Aristophanic texts do resonate. For example, philosophers and classicists have often highlighted the similarities of *Assemblywomen* and *Republic* V,[1] as Freyd-

berg does in Chapter 3. But the modern consensus, with one notable exception,[2] has Aristophanes influencing Plato, if influence is acknowledged at all. By not engaging with such alternative and arguably "mainstream" interpretations of the intertextuality on which his conclusions rest, Freydberg deprives his readers of a rich field of conclusions about philosophy and comedy — such as Andrea Nightingale's proposal that Plato may be "more indebted to comedy than to any other literary genre," and that he took some of Aristophanes's political ideas "much more seriously than Aristophanes did" (172).[3]

With these provisos in mind, the connoisseur of comedy and intellectual history will find food for thought embedded throughout Freydberg's four central chapters. In Chapter 1, Aristophanes's notorious on-stage lampooning of Socrates emerges as a case study in the "excess" of *logos*, designed to help Aristophanes's audience "on the page or on the stage" (54) to avoid its pitfalls. A delightful volte-face frames the comic protagonist Strepsiades as the closest thing to the "Platonic" Socrates — who finds himself faced with a twisted caricature who carries that name. In performance, much could be done with the implication, not fully spelled out here, that Strepsiades is the "real" Socrates on stage. Chapter 2 consciously de-emphasizes the historical role of Aristophanes's nemesis, Cleon, in the *Wasps* (56), and chooses to focus instead on issues that "transcend" history, particularly the interplay of reason, *logos*, and madness (107). Freydberg's third chapter brings a wider range of modern philosophical perspectives to bear on the "impossible erotic life" and gender relationships of *Assemblywomen* (157), and offers the unusual conclusion that the play should be presented as describing a kind of "bliss," in the spirit of Hegel's *Seligkeit*. Finally, Chapter 4 argues that the heroine of *Lysistrata* functions like the Socrates of the *Republic*, as a liberator of humanity from captivity in the "cave"— an enticing assertion, which could also be further explored.

Each chapter of *Philosophy and Comedy* delivers a novel interpretation of the Aristophanic text, viewed through the lens of Plato, or rather through the lens of a certain interpretation of Plato. So long as the reader appreciates that this is what is going on, and digests the historical implications of Freydberg's approach with a grain of salt, there is something to be gained from following the author through this close examination of four deeply influential texts of Western comedy.

Notes

1. See recently R. Tordoff, "Aristophanes's *Assembly Women* and Plato, *Republic* Book 5" in R. Osborne, ed., *Debating the Athenian Cultural Revolution* (Cambridge University Press, 2007), with bibliography. For a perspective on the philosophical implications of the relationship, see Malcolm Schofield, *Plato: Political Philosophy* (Oxford University Press, 2006):229–231.

2. H. Thesleff, "Platonic Chronology," *Phronesis* 34 (1989):1–26.

3. A. W. Nightingale, *Genres in Dialogue: Plato and the Construct of Philosophy* (Cambridge University Press, 1995).

MICHAEL J. GRIFFIN
The University of British Columbia

Margaret Jane Kidnie. *Shakespeare and the Problem of Adaptation.* London and New York: Routledge, 2009. xii + 216 pp. Paperback $39.95.

Here is a true story. Early in his course on Shakespeare, Professor A asks the students if they have brought the play to class. Most of them wave their single editions in the air or hoist aloft their hefty one-volume complete Shakespeares, but the professor shakes his head and says, "No, you haven't got the play; you have the text of the play." In an apocryphal ad-

dition to this tale, at that very moment Professor B bursts into room and corrects his colleague: "No, they haven't got the text of the play, they have various attempts to recover it." For Professor A, the "play" somehow exists In Performance, but which performance(s), and how are he and his students to decide whether any given performance is an authentic interpretation of the play or whether it contains so many unscripted directorial interventions, including cuts, silent emendations, speech reassignments, and invented stage directions, that it might more accurately be termed an adaptation? And how are they to classify partial or complete rescriptings of Shakespeare's plays? For Professor B, performances are irrelevant distractions from his real goal of recovering the text as Shakespeare actually wrote it, a text purified of the corrupting influences of copyist, playhouse, and printing shop (leaving aside the question of whether or when he might have rewritten or revised an earlier version).

Margaret Kidnie has good advice for both professors: Lighten up! She instructs Professor A that the line between a staged interpretation (and all productions are by their very nature interpretations) and a version that is divergent enough to be called an adaptation is fuzzy and porous. She advises Professor B that his quest for the authentic authorial Shakespearean text is a wild-goose chase based on suppositional narratives about the relation of manuscripts of plays to printed editions of plays. The fallacy shared by both professors is the assumption that a single true version of The Work in question exists somewhere else, just out of reach. For Kidnie, The Work, as defined in Chapter 1, is always somewhat amorphous because it is always in flux, always being modified by new interpretations and editions. The question of whether or not any given production or text is a true instance of The Work will inevitably arise to produce what Kidnie calls "crises of work recognition," but she sees little value in policing the boundaries and instead urges us to examine "the surrounding contextual circumstances to determine, how, at this moment and for a particular community of users, the work is being defined (and redefined) as a conceptual tool" (134). In the central chapters of the book, Kidnie examines test cases ranging from live Royal Shakespeare Company productions to radically revised texts by two Canadian dramatists to a rescripted BBC television series.

In Chapter 2, Kidnie contrasts the reception of two RSC productions: Matthew Warchus's 1997 *Hamlet* and Gregory Doran's 2003 *All's Well That Ends Well*. Warchus's Hamlet was attacked by most reviewers for its severe cutting as well as its use of cinematic storytelling techniques, even though many of these filmic devices had been employed in earlier English stage *Hamlets*. Reviled as an attempt to popularize, or worse still, Americanize, Shakespeare, Warchus's production caused "a crisis of recognition." Many critics denied it to be a true instance of The Work and dismissed it as a mere adaptation. Doran's *All's Well*, by contrast, was seen as traditional, orthodox, and thoroughly English, and hence as a true instance of The Work, even though Doran cut 10 percent of the Folio text and made other major directorial interventions. Kidnie argues that the reception of Doran's *All's Well* was the result of the RSC's marketing and advertising strategies, as well as its casting of Judi Dench as the Countess of Rossillion. "Work recognition," Kidnie concludes, "in practice depends in large part on the contextual influence of historical, national and even institutional circumstances" (41).

In Chapter 3, Kidnie takes up two Canadian plays which at first glance seem quite distant from The Works: Djanet Sears's *Harlem Duet* and Robert Lepage's *Elsinore*. Rather than pigeonhole them as adaptations, Kidnie uses them to interrogate the relationship of adaptation to The Work. Many adaptations, she argues, are intended as critiques of The Work. Those informed by postcolonialism or feminism "talk back" to Shakespeare, challenging the ideological assumptions of the original from the perspective of the present. As "canonical counter–discourses," such adaptations thus become so entangled with the Shakespearean Work that they in turn influence subsequent stagings of the original and so enlarge our conception of The Work. Here, Kidnie argues, the line between adaptation and interpretation all but disappears, as both text and adaptation become part of a single complex organism.

In Chapter 4, Kidnie turns to a four-play BBC television series, *ShakespeaRetold*, which aired in 2005. Here, although the Shakespearean titles were retained and the series marketed as "four modern *interpretations* of Shakespeare's plays" (my emphasis), the fact that each play was completely rewritten and updated to contemporary England would seem to place them squarely in the category of adaptation. But here again Kidnie sees the boundary as blurred. She argues, for example, that the *Macbeth* of *ShakesepeaRetold* complicates "work recognition" by occasionally using "language that in its patterning and stylization seems overtly literary — or more specifically "Shakespearean'" and that plays off against the normative flatter, more prosaic, standard television dialogue (119). Similarly, the *Much Ado About Nothing* of *ShakespeaRetold*, set in a television studio, uses tricky camera work and other techniques of visual narration to undermine the audience's ability to make sense of what it sees, just as the play dramatizes the characters' confused perceptions. Finally, *A Midsummer Night's Dream* of *ShakespeaRe-told* used interactive technology to permit the viewer to access supplementary materials such as interviews with performers and scholars. Kidnie suggests that the intertwining of analog and digital modes of transmission accords with the mobius-like interweaving of planes of illusion within the world of the play. She also regards *ShakespeaRetold* in general as invoking a traditional sense of the value of Shakespeare to offset rapidly changing television aesthetics and describes its *A Midsummer Night's Dream* in particular as part of a deliberate campaign to use Shakespeare to lead British viewers gently into the digital age.

In her final chapter, she follows Paul Werstine and Barbara Mowat in urging editors of Shakespeare to abandon the quest for texts which never existed, and instead to publish editions of texts which *did* exist, e.g., Folio and quarto texts or later acting scripts, but to expand their readers' sense of The Work by making their emendations and annotations reflect the rich bibliographical, performance, and cultural histories of Shakespeare's plays.

Kidnie has written a very valuable book. Her conception of The Work as flexible and protean enables her to make three valuable contributions: (1) she releases editors of Shakespeare from the impossible mission proposed by the New Bibliographers, (2) she moves the discussion of Shakespearean adaptation beyond the taxonomies of earlier theorists, and (3) she transcends the bickering over "work recognition" by exploring the murky frontier and the complex interrelations between interpretations and adaptations.

MICHAEL SHAPIRO
Loyola University Chicago

Mary Trotter. *Modern Irish Theatre.* Cambridge: Polity, 2008. Pp. 256. Paperback $24.95.

Shaun Richards (editor). *The Cambridge Companion to Twentieth-Century Irish Drama.* Cambridge: Cambridge University Press, 2004. Pp. 304. Paperback $32.99

John P. Harrington (editor). *Modern and Contemporary Irish Drama*, 2nd ed. New York: Norton, 2009. Pp. 633. Paperback $20.67.

Three recent additions to the field of Irish Studies offer an impressive, expansive, and inclusive look at modern and contemporary Irish drama.

Mary Trotter's *Modern Irish Theatre* successfully traces the "history of Irish drama over the long twentieth century as a communal and community-building art form [and offers] an introduction to some of the major trends that have shaped modern Irish theatre's cultural legacy since the 1890s" (2). The book is engaging and expansive, serving as a fine introduction to the cultural history of modern Irish drama. In "Part I: Performing the Nation, 1891–1916" Trotter begins with an exploration of Irish drama's origins in the cultural nationalist movement, and rightly identifies the contrast between the "high modernist leanings of the Abbey's directors [and the] rise of an Irish realist aesthetic that engaged with local communities and concerns" (3). On the one hand, the modernists sought to eradicate the stereotypical stage Irishman in two ways. First, by presenting "images of an Irish 'folk' with the qualities upheld by the movement — spiritual, morally upright, healthy and, in order to appear as far removed from the British influence as possible, living in an idealized, rural, Irish language-speaking West" (15), and second, by dramatizing stories "from pre–Christian, ancient Irish mythology, proving that Ireland had possessed a rich cultural heritage before the encroachment of British imperialism" (16). On the other hand, rather than "imagining an idealized past, many Irish realist playwrights attempted to present the personal and political challenges of the present, such as poverty, emigration, and sectarianism, and their roots in British imperialist policies" (36). Trotter thus traces the rise of an Irish realist theatre aesthetic across the island — from the Abbey's own Padraic Colum and William Boyle, to the Cork realists Lennox Robinson and T.C. Murray, to the Northern voices of Rutherford Mayne and Gerald MacNamara — that came to "overshadow, but not obliterate, verse plays and plays written on themes from Irish legend" (11). Trotter reminds us "it was Yeats's vision, not that of the larger movement, that was being broadcast as the mirror up to Irish culture" (31).

"Part II: War and After, 1916–1948" offers a much needed and often overlooked discussion of Irish drama's response to war by "addressing the conflict between the imaginative individual and a repressive culture" (3). The most significant venture of this chapter is the identification that the "legacy of war and the Irish Free State's deeply conservative social policies of the 1920s to the early 1950s have led some theatre scholars to consider this period an artistic wasteland, skipping from O'Casey's Dublin trilogy to Brian Friel's *Philadelphia, Here I Come!* in the bat of an eye" (65). Trotter refocuses our eyes on this so-called wasteland and unearths a rich cultural history of mid–twentieth-century Irish performance that resists the "suffocating moral code" (66) of the conservative Fianna Fail government as well as the now institutionalized and nationally subsidized Abbey Theatre. She offers a refreshing overview of voices such as George Shiels, Teresa Deevy, Mary Manning, Paul Vincent Carroll, Austin Clarke, and the Longfords, not merely as the precursors of what is to come, but as significant playwrights in their own right who explore the subcultures of gender, sexuality, politics, class, and modernization.

Trotter next "considers the impact of the establishment of the Irish Republic, economic reforms, European artistic influences, and the rise of sectarian violence on the Irish theatre mid-century" (3) in "Part III: Rewriting Tradition, 1948–1980." Emigration, industrialization, urbanization, economic expansion, and other extreme socio-political changes such as the Troubles led many in the Irish nation — a nation "built on an idealized image of its culture as ancient and racy, of the soil" (116) — to shift their cultural goals and pursue modernization rather than tradition. This shift is to be expected when we consider the movement from isolationism in the 1940s toward globalization in the 1950s. Trotter rightly credits this movement as the start of a new generation of Irish dramatists who — affected by the anxiety accompanying the above changes — will use "the stage as a laboratory for investigating cultural crisis and imagining new solutions" (118). Unlike the previous chapter, there are no surprises in her selection of playwrights. Yet Trotter freely admits her discussion of Beckett and Behan, as well as the "second wave" playwrights Keane, Friel, Kilroy, Murphy and Leonard, "does not attempt to overview their long, influential, and prolific careers but, rather, to situate their origin in the context of other cultural and political movements and events of the time, thus pointing to their influence in future decades and on later playwrights" (136).

The final and strongest section, "Part IV: Re-imagining Ireland, 1980–2007," begins with the recognition that the dominant political discourse of the prior decades asserted a fragile and false cultural identity that claimed unity, community, and legitimacy through a fusion of nationalism, Catholicism, and Gaelic romanticism. Trotter asserts that "this narrow and singular understanding of the Irish people was not only oppressive, but untenable" and ultimately led dramatists from both the Republic and Northern Ireland to generate "new work intended either to create an imaginative space inclusive of all Irish difference, or to address the particular needs and concerns of a smaller, overlooked social group" (153). Thus we have, on the one hand, the death of the ubiquitous realist peasant kitchen play and, on the other hand, the birth of new companies such as Field Day and Charabanc that transgressed "the boundaries of urban/rural, North/South, Catholic/Protestant, Nationalist/Unionist" (158) and arguably transcended them. Trotter writes: "The plays and polemics of Irish theatre in the 1980s may not single-handedly have brought on the peace talks in the late 1980s, but they did open up an imaginative space for considering ways to move beyond past traumas and towards forgiveness, reorganization, and new possibilities" (175). It is in this space, however, that contemporary playwrights like Martin Lynch, Anne Devlin, Christina Reid, Jimmy Murphy, Enda Walsh, Marina Carr, and Conor McPherson represent the transformations of urban Irish life with "an apparent absence of interest among [their] characters in a sense of identity beyond their immediate desires or their loose alliances with similarly disenfranchised souls" (184).

Trotter's conclusion, "What is an Irish Play?," turns to the 2007 production of *The Playboy of the Western World* as updated by Roddy Doyle and Bisi Adigunher as a reflection on "the drastically new demographic make-up of twenty-first-century Ireland, with a majority of its population living in the cities, and the image of Ireland once reflected by the idealized peasant increasingly being supplanted by characters who are working-class urbanites" (195). In this version (produced one hundred years after the original), the time

is contemporary, the setting is a Dublin pub, and Christy Mahon is a Nigerian immigrant. Trotter cites this production as an example of the growing concern that Irish theatre is losing its identity. "On the one hand, artists and audiences continue to find meaning in the century's canonical works, and these plays often tour in other countries, or are produced by theatre companies abroad. On the other hand, much contemporary theatre seeks to break away from these tropes of the classic Irish play by commenting ironically upon them ... or by ignoring them in favor of new performance models that address new issues" (196).

Trotter's book, as a whole, achieves what it sets out to do: namely, "to reveal the dynamic, even symbiotic, relationship between Irish theatre and Irish culture" (2). Its strength is providing a succinct, brisk, engaging survey of Irish theatre since 1890. It is (as advertised) a cultural history rather than a critical exegesis. And while the book falls short of providing an original answer to "What is an Irish play?," Trotter's *Modern Irish Theatre* provides ample material for readers to originate answers of their own.

In *The Cambridge Companion to Twentieth-Century Irish Drama*, editor Shaun Richards assembles an impressive, extensive, and significant collection of nineteen essays regarding the whole range of Irish drama from the past century. What is most commendable, however, is Richards's choice to include (and begin with) an article by Stephen Watt on nineteenth-century Irish melodrama. Watt reminds us that the Irish Literary Theatre's fantasy of an autochthonous birth really attempts to cover up its origins in the embarrassingly understudied popular drama of the day. This essay sets up a theme for the collection; that is, exploring the tensions between traditional and popular drama, between state-supported and community-generated theatre, between the Abbey and everyone else. To be expected are the major playwrights and themes: the ideology of Yeats and Lady Gregory, the imagination of Synge, the Irishness of Wilde and Shaw, the disillusionment of O'Casey, the countertradition of Beckett, the sense of place in Friel, and the role of loss in Murphy. These essays all survey the writers and their craft with insight and depth, serving as appropriate and accessible companion pieces to their plays. What truly delights, however, are the less expected essays on design, history, and revival. Richard Allen Cave, in his "On the Siting of Doors and Windows: Aesthetics, Ideology and Irish Stage Design," convincingly reveals the relationship between the early Abbey's aesthetic focus on minimalism and its limited budget. Claire Gleitman, in "Reconstructing History in the Irish History Play," argues that contemporary Irish dramatists are not narcissistically focused on the past, but rather "they offer a rich analysis of the ideological and psychological imperatives which control the ways in which history is remembered, transmitted and employed, and its potent power to whisper persistently (and sometimes perniciously) in the ear of the present" (219). In "The Revival Revised," Brian Singleton exposes the traditional Abbey Theatre audiences who "[decry] all attempts to break away from naturalism as the dominant theatrical form" and place an unfair expectation on Irish dramatists to "uphold the tradition of writing the nation" (258). Singleton beautifully investigates and recreates such notable departures as director Garry Hynes's production of *The Plough and the Stars* and the theatre company Barabbas's production of *The Whiteheaded Boy* not so much as "recent attempts at revival of an original Revival, but more exponents of the art of theatrical recovery" (270). Finally, were it not for Cathy Leeney's excellent "Ireland's 'exiled'

women playwrights: Teresa Deevy and Marina Carr," this collection would be negligent in its representation of female Irish dramatists and theatre practitioners. Then again, this essay draws attention to the fact that more attention must be paid to valuable Irish female voices on and off stage, in and out of print.

To call the Norton Critical Edition of *Modern and Contemporary Irish Drama* a second edition is a bit of a misnomer. On the one hand, it is a welcome reissue of John P. Harrington's 1991 classic collection of plays, playwrights, and criticism from Yeats to Friel. On the other hand, it has been updated and expanded to such a degree that it reads like a new, insightful compilation in and of itself. Of the fourteen plays in the collection (including works by Yeats, Lady Gregory, Synge, Shaw, O'Casey, Beckett, and Friel), four are new additions: *The Pot of Broth* by Yeats and Lady Gregory, *At the Hawk's Well* by Yeats, *The Weir* by Conor McPherson, and *By the Bog of Cats* by Marina Carr. It did not go unnoticed by this reviewer that, between the editions, Lady Gregory is finally credited for her authorial stake in *Cathleen Ni Houlihan*. The extensive "Backgrounds and Criticism" section now includes essays by notables Colm Tóibín, Nicholas Grene, Terence Brown, Paige Reynolds, Declan Kiberd, Christopher Murray, Susan Cannon Harris, Antoinette Quinn, James Knowlson, and Anthony Roche. Four of the five entries for the section on Samuel Beckett are new, as are the sections dedicated to Conor McPherson and Marina Carr. True standouts here are Eamonn Jordan's "Pastoral Exhibits: Narrating Authenticities in Conor McPherson's *The Weir*" and Melissa Sihra's "A Cautionary Tale: Marina Carr's *By the Bog of Cats*." Jordan explores "the links between story-telling, the ghost story, memory, and the past, and between identity and narrative formation, within the frame of the pastoral" (572) and effectively argues that McPherson's play "overlaps with something else—wake rituals" (576). Through story-telling, the characters attempt (and fail) to distance themselves from and contain Death. Jordan writes, "In pastoral, loss, or a communal acknowledgment of it, to put it more accurately, is ultimately the key ingredient. In the lived world, loss has less and less currency or value" (576). Sihra—writing on Big Josie Swane (the unseen character in *By the Bog of Cats*)—tackles the traditional view of mother figures in Irish drama as personifications of the Irish nation. Sihra writes, "The nation as female is now depicted as an overweight, erotic, foulmouthed transgressive energy who, according to [the character] Xavier Cassidy was 'loose and lazy and aisy, a five shillin' hoor,' in contrast to Yeats's martyric wanderer" (582). Sihra's argument that "Carr replaces familiarity and comfort with estrangement and unease, thus offering the necessary objectivity for self-scrutiny," is not only perceptive and correct, but also serves as a tidy summary of much contemporary Irish drama.

Also of note is a new section "On Theatre in Ireland" with essays on postcolonialism and women in Irish theatre history. The gem, however, is a brief but fascinating look at paratheatrical events such as "parades, processions, funerals, festivals, protest marches, sporting events, dramatic interludes, and political meetings" (613) by Joan Fitzpatrick Dean in "Pageants, Parades, and Performance Culture." Dean argues that the "impulse to perform identity by participating in an original, rather than canonical, work" (621) both fosters community and collaboration while offering an alternative to the persistent, elitist, traditional dramaturgy lingering around the Abbey stage.

Most notably absent is the first edition section on Brendan Behan. A handful of seminal essays has also been removed from the new table of contents, but I am sure it was a matter of space rather than choice. While I do miss some of those entries that made the first edition the "go to" collection, I am reminded of Shaw's line: "You have learnt something. That always feels at first as if you had lost something."
KELLY YOUNGER
Loyola Marymount University

Emily Roxworthy. *The Spectacle of Japanese American Trauma: Racial Performativity and World War II.* Honolulu: University of Hawai'i Press, 2008. Pp. viii + 231. Hardcover $35.00.

Tracing the long-standing American practice of viewing Japan through a lens combining Orientalism with anti-theatricalism, Roxbury suggests that the internment of Japanese Americans during World War II was shaped by racial performance on both sides. She maintains that since the time of Admiral Perry's "black ships," Americans have seen the Japanese as "natural born actors" who are either adept at masking their true feelings or whose masklike personas cover a core of nothingness. Either case renders them antithetical to the supposedly sincere, "anti-theatrical" nature of Americans. Roxworthy highlights the Catch 22 of what she calls Japanese Americans' "performative citizenship." If they dressed and acted like White Protestant Americans, they were accused of mimicry and insincerity; if they looked and behaved like Japanese, they were exoticized, infantilized, or demonized. During World War II, they were required to "perform patriotism" by placidly allowing themselves to be incarcerated as enemy aliens, signing loyalty oaths, and joining the military to fight for the country that criminalized them.

More than two-thirds of this book deals with the performative aspects of anti–Japanese racism. This emphasis on social performance sometimes highlights American theatricalism rather than anti-theatricalism. For example, Roxworthy suggests that Americans felt the need to "out–Herod Herod" in dealing with Japan, popularly imagined as the world's "most esthetic nation." She chronicles a century of American theatricalist display, from Perry's black-face minstrel shows to the spectacle and trauma of the atomic bombs. In discussing the FBI's carefully choreographed and rehearsed round-ups of Japanese Americans, which began mere hours after Pearl Harbor, she demonstrates how J. Edgar Hoover had transformed his agents from highly melodramatic G-Men to "gentlemanly," straight-laced, anti-theatrical bureaucrat/scientists prosecuting "public enemies." Her indictment of the media (especially the Hearst empire) as role-playing, hysterical divas is equally riveting. However, Roxbury seems naively convinced that the puritanical, anti-theatrical American public was oblivious to the blatantly theatrical practices of the government and media, while simultaneously outraged by "insincere" Japanese theatricality.

Roxworthy's most important contribution is her analysis (in the last two chapters) of the double nature of internment camp performance. At California's Manzanar and Tule Lake camps, Issei (first-generation Japanese), who were forbidden American citizenship by prewar immigration law, performed in and attended traditional Japanese festivals, music, dance, story-telling, and theatre presented in Japanese. In doing so, they emphatically practiced "performative citizenship" of (and cultural allegiance to) Japan. In contrast, Nissei (their American born — and thus already citizen — children) performed and attended "all American" (and often patriotic) entertainments in English, including tap dancing, jitter-bug, American

folk music, baton twirling, Carmen Miranda impersonation, improvisational cabaret, and plays. This generational and performance divide erupted in sometimes violent political/cultural differences.

Despite camp censorship and governmental control, Issei performed and attended Japan-centric, anti–American *kabuki* plays that, after the war, would be forbidden by Occupation censors in Japan. Roxworthy does not explain this paradox, suggesting only that at least one camp administrator was incompetent. Nor does she explain how bulky, "enemy" musical instruments, costumes and wigs ended up in the camps. The internees had been forced to relocate with minimal luggage or notice. As she notes, carrying "Japanesey" items would have cast suspicion on their loyalty.

If the anti-theatrical prejudice was largely responsible for anti–Japanese prejudice, why were internee cultural performances allowed and even encouraged? Roxworthy seems unaware of the paradox. While offering more information on internee cultural performances than any previous study, Roxworthy seems oddly uninterested in scripted plays. Although she mentions that Tule Lake's Nissei Little Theatre presented "high-minded productions of Western realist dramas (including Chekhov) and highly civilized English-language comedies" (174), she gives no titles or details. We might well ask how Chekhov was perceived by both internees and camp administrators. What would the cross-racial casting of disenfranchised Japanese internees playing Russian gentry in a society on the verge of collapse suggest? Roxworthy misses a great opportunity by failing to consider these and other plays.

Roxworthy displays a penchant for misstating (or failing to clarify) facts, in order to support her thesis. For example, in discussing the *kabuki* play *The Three*

Kichisas and the New Year's Visit to the Pleasure Quarter, she maintains that the titular bandits share the same surname. However, Kichisa is their shared personal name. This mistake dilutes her argument. She states: "Parallel to the manner in which Japanese Americans found themselves spectacularly lumped together in their suspect status because of the assumed association of their shared heredity, Ojō, Oshō, and Obō are yoked in public notoriety by their shared surnames..." (146). Japanese surnames helped the FBI differentiate "enemy aliens" from otherwise visually similar "non-enemy" East Asians. The Kichisas, however, share only their personal name. Roxworthy continues: "Aware that the practice of Japanese culture rendered them un–American in the performative logic of U.S. citizenship — as the surname "Kichisa" enveloped the three bandits in their shared notoriety — the remaining factions of performers at Manzanar yoked their fates together, not in resigned acceptance of the dominant policies that enforced their exile, but in reasoned resistance to them" (147). What might have been a significant thesis of internee resistance (a major shift from previous scholars' work) is deflated by a factual error. Far more serious is the following argument. She states that the performance "...compelled audiences to at least partially identify with the unapologetic criminal anti-heroes whose intertwined fates generated the dramatic plot. It is significant that the Manzanar cast for *The Three Kichisas*—particularly the internee-actors who played the bandits Ojō Kichisa, Oshō Kichisa and Obō Kichisa — remained anonymous in the published program for the 20–21 January 1945 shows" (145–146). One page earlier she notes that "one chanter-*shamisen* team performed a *jōruri* rendition of *Taikōki jūdanme*...; the other group performed the Kabuki play *San'nin Kichisas* (The Three Kichisas)" (144). This

phrasing suggests two two-man teams. If so, all roles would have been voiced by a single *jūruri* chanter accompanied by a *shamisen* player, thus explaining the "missing" cast list. Roxworthy's failure to clarify the situation nullifies what might have been a powerful argument.

In the final chapter, she discusses internees' performance of other races. Her application of Eric Lott's concepts about blackface masking (*Love and Theft*, 1993) suggests that she will provide evidence that performing maligned "Others" signified internee resistance. Once again, factual mistakes distort the argument. Roxworthy writes, "...the Little Theatre's plan to stage an African American folk play — Paul Green's 1926 one-act *White Dresses*[1] (subtitled *A Tragedy in White and Black*) — with the conscious artistic decision that white actors embody black Southern characters originally created by a black playwright, sheds some light on Ozaki's (the Japanese American actor/director) contemporaneous motivation for performing a "negro folk song" in his bid to impress the white panel judging the hidden talents competition" (170). Pulitzer Prize winner Paul Green (1894–1981) was a white Southerner. By misstating his race and the provenance of the play, she undermines her entire analysis. The Caucasian actors would have been camp secondary school teachers, employees of the United States government. A white-written play about African Americans, directed by a Japanese American internee, and performed by white actors holding positions of authority over the director, would have made a fascinating analysis, if Roxworthy had gotten her facts right.

Roxworthy seems unaware that theatre historians need concrete evidence. She casually drops what could be a minor theatre history bombshell. Citing the memoir of a single internee, she maintains that "...visiting Kabuki artists from Japan had been trapped on tour in the United States when war broke out, so these highly respected professional actors found themselves interned at Tule Lake, where they performed 'on a grand scale' for appreciative audiences and taught kabuki performance techniques to other internees" (158). If true, "Wow!" But it appears that Roxworthy may have misread her source. The original states that these actors were former traveling performers who had toured the Japanese countryside (not the USA). Many such minor semi-professionals had emigrated to Hawaii in the early twentieth century, where they taught and performed for other Issei.[2] Certainly Japan's wartime press, which constantly vilified the American internment camps, would have mentioned the arrest of high level professional *kabuki* actors. If Roxworthy's interpretation of this anecdote could be supported by evidence, the history of *kabuki* performance in America would need to be rewritten. As a performance scholar, Roxworthy is obliged to verify such an extraordinary statement.

This book begins on a promising note, using an intriguing combination of theories including Orientalism, the antitheatrical prejudice, trauma studies, spectacularism, and performativity. Despite presenting important new material, the author's tendency to make factual errors and her failure to offer specifics make this book of questionable value to scholars.

Notes

Acknowledgment: I am grateful to James R. Brandon for helping me attempt to determine if there is evidence that a professional *kabuki* troupe was in fact interned, and for tracking down a copy of the Shirai book.

1. The correct date for the premier of Paul Green's *White Dresses* is 1923.

2. The paragraph that Roxworthy cites reads: "Music and drama were important as entertainment. The mess hall in each block often served as a Kabuki theatre. Before the war, there were many amateur Kabuki groups in the Japanese community. These groups had many kinds of wigs, costumes, and stage props such as swords and rifles. They brought these and other items from outside the camp. Professional dramatists who had come to the United States before the war were stuck at Tule Lake with us. These ex-*dosa mawari* had staged shows all over the Japanese countryside. Not only were they excellent performers, they were also fantastic teachers. Thanks to them, we were able to stage Kabuki plays on a grand scale. The most popular were *Chushingura, Konjikiyasha,* and *Hototogisu*" (Shirai 141).

References

Lott, Eric. *Love and Theft: Blackface Minstrelsy and the American Working Class.* New York: Oxford University Press, 1993.

Shirai, Noburo. *Tule Lake: An Issei Memoir.* Trans. Ray Hosoda. Sacramento, CA: Tom's Printing, 2001.

CAROL FISHER SORGENFREI
University of California, Los Angeles

Neilesh Bose, ed. *Beyond Bollywood and Broadway: Plays from the South Asian Diaspora.* Bloomington, Indiana: Indiana University Press, 2009. Pp. 520. Paperback $29.95.

Neilesh Bose's edited volume of plays from the South Asian diaspora is a welcome beginning to what will hopefully become a long list of publications on diaspora theatre. The primary challenge with a project like this lies in selecting the plays to be included, and Bose has done a commendable job, offering a wide variety of perspectives and genres. These are not just plays with South Asian themes or Indian plays that have international appeal. What holds the eleven plays together is that they are all *by* and *about* people of the South Asian diaspora, from four countries that have very different histories of migration and relationships with the subcontinent: the United States, Canada, the United Kingdom, and South Africa. This collection encourages the consideration of

"South Asian diasporic drama" as a cohesive object of study, with its own emerging performance aesthetic. The plays that fit this description express diverse sociopolitical and aesthetic concerns, but as Bose convincingly demonstrates, this theatrical tradition, especially since the mid-to-late 1980s, is beginning to establish a voice that is separate from both the theatrical traditions of India and the host cultures.

The organization is helpful and straightforward, beginning with a brief general introduction to explain the selection process. This is followed by four sections, each of which includes an introduction to the migration history of South Asians to a particular country along with a history of the diaspora community's theatrical endeavors there. This introduction is followed by three plays from that country (except for Canada, which has two), each of which has its own brief introduction with information about the playwright and performance history. The introductions also give a sense of the production context by citing critical responses to the plays as well as quoting from interviews with the playwrights. Context is especially important in an anthology such as this, where the very structure promotes comparison.

It is clear from the volume that there is no single "diaspora" narrative, and that the real project is to put these various diasporas and the way they reflect processes of identity formation on stage "into conversation with one another" (5–6). Bose complicates the comparative project by providing complexity, reminding readers that people immigrated to these four nations at different times for different reasons. Additionally, relationships between the host countries and migrants are continually changing. It is also important to note that these four migration histories did not happen in isolation, but influenced and overlapped with one another. For example, in the late 1960s to early 1970s, many Indians who were forced to leave East Africa immigrated to the UK. These "twice-migrants" have a different relationship to the UK and to the immigrant experience than those who came directly from India, and Bose deliberately includes a play (Jatinder Verma's *2001: A Ramayana Odyssey*) from this perspective. These dramas are records of varied immigration experiences, and the medium offers a different entrée point into the South Asian diasporic experience than film or literature. The multiple identities and readings in the plays reflect the complex and multiple identities of South Asians in the U.S., Canada, the UK, and South Africa, and their various literary, cultural, and actual journeys.

These plays compete both with entertainments in the host countries and those imported from India. Troupes such as Salaam Theater, South Asian American Theater, Teesri Duniya Theater, Rasikarts, Tara Arts, the Asian Theater Cooperative, Shah Theater Academy, and Durban Academy of Theater Arts are starting to gain recognition outside of diaspora communities to appeal more broadly to Americans, Canadians, the British, and South Africans. In many ways, the diaspora plays are no different from non-diaspora plays, but they tend to include a bit of the immigrant experience and minority culture, which adds a fresh perspective to the host country's theatre scene. Rana Bose's *The Death of Abbie Hoffman*, for example, includes few references to South Asia, instead focusing on radicalism, and demonstrating that diasporic South Asians in theatre do more than just represent themselves, but also engage with larger theatrical and critical issues.

In this volume, Bose has included realistic plays containing social criticism (*Song for a Sanctuary, Working Class Hero, Bhopal*), those that incorporate Indian dance traditions (*Strictly Dandia, Looking for Muruga*), those that engage western or Indian classics (*Merchant on Venice, 2001: A Ramayana Odyysey*), and an absurdist play (*The Death of Abbie Hoffman*), among others. These plays engage stereotypes of South Asians, but move beyond them or offer sympathetic views (*Sakina's Restaurant*). Hanif Kureishi's *Borderlines* is not included in this volume, but Bose uses it continually as a reference point.

These diasporic plays include South Asian references, themes, and characterizations. The most common themes in the plays represented here are race, class, and intergenerational conflict, and they are approached from a variety of sociopolitical and aesthetic positions. Many plays depict the racial harassment and discrimination often faced by South Asians of all educational and economic levels in their adopted countries. Others, such as *Merchant on Venice* and *Strictly Dandia*, engage with issues of racism within the South Asian community. The plays from South Africa, in particular, expose the hypocrisy of South Asians' complaining about the discrimination they face from Whites while themselves discriminating against Blacks.

Beyond Bollywood and Broadway provides an excellent model of the diversity not only of aesthetic traditions and sociopolitical perspectives, but of the variety of ways that Indians in the diaspora relate to the homeland and what Bose refers to as the "colonial modern" experience (11). Some of the plays that do this especially well are *Chaos Theory, Bhopal*, and *The Lahnee's Pleasure*. The plays depict complex, conflicted characters and stories, and their very richness is what makes them such a pleasure to read together in a single volume. While each region, indeed, each play, stands alone, there are obvious points of overlap and broad themes that should provide both fruitful scholarship and cross-cultural productions.

The South Asian diaspora and its theatrical traditions are, however, far larger than the four nations that Bose has chosen to represent. Bose has chosen these countries both for linguistic reasons and because of their fairly established diasporic theatrical traditions, which have often developed with little to no institutional infrastructure (with the possible exception of the UK). Additionally, these plays were all originally written in English, and diaspora communities have long traditions of Indian language theatre for internal consumption. Translations of these plays would make another excellent addition to South Asian diaspora theatre scholarship. In the case of South Africa, Bose has chosen to include three classic plays, all of which were written during apartheid. While he acknowledges that there is an active post-apartheid (post–1994) theatre tradition in South Africa, readers are not given an example in this anthology. It is clear that Bose had difficult choices to make, and that each of the four nations could easily have had its own volume.

By any estimation, *Beyond Bollywood and Broadway* is an amazing start to a discussion of South Asian diaspora theatre, and I hope that Bose and other scholars will continue the conversation. This is a book that should be read by anyone interested in postcolonial migration, diaspora communities and arts, or theatrical traditions in any of these countries.

KRISTEN RUDISILL
Bowling Green State University

Jon D. Rossini. *Contemporary Latina/o Theater: Wrighting Ethnicity.* Carbondale: Southern Illinois University Press, 2008. Pp. 253. Paperback $37.50.

Jon D. Rossini's book, *Contemporary Latina/o Theater: Wrighting Ethnicity*, is an indispensable addition to theatre and ethnic studies. Rossini addresses a wide range of readers in his study of "theatricality as a means of understanding, exploring, and rethinking ethnicity" (1). The often highly theoretical work provides scholars and students with key figures and performances that have irrevocably shaped Latino theatre. Rossini inquires, "What does it mean to represent a Latino, and how can playwrights create the texts in which this question can be explored?" (21). Framed by immigration and translation debates, his introduction contains an historical overview of contested terminology (Hispanic, Chicano, Latino, etc.) surrounding the field. The debates, and the performances herein, are consistently anchored within politics, social constructions, and cultural histories. Rossini's research illustrates how playwrights "correct and create" representations of ethnicity by reconceptualizing them through wrighting, a practice that involves "writing and righting" (10). Each performance included in the book is situated in its own meticulously researched historical moment, as Rossini succinctly traces the politics from which each project emerged.

Following the introduction, the book's second chapter provides close readings of Miguel Piñero's *Short Eyes* and *The Sun Always Shines for the Cool*. Rossini begins his discussion with a poem, a quote, and a narrative description of an event; this engaging entrée instantly situates Piñero's dramas in a Nuyorican cultural identity, from which Piñero wrights "art out of life" (32). The inversion of ethnic relations within the prison environment in *Short Eyes* is, according to Rossini, a "microcosmic mirror for exploring codes of interethnic interaction in the broader social macrocosm" (32). Rossini argues that Piñero wrights criminality by shifting it from ethnic bodies to that of a white, middle-class family man. However, the author also insists that Piñero "makes it clear that if the individual and the com-

munity are to survive, identity cannot be predicated upon destruction and dehumanization of the other" (40). Piñero's wrighting of masculinity and the code of respect that informs community are central to Rossini's discussion of *The Sun Always Shines for the Cool*. Rossini examines, in detail, the characters of the play who wright, "when forced through a combination of ethnoenvironmental factors to perform" (50), by playing out identities and widening the bounds of liminal space.

El Pachuco and Luis Valdez's wrighting of this ambivalent figure are the focus of Chapter 3, and criminality resurfaces in Valdez's *Bandidos!* and *I Don't Have to Show You No Stinking Badges* in Chapter 4. While a great deal has been written about *Zoot Suit*, Rossini reexamines the ethnic identification of the pachuco as "a creative space for the formation of an identity in between cultures" (59). Rossini analyzes style as a means of control that offers agency and makes space for possibilities on stage and off, as well as the corporeal iconography and spiritual function of El Pachuco (and Edward James Olmos) to facilitate transformations. Rossini insists that *Zoot Suit*'s multiple endings "rewrite history beyond the scope of partial facts" (76) and demand that audiences seek alternative futures. In Chapter 4, Rossini investigates Valdez's "process of wrighting an alternative relationship between Chicano identity and community" (77) through his use of melodrama that exposes myths, ideologies, and representations in *Bandido!* Expanding on the work of scholars like Jorge Huerta, Rossini contends that Valdez employs this reductive genre to depict, rather than to resolve, cultural anxieties about ethnicity. "The very act of revealing this anxiety is productive"(79), according to Rossini, who includes ample detail to establish Valdez's wrighting of historical amnesia. *Badges*, according to Rossini, explores everyday televisual representations of Latino ethnicity "to once again work in and against an established genre" (95). The author traces how Valdez's play complicates restrictive sitcom stereotypes, asserting that these roles reinforce Latinos as a visible, permanent part of middle-class America. Asserting control over the means by which one's ethnic badge is worn (as cholo, etc.) is a central concern for Rossini, who addresses several different versions of Valdez's text and its productions. Rossini contends that Valdez critiques and subverts the "representational machinery" of Hollywood by stretching its stereotypes "to the point of meaninglessness" (109) in order to offer alternative representations.

Chapter 5, "Wrighting the Borders in the 1990s," departs from the structure of the previous chapters. It provides a thematic overview of complex United States-Mexican border discourse, its lived realities, and several means of performing these realities. Works by Guillermo Gomez-Peña, Teatro de la Esperanza, and Teatro Visión provide a backdrop for Rossini's in-depth discussion of the border agent in pieces by Culture Clash, John Leguizamo, Rick Najera, Guillermo Reyes, and Octavio Solis. Rossini uses these performances to illustrate a "change in thinking about ethnic representation during this decade, a movement away from exploding stereotypes to representational choices that resist the potential imposition of stereotypes" (131). Ultimately, he argues for the transformable space of the theatre as an "effective material metaphor" (146) for performing the geopolitical border.

Rossini returns to his single-playwright model in Chapter 6, on the aesthetics of wrighting in the work of Puerto Rican playwright José Rivera. Here Rossini foregrounds the "critical tendency to attempt to codify any departure from traditional realism" (147), a propensity that inscribes Latino playwriting as a cultural product rather than an intellectual endeavor. For Rossini, Rivera's "integrated and symbiotic" (149) plays have their own logic, one that extends the notions of character and community. Through rigorous readings of *Marisol*, *Each Day Dies with Sleep*, and *Cloud Tectonics*, Rossini endorses Rivera's creation of alternative realities, where the violence of capitalism, the transformational power of love, time-specific identities, and dreams reign. He pinpoints the relationships between Rivera's characters as the playwright's way of wrighting ethnicity, making the theatre a space where the possibility for a community "coming into being" (175) exists because audiences witness acts of being.

The book appropriately concludes with a chapter on "Cherríe Moraga and the Wrighting of Community" (176). For Rossini, Moraga's primary project is to "remind her audience of the fantasy of cultural solidarity that obscures the real heterogeneity of Latino identity" (176). Hence, he closely reads Moraga's *Heroes and Saints*, *A Circle in the Dirt*, and *Watsonville* for their interrogations of a communal reality. Rossini highlights Moraga's departure from artists like Piñero and Valdez through her adamant refusal to "grant the forces of oppression and repression any visibility" (190), enacting resistance through staging. Moraga's insistence that witnessing in the theatre inevitably creates room for an inclusive community, "a generative community, one capable of wrighting itself" (196) extends Rossini's initial concept of the (utopian?) potential of the theatre. He argues that, in Moraga's work, the political ideals of community-based theatre are palpable even in her single-author plays, and that she wrights ethnicity beyond stereotypes and borders, by "creating new models in the process of correcting old ones" (209).

Rossini's book contributes to the field because it extends the study of each of these plays and playwrights by making ethnicity central. His comprehensive analyses do not reinvent our ideas about contemporary Latino/a theatre, but considerably broaden them. He deepens an ongoing discourse about how these playwrights expose structures, put forth alternatives, and transform relationships between spectators and actors. The sheer number of Latino/a playwrights and plays considered in conversation in this book is significant, useful, and pioneering.

YAEL PRIZANT
University of Notre Dame

Sharon Friedman, ed. *Feminist Theatrical Revisions of Classic Works: Critical Essays*. Jefferson, NC: McFarland, 2009. Pp. 300. Paperback $45.00.

I was among a crowd of people hoping to win Sharon Friedman's new collection of essays, *Feminist Theatrical Revisions of Classic Works,* at the 2009 Comparative Drama Conference book raffle. While I lost out there, I definitely won when asked to write the review of this book. It is everything I had expected it to be: a perceptive and broadly conceived overview for those who wish to become acquainted with the kinds of adaptations created by women in theatre over the past thirty years, and an insightful critical reference for those familiar with feminist revisionist theatre.

Friedman's introduction provides a solid grounding for the collection's ethos. The essays in the volume focus on productions that *interpret* the original classic text in adapting it. Thus, the subjects of the critical essays are subversive "revisions" informed by feminist theory and practice. Friedman organizes the volume logically, by the period and genre of the source play, myth, or text. Her divisions — Classical Theater and Myth, Shakespeare and Seventeenth Century Theater, Nineteenth

and Twentieth Century Narratives and Reflections, and Modern Drama (which is disappointingly less extensive than the other divisions) — are then organized chronologically according to the revisionist production, providing readers an overview of feminist aesthetic strategies and developments from the 1970s to the present. For newcomers to feminist theatre and theory, early in the introduction Friedman provides a succinct overview of broad movements within feminist thought: liberal humanist feminism, radical cultural feminism, materialist/socialist feminism, and postmodern feminism. However, what is particularly laudable is Friedman's open vision of feminist work and inquiry, which refuses to limit, dismiss, or devalue the varying political aims and wide array of practices of contemporary feminisms and theatrical productions informed by those feminisms.

Several essays in the collection, including the first, Julie Malnig's "All is Not Right in the House of Atreus: Feminist Theatrical Renderings of the *Oresteia*," manifest Friedman's ethos as revealed in the introduction. Malnig's essay examines two re-visionings of the Oresteia myth: *Electra Speaks*, by Women's Experimental Theater (WET) in 1980, and Ellen McLaughlin's 1995 *Iphigenia and Other Daughters*. Ostensibly, her focus is to compare and contrast the productions, tracing their thematic concerns and aesthetic strategies to the prevailing movements in feminist and theatrical theory of their cultural moment. Ultimately, however, Malnig quite usefully argues that we not see feminist performance in stages that have a "progression," thus devaluing prior work. Instead, Malnig (like Friedman) uses the term "development," because most feminist works inhabit more than one ideological stance. For example, key projects from the primarily cultural feminist production *Electra Speaks*, such as "exploration of female as subject ... [and] validating women's experience"(27), are still important aims within a primarily poststructuralist feminist text such as *Iphigenia and Other Daughters*, which also paradoxically undermines the notion of a unified female self or subject. Carol Martin's essay "The Political Is Personal: Feminism, Democracy and *Antigone Project*" foregrounds this same acceptance that the varying aims of feminism, while often contradictory, are all still vital. Martin analyzes the 2004 production of five one-act revisions of Sophocles's *Antigone* by the Women's Project, highlighting the paradox at the center of Antigone as heroine, *The Antigone Project*, and indeed at the heart of feminism: "devoted to the individual voice, which always acts in the context of the collectivity of history" (90). Indeed, many of the essays in Friedman's edition deftly — and consciously — walk the tightrope of liberal humanist feminism's attempt to move women into mainstream culture, cultural feminism's desire to validate a uniquely woman's experience, and postmodern materialist feminism's contention that identity is a shifting construct of the ideologies of material culture (thus negating conceptions of a core self or identity and critiquing mainstream culture).

Nevertheless, regardless of the reader's political inclination, the dazzling variety of the dramatic texts and productions encompassed by the volume will be a delight to any serious student of drama and theatre. In addition to introductions to lesser-known productions such as *The Antigone Project* or *Iphigenia and Other Daughters,* included in the volume are analyses of works by authors and directors who are perennial favorites of academe and often taught in English and Theatre departments. Friedman's own contribution to the volume, "The Feminist Playwright as Critic," examines revisions of *Othello*

by Paula Vogel, Ann-Marie MacDonald, and Djanet Sears; Maya E. Roth focuses on Timberlake Wertenbaker in "The Philomela Myth as Postcolonial Feminist Theater"; and Cheryl Black chronicles several productions by Director JoAnne Akalaitis in "Transgressive Female Desire and Subversive Critique in the Seventeenth Century Canon." Too, while some of the revisions analyzed in the volume remain very close to the source text, as in Akalaitis's productions of *The Rover* and *'Tis Pity She's a Whore*, which, according to Black, rely on Akalaitis's subversive staging to interpret and counterpoint the primarily original language, other revisions are, in Leonora Champagne's characterization, "explosions of the classic text that challenge the author's authority" (169). Champagne's "Outside the Law: Feminist Adaptations of *The Scarlet Letter*" examines plays by Phyllis Nagy, Suzan-Lori Parks, and Naomi Wallace that rewrite the narrative around more transgressive characters (such as the witch Anne Hibbens or Pearl) or re-invent time and place in order to deconstruct, invert, and/or undermine the novel and its themes, focusing on contemporary issues such as welfare, female sexuality, homosexuality, and abortion.

Further, the variety of critical theories both informing the feminist theatrical revisions of classic works and brought to them by the essayists will engage and enrich any academician, reminding us of what we have internalized and inviting us to new critical discourse. Of course, the volume does examine plays by women that were not billed as feminist productions; yet, as Andrea J. Nouryeh clearly delineates in her essay "Mary Zimmerman's *Metamorphoses*: Storytelling Theater as Feminist Process," Zimmerman's production was unconsciously influenced by feminist ideologies, theatrical strategies, and aesthetics from the 1970s through the

1990s, foregrounding women's voices and bodies and ultimately "produc[ing] a theater piece that undermines fixed notions of gender and the concept of an immutable identity" (62). Nevertheless, most of the revisions discussed in the volume were conscious products of feminist ideology. Wertenbaker's *The Love of the Nightingale* is a product of postcolonial ethics (Roth), and Vogel, MacDonald, and Sears produce "dramas of ideas" grounded in "critical approaches from feminist and gender studies, literary criticism, and performance and cultural studies" (Friedman 113). Additionally, the materialist feminist analyses of Women's Theatre Group and Mabou Mines when revisioning *King Lear* in their respective productions *Lear's Daughters* and *Lear* are delineated in Lesley Ferris's "Lear's Daughters and Sons." Playwright Chiori Miyagawa (whose *Red Again* for *The Antigone Project* is analyzed in Martin's essay) even outlines the postmodern minimalist theoretical underpinnings to her own *Awakenings,* a revision of Kate

Chopin's *The Awakening,* in "A Mystical Place Called Grand Isle." And all of the essayists in the volume partake equally in the critical discourse, viewing the revisions through a variety of paradigmatic approaches. Kristin Crouch's "Expressions of 'Lust and Rage'": Shared Experience Theatre's Adaptation of *Jane Eyre*" is an excellent reminder of the classic feminist theories of Helene Keyssar, Sandra Gilbert, Susan Gubar, and Adrienne Rich. Sandee K. McGlaun compellingly applies rhetorical and semiotic theories in "SITI Company's *Room*: Theatrical Performance and/ as Feminist Invitational Rhetoric," and Deborah R. Geis incorporates cutting edge gender and queer theory in "Deconstructing (A Streetcar Named) Desire: Gender Re-citation in *Belle Reprieve.*"

Overall, *Feminist Theatrical Revisions of Classic Works* is a wonderful text for anyone interested in feminist revisionist theatre.

LAURA SNYDER
Stevenson University

Index